Prosperity Lost

Prosperity Lost

Philip Mattera

Addison-Wesley Publishing Company, Inc.
Reading, Massachusetts   New York   Menlo Park, California
Don Mills, Ontario   Wokingham, England   Amsterdam
Bonn   Sydney   Singapore   Tokyo   Madrid   San Juan
Paris   Seoul   Milan   Mexico City   Taipei

Many of the designations used by manufacturers and sellers to distinguish their products are claimed as trademarks. Where those designations appear in this book and Addison-Wesley was aware of a
trademark claim, the designations have been printed in initial capital
letters (e.g., Maypo).

Library of Congress Cataloging-in-Publication Data

Mattera, Philip.
 Prosperity lost / Philip Mattera.
  p. cm.
 ISBN 0-201-19897-5
 ISBN 0-201-56772-5 (pbk.)
 1. Poor—United States. 2. Cost and standard of living—United
States. 3. Working class—United States. 4. United States—
Economic policy—1981– 5. United States—Economic
conditions—1981– 6. Competition, International. I. Title.
HC110.P6M33 1990
330.973′092—dc20   90-31577
                      CIP

Cover design by Mike Fender
Text design by Joyce C. Weston
Set in 11-point Berkeley by Shepard Poorman

1 2 3 4 5 6 7 8 9-MW-9594939291
First printing, July 1990
First paperback printing, September 1991

· CONTENTS ·

· ACKNOWLEDGMENTS ·

This book would not have been possible without a wide range of statistics and analysis assembled by various government agencies, non-profit research organizations, and public interest groups. Among those bodies whose work I drew on the most are the Center on Budget and Policy Priorities, the Economic Policy Institute, the Employee Benefit Research Institute, the Children's Defense Fund, the U.S. Bureau of Labor Statistics, and the U.S. Census Bureau.

Randall Dodd, Kim Fellner, Hardy Green, Sam Hirsch, and Kathleen Maloy were kind enough to read and comment on various chapters. My appreciation goes to Ray Rogers and everyone else at Corporate Campaign, who showed great patience during the time I was struggling to finish the manuscript. Thanks to Martha Moutray and Jane Isay at Addison-Wesley for their help in shaping the book and their willingness to support a project somewhat out of the mainstream. My agent, Edythea Ginis Selman, was an endless source of energy and encouragement.

My deepest appreciation goes to my family, who have remained supportive of what must still seem to them a bizarre career choice: book writing. My wife, Donna Demac, and our son Thomas, who entered the world while this book was being written, have kept my personal quality of life very high even as general living standards have been eroding. Special thanks to Donna for keeping me and my writing on track and putting up with my inability to leave the keyboard at a reasonable hour.

Prosperity Lost

What's wrong with this picture?: a photograph of Michael Boskin, chairman of the Council of Economic Advisers, and a handful of other U.S. officials arriving in Warsaw, published in various newspapers at the end of November 1989. The aim of the delegation's visit was to encourage the Solidarity-led government of Poland to pursue a free-enterprise course—in other words, to emulate the U.S.—in dealing with the country's economic troubles.

In economic matters the Bush administration has not been inclined toward boldness, but this offer of advice to Poland was an act of great chutzpah. While the administration has been uncertain as to what political stance to take toward the developments in Eastern Europe, the assumption both within the federal government and among most observers is that those developments have vindicated economics American style. As Mobil Corporation, for example, gloated in one of its op-ed page advertisements in late 1989: "We snap on the TV and find thousands of people in some foreign square shouting for free markets."* We Americans should be thankful, the message goes, for we have what the victims of communism are so fervently seeking.

It is undeniable that the state-dominated economies of the Soviet bloc have been just as discredited as the authoritarian political structures of those countries. Yet the crisis of communism does not necessarily imply the moral triumph of capitalism, particularly in its American manifestation.

In fact, there is something almost comic about those responsible for

---

*Sources of quotes and additional information, keyed to page numbers, may be found in the Notes section. See page 211.

U.S. economic policy presuming to have the solutions to the difficulties of another nation, even one as desperate as Poland. These are the people, after all, who preside over the economic management of a country that is now the world's largest debtor, a country suffering from chronic industrial decline, a country that says it cannot afford to eliminate afflictions like homelessness, inadequate health care, and pollution. It is also a country where, as is less well known, average wage levels (adjusted for inflation) have been stagnant for years and distribution of income grows increasingly unequal. As for economic advice, the U.S. belongs on the receiving rather than the giving end.

The passion for change seems to be blinding many citizens of Eastern Europe to the flaws in what they take to be the only alternative to their despised system. In Poland, for example, Solidarity was determined to embark on the capitalist road even before the U.S. government delegation arrived. Heeding the words of its economic counselor, Harvard professor Jeffrey Sachs, Solidarity concluded that the cure for Poland's ills lay in an abrupt transition to a market-oriented system. This meant a "cold bath" treatment of privatizing state enterprises, slashing price subsidies, and allowing troubled firms to lay off workers or go bankrupt. Over the short term this will cause living standards to decline; "real wages will have to fall," the Harvard economist admitted.

The gamble Solidarity is taking is that the dislocations will be temporary and that once the economy is largely free of state control, the country will prosper. In other words, the assumption is that when the Polish system begins to resemble the American one—with a reduced public sector, managerial freedom, and a competitive labor market—all will be fine. While Professor Sachs may have been too caught up in his experiment to recognize the flaws in this hypothesis, a columnist for the *Wall Street Journal* was more clear-sighted: "The most difficult challenge for the new government," he wrote of Poland, "is to persuade workers educated in a Marxist system to accept the hardship of a tough anti-inflation plan or the vagaries and inequities of a capitalist economy." The irony is that the Soviet bloc is embracing the Western economic model just at the time when those vagaries and inequities are growing worse.

Poles and other East Europeans will have to find out for themselves whether they made the right decisions in their economic strategy. In the U.S. we also face momentous choices, though of a different nature. Although the current fashion is to portray America as an economic nirvana, there is a crisis here comparable in severity to that of the Soviet bloc. The rough seas that disrupted the meeting of Bush and Gorbachev off the coast of Malta in December 1989 can be seen as a symbol of the underlying economic instability of both men's countries.

In the U.S. the problem is not simply the fact that the economy seems to be heading for a recession. The American disease is more than the ups and downs of the business cycle. Despite the presence of the country's longest peacetime expansion—which reached an age of 85 months at the end of 1989—the economic situation of most people got worse during the Reagan era. Recession and expansion are merely technical terms relating to trends in the gross national product. What marked the 1980s was the deterioration of conditions in fundamental rather than cyclical terms. The result has been a quiet erosion of living standards for all but the wealthiest parts of the population. The aim of this book is to document this dismal trend and to suggest ways to regain our lost prosperity.

For 40 years, and especially during the Reagan era, one of the major obstacles to a more humane economy in the U.S. was the perceived need to keep the country on a virtual war footing, to defend against a supposedly aggressive Soviet empire. During the 1950s up to 70 percent of annual federal outlays were in the "national defense" category. The rise of entitlement programs has lowered that relative share, but more than 25 percent of expenditures are still going to the military. In fiscal year 1990 these outlays amounted to some $300 billion. The gargantuan appetite of the military sector has preempted many social needs and contributed to the weakening of civilian industry.

The waning of the cold war has put the economic problems of the U.S. in a new context and created exciting possibilities. The events of 1989—the opening of the Berlin Wall, the toppling of the old regimes across Eastern Europe, the disarmament initiatives of Gorbachev— appeared to have finally placed substantial reductions in the military budget on the mainstream policy agenda. Before the end of that year Defense Secretary Dick Cheney had seized the initiative, ordering the armed services to draw up plans for cutting $180 billion in spending over several years.

As peace breaks out, it is no longer utopian to imagine a dramatic reordering of domestic priorities. The federal government could finally abandon its preoccupation with fighting real or imagined foreign enemies and redirect its attention to those more malevolent domestic foes: poverty, hunger, homelessness, and other forms of privation.

Yet as soon as people began to speak of a "peace dividend" resulting from the new pacific relationship with the Soviet Union, the Bush administration and prominent conservatives quickly moved to dampen these expectations. Unregenerate cold warriors like Vice President Quayle and former Defense Secretary Caspar Weinberger argued against any shrinking of the military security blanket, while those who accepted the need for cuts insisted that the savings would not provide a windfall for social spending. "We can't do that," Bush himself insisted. "We've got enormous budget problems." Republic Senator Pete Domenici warned: "Those who are looking for an instant pot of gold at the end of the rainbow are going to be disappointed in the short term, for sure."

The peace dividend did indeed begin to disappear when, upon closer examination, it turned out that the military cuts being considered were not very substantial. Cheney's $180 billion was calculated in relation to previously planned spending increases over several years (the exact number was unclear), which meant that the actual decline over current levels would be only a few percentage points. A political cartoon at the time showed a senior military officer kneeling in front of an embankment of money bags labeled "U.S. defense spending" and pleading with Cheney: "Please don't let them tear down our wall." It appears that the Bush administration, left to its own devices, will at best put but a few small chinks in that structure.

As in Eastern Europe, the lesson is that people cannot wait for those in power to make a final break with the old ways. Once the streets of American cities begin to resemble the scenes of protest in Prague, East Berlin, Sofia, and Bucharest, then we may begin to see the emergence of the perestroika the U.S. so desperately needs.

A key cause of discontent in the Soviet bloc was the practice within Stalinist economics of promoting rapid industrialization at the expense of consumer goods. "It was necessary to accept sacrifices, and to impose the severest economy in everything," Stalin himself wrote in 1939. "It was necessary to economize on food, on schools, on manufactured goods so as to accumulate the indispensable means for the creation of industry." For decades apologists for capitalism cited this Soviet approach to economic growth as one of the cardinal sins of

4

communism. The free-market system, by contrast, was praised for delivering both the goods and political liberty.

One of the many ironies of today is that while people in the Soviet bloc are rising up against such policies and embracing Western economics, there are prominent voices in the U.S. advocating that some Stalinist-type policies be adopted here. This is in effect the message of influential figures like Peter Peterson, investment banker and Commerce Secretary during the Nixon administration, who say that America's trade and budget deficits and mounting international debt require a shrinking of supposedly swollen living standards and an expansion of capital investment. Saying that the "root malady" of America's problems is a "national preference for consumption over production," Peterson has written that it will take at least 20 years of austerity—including reduced real wages and government spending—before the U.S. will have its house back in order.

An insistence that the U.S. has to go back to living within its means can also be heard from other quarters. In a 1989 volume called *Critical Choices,* containing advice for the new administration, economists of the supposedly liberal Brookings Institution warned that one way or another, total demand will have to be brought back in line with growth in productivity. Ironically, the chapter entitled "Improving Living Standards" contained forecasts that implied just the opposite, at least over the next decade.

The problem with the austerity crowd is that they advocate sacrifices from those portions of the population, primarily workers and the poor, who did not participate in what Peterson called the "consumption bacchanalia" of the 1980s and who are least able to live with less. In fact, they were experiencing austerity even before Peterson began his crusade, and there is no evidence that their suffering made the U.S. economy any stronger.

Between the new smugness about capitalism, the resistance to diverting military spending to social needs, and the calls for austerity, it will be a major challenge to put the U.S. back on the road to mass prosperity. Before we can even begin that journey, we need to understand how and to what extent American living standards have eroded. The following chapters attempt to accomplish that task.

April 22, 1990

ONE

The Big Squeeze

BACK in 1982 Ronald Kistler and Michael MacKay were trying to get somewhere in the world. Where they ended up was on the ledge of a billboard in Allentown, Pennsylvania, where each of them remained for 261 days in a quest for the American Dream: a home of his own, and perhaps a bit of fame.

Kistler, an unemployed baker, and MacKay, who worked at a halfway house for retarded children, had entered a contest sponsored by a local radio station and a mobile home dealer. Three contestants, whose names were chosen at random from half a million entries, were equipped with tents and other necessaries and placed on the ledge. The one who endured the longest in front of the billboard, which was adorned with the names of the sponsors, WSAN and Love Homes, was to win a furnished two-bedroom mobile home known as the Cozy Cottage, retail price $18,000.

The third contender was disqualified after being arrested on drug charges, but Kistler and MacKay persevered, much longer than the sponsors had anticipated. The contest had generated extraordinary publicity—among the coverage were spots on French and Australian television—and after nearly six months WSAN and Love Homes declared both men winners and awarded each of them a Cozy Cottage, with automobiles thrown in for good measure.

The contest had put a roof over the Kistler and MacKay families, but otherwise little changed for the two men. Talk about TV and book deals evaporated, and they were thrown back into the uncertain labor market of the 1980s. It took MacKay several years to find a steady job, while Kistler had to change occupations in order to find employment—as a painter for a realty company owned by the proprietor of the radio station.

Looking back, MacKay said to a reporter that the contest had nothing to do with hard times; for him it was simply a test of personal fortitude. Yet the whole episode was a fitting symbol of America in the 1980s. The willingness of people to endure physical discomfort and indignity for the sake of having a place to live attests to an underlying economic desperation while at the same time recalling the dance marathons of the Depression.

The transformation of home ownership from a right for everyone, as it all but was in the 1950s and 1960s, into a prize available to fewer Americans—and in devalued, Cozy Cottage form at that—symbolizes a halt to widespread upward social mobility. The contest began during a severe recession, but the experiences of Kistler and MacKay in the years following 1982 suggest that even those designated as winners have not been able to escape the stagnation of living standards that has persisted during the years of "official" economic recovery. What had once been an easy passage to middle-class security now requires jumping through hoops—a trick that increasing numbers of Americans are unable to perform.

The End of Mass Prosperity

The 1980s might be labeled the Decade of Denial. For most of that 10-year span America was simply unable to come to grips with the reality of the economic changes taking place. It is true that in the early part of the decade there was still a passing sense of economic crisis, especially with the arrival of the first double-digit unemployment rates since the 1930s. And there has been a lot of handwringing about the growth of the federal deficit and the decline of U.S. competitiveness in world markets. Yet once the official recession was over, the propaganda machine shifted into overdrive. Public officials and the media repeatedly depicted the era as one of widespread affluence. The young were presented as yuppies using fat salaries to indulge in faddish restaurants and imported luxury cars; the old were supposed to be enjoying a lush retirement thanks to generous Social Security benefits, private pensions, and savings. And just about everyone in between was said to be doing better than ever. We were force-fed the idea that our economy was the envy of the world and that in many countries people were risking their lives in order to live like Americans. Any doubts were warded off by Bobby McFerrin's hit song, "Don't Worry, Be Happy," the anthem of the feel-good era ushered in by Ronald Reagan and opportunistically extended by George Bush.

The propagandists were right about one thing: the *image* of life in America was marvelous. But the reality was something else. Behind the hype, the eighties saw acceleration of a trend that is nothing to celebrate: the United States has ceased to be a solidly middle-class society. Instead of a country dominated by a growing mass of citizens of moderate but comfortable means, America is becoming a land in which much of the population is experiencing declining conditions of life while a small minority is amassing a disproportionate share of income, wealth, and influence.

Social inequality is nothing new to this nation, but what the recent period has witnessed is a reversal of the widely trumpeted accomplishments of the first 25-year period after World War II. During those years America was said to have achieved something unprecedented in human history: mass prosperity.

"All history can show no more portentous economic phenomenon than today's American market," proclaimed a book written by the editors of *Fortune* magazine in 1955. "The whole world also marvels at and envies this market. It is enabling Americans to raise their standard of living every year." As late as 1969 a federal government report was bragging:

> The most obvious fact about American income is that it is the highest in the world and rising rapidly. In terms of gross national product per capita—or any other measure of the average availability of goods and services—the United States far outranks its nearest competitors.

Among social scientists one of the hot topics was how society would deal with a situation in which everyone supposedly had all their material needs met. Robert Theobald wrote a book in 1961 on "the challenge of abundance," while economist Roy Harrod could talk of "the possibility of economic satiety" and warn of the need for people to use their wealth and leisure wisely.

Ideology and hyperbole aside, there was genuine progress in the fifties and sixties. All the main indicators of economic well-being— gross national product per capita, real (inflation adjusted) earnings, disposable income, consumer spending, prevalence of indoor plumbing—were rising smartly.

As important as improvements in the absolute standard of living was the sense that relative conditions had been transformed as well. A parade of sociologists and economists appeared on the scene to announce that, thanks to the new affluence, class differences were evaporating. Simon Kuznets produced an influential study showing that the portion of national income going to the rich was declining. Robert Nisbet declared the concept of social class "nearly valueless" in analyzing the contemporary U.S. The editors of *Fortune* hailed the arrival of "a huge new moneyed middle-income class."

The subtext of much of the fifties and sixties literature on class convergence and the "end of ideology" was an attack on Marxism. Conventional social scientists, having been on the defensive during the economic disaster of the 1930s, came out fighting once again. Now that capitalism was delivering the goods for all, they felt confident in announcing the demise of their adversary.

Reports of the death of Marxism and claims about attaining economic equality were both greatly exaggerated, but the apostles of affluence did have a decisive effect on the language of social analysis. The term *working class* was all but eliminated in polite discourse, tainted as an artifact of leftist ideology. *Middle class* was enlarged to fill the void— a term coined in Europe to designate merchants and property owners as distinct from the aristocracy, and which in the U.S. had previously referred to managers and professionals, had become a rubric of nearly universal proportions.

The idea of an all-encompassing class spread from the academic world to the general public. It became commonplace for an extremely wide range of Americans—from those just above the poverty line to well-paid blue-collar workers to near-millionaires—to identify themselves as part of the proud middle class.

While general living standards were rising steadily, this collapsing of distinctions was a problem mainly for those on the Left, who tried, with little success, to make people see that the social hierarchy had not in fact disappeared. But in more recent years, as real incomes have been faltering, the legacy of this middle-class universalism has been widespread anxiety and frustration. A large part of the population still considers itself middle class, which is equated with security and stability, yet feels it is not living as well as in the past. Americans raised to believe they lived in the richest country in the world cannot understand why some of the basic elements of the good life—home ownership, decent health care, college education for the kids, adequate leisure time—seem increasingly out of reach. Two-income couples cannot figure out why they are unable to attain the same living standard their parents had achieved with only one breadwinner. People told that they were enjoying one of the longest periods of economic recovery puzzle over why, as in the looking-glass world visited by Alice, they must run as fast as they can just to stay in place.

The lingering amnesia about class differences makes it difficult for people to see that the rules of the game have changed. At one time it may have been true that, to paraphrase the famous comment by auto-executive-turned-government-official Charles Wilson in the 1950s, what was good for General Motors and the rich was good for the country. By the 1980s such a claim was unthinkable. While corporate profit rates were climbing, the stock market booming (with some notable exceptions), and the likes of Donald Trump growing ever wealthier, living standards for much of the population were eroding. In a return to the conspicuous consumption of the age of the robber baron, publisher Malcolm Forbes felt comfortable throwing himself a multi-million-dollar birthday bash while poverty and homelessness made the streets of many American cities look like something out of Dickens. As the once-mighty middle class split between those few fortunates who rose to the top and the rest who lost ground, class convergence turned into class divergence. To borrow an observation once made by a Brazilian statesman about his country, America is doing fine—most Americans not so fine.

Family Incomes in Trouble

More than any other measure, income is the variable that captures changing conditions in a society such as ours. Wages, salaries, interest, dividends, royalties—these are the yardsticks by which most Americans judge their level of well-being. So income is the place to begin in documenting the erosion of American living standards.

The traditional figures to look at are the family income data compiled by the Census Bureau from information provided by a sample of households interviewed in the Current Population Survey. The key figure is the median annual family income adjusted for inflation. When all pretax incomes are placed in order of size, the median is the value that divides them in half; that is, half the incomes are above and half below the median. The median is considered more representative than the average, which can be skewed upward by a few incomes at the extreme upper end.

From 1947, the first year for which data are available, to the early 1970s, a curve charting real median family income arches up impressively, especially during the 1960s. Expressed in 1987 dollars, the median rose from $15,422 in 1947 to $30,820 in 1973. This represented growth of more than 30 percent from 1947 to 1957 and almost 35 percent in the following decade.

With the onset of economic crisis, 3 percent annual growth quickly vanished. The median remained stuck at about $30,000 throughout the 1970s and began sinking in the early 1980s. The much-vaunted Reagan recovery had a limited impact. By 1987, the most recent year for which complete information is available as of this writing, the median had inched up only to $30,853—just a few dollars above the figure of 14 years earlier. Frank Levy, one of the most rigorous analysts in the income field, has argued that this "sudden break in trend—26 years of income growth followed by 12 [as of his writing] years of income stagnation—is the major economic story of the postwar period."

In these data, as in most other economic statistics, the figures for blacks and other minorities are even worse than those for whites. From 1977 to 1987 the median income for black families rose nine-tenths of 1 percent, while for whites the rise was 2.8 percent. In 1987 the black median was only 56 percent of the level for whites, compared to 59 percent two decades earlier.

The statistics on families in general are dismal enough, but the news is bleaker when one looks at the results for specific types of families. First consider the number of earners. Whatever meager gains there have been in median income during the 1980s have been enjoyed by families in which both husband and wife are working outside the home. Traditional one-earner families have increasingly fallen behind; by 1987 they had a median income only about two-thirds that of two-income couples.

What this demonstrates is that the only way families have been able to keep up has been to send someone else out to work, a phenomenon clearly illustrated in the rising labor force participation rates for women, including mothers of young children. When families run out of people to hand over to the labor force, those already employed are compelled to take on extra work. The Bureau of Labor Statistics reported in late 1989 that the proportion of employed persons with two or more jobs had reached 6.2 percent, the highest rate of multiple jobholding in more than three decades. One of these moonlighters is Leroy Montgomery, a maintenance worker in Baltimore who holds two full-time jobs to make ends meet. Aside from a short visit with his two daughters between jobs, Montgomery spends virtually all of his waking time, some 16 hours a day, on the job.

The need for families to work increasing hours for the same real income, often called the "sweat factor," has put countless couples in a severe squeeze regarding time as well as money. Mothers and fathers (especially mothers) run themselves ragged trying to meet the requirements of both home and workplace. As a result, surveys find that Americans have declining amounts of leisure time. Lives filled with more work and stress yet less money are a glaring symptom of an economy in decline.

Unlike the golden 1950s and 1960s, when parents prospered along with everyone else, in recent years families with children have had a much harder time of it. The Census Bureau does not regularly publish figures on families with children as a group, but a 1986 study by Sheldon Danziger and Peter Gottschalk separated out the data. They found that the average real income for families with children sank more than 8 percent from 1973 to 1984. For black families the drop was nearly 11 percent.

Among families with children, the poorest are those headed by a single parent, a category swollen by high divorce rates. Median incomes for female-headed families have been stagnant for more than 20 years, and in 1987 their median was only $14,620, or 42 percent of the figure for married couples.

Yet more ominous for the future is the deteriorating economic condition of young families. The Children's Defense Fund labeled "an economic disaster" the fact that families with children headed by persons under the age of 25 suffered a 26 percent drop in median income from 1973 to 1986, likening it to the decline in living standards experienced by families as a whole during the Depression. The Fund also argued that the inadequate income of young people was one of the main causes of the fall in marriage rates and the rise in out-of-wedlock births.

"Young Americans," said a report published by the Fund, "now are less able to build the foundation for their own economic security, form stable families, provide adequate support for their children, or have hope and confidence in the future." The report found that families headed by college graduates had done better than the rest, but they account for fewer than one in four young families.

Economist Frank Levy has a graphic way of showing how stagnating incomes for young people contribute to the process of intergenerational downward mobility. Consider, Levy writes, a typical father in his mid-40s and his 18-year-old son who is preparing to leave home. In the 1950s and 1960s, Levy says, such a young man by age 30 would have been earning about 15 percent more in real terms than his father had been making when the son left: "The young man would have known early in life that he would live at least as well as he had seen his parents live." Today the average 30-year-old man earns several thousand dollars *less* than his father earned a dozen years ago.

Studying the Finger

It has been said that when critical thinkers point their finger at reality, orthodox thinkers study the finger. That is, in effect, what has happened in the debate on changes in living standards. Once the signs of income stagnation became clear, some analysts began to argue that the Census Bureau data were overstating the problem. Among the arguments were that the Consumer Price Index used to adjust for inflation had exaggerated housing costs in the 1970s, that the Census figures failed to account for reduced living costs that had supposedly resulted from declines in average family size, and that limiting the calculations to cash income overlooked the growing importance of in-kind items like food stamps, Medicare, employee benefits, and executive perks.

Various studies have used such adjustments to claim that family incomes have been rising rather than stagnating since the early 1970s, although this involves the dubious step of including childless individuals as a type of family. Among the more careful of these revisions was a study conducted by Stephen Rose and David Fasenfest for the Economic Policy Institute. Using a revised form of the Consumer Price Index and adjusting for family size, they concluded that average family income had risen 7.3 percent between 1979 and 1986. That rate of 1 percent a year is well below the standard of the earlier postwar period, and one-third of the increase was attributable to the increased earnings of wives and another third to increases in property income rather than earnings. Since the study used averages rather than medians, the high levels of investment income of the wealthy helped to elevate the figures. Overall, the revisionist approach may make the trends of recent years seem less catastrophic, but they do not adjust out of existence the reality of faltering living standards.

Trickling Up

One disturbing trend that the revisionist analyses do not diminish at all is that family incomes are becoming increasingly unequal. In recent years the distribution of income, that is, the way incomes are apportioned among the entire population, has been shifting noticeably in favor of the rich.

The way this is determined is by ranking all incomes from lowest to highest and dividing them into five groups, or quintiles. The trends in how much of total income is received by each quintile reveal the relative positions of the rich, the poor, and those in between. Even seemingly small changes in the portion held by a quintile, say 2 or 3 percentage points, indicate substantial shifts in the distribution of income.

When looking at the Census Bureau quintiles, the first thing one notices is that for most of the postwar period the distribution remained remarkably stable. Amid the relatively rapid growth of real incomes, the relative position of the different income groups did not change much, indicating that each was rising in proportion to the others. The accompanying table illustrates the percentage shares of the quintiles and the very top of the income pyramid.

	1st (poorest)	2nd	3rd	4th	5th (richest)	top 5%
1947	5.0	11.9	17.0	23.1	43.0	17.5
1957	5.1	12.7	18.1	23.8	40.4	15.6
1967	5.5	12.4	17.9	23.9	40.4	15.2
1977	5.2	11.6	17.5	24.2	41.5	15.7
1987	4.6	10.8	16.9	24.1	43.7	16.9

While the claims made in the 1950s of massive shifts toward income equality were far from true, there was some movement in that direction. Starting in the 1970s, however, the process suddenly switched into reverse. From 1977 to 1987 the bottom 80 percent of families lost about 2 percentage points of income share, equivalent to tens of billions of dollars, which went into the pockets of the richest quintile.

The lion's share of this gain was enjoyed by the top 5 percent of families. The increasing lopsidedness of income distribution is seen most clearly in the fact that in 1982 the share of this tiny elite began to exceed that of the entire bottom 40 percent of families—the first time this milestone of inequality had been reached in three decades. In the past, income inequality lessened during periods of economic recovery; not so in the Roaring Eighties, when the benefits of the boom never quite made it to the majority of the population.

Back in 1975 *Business Week* warned its readers about an ominous move toward economic equality: "Business for its part sees the egalitarian push as a threat—not just to its pay scales but to the fundamental principles of a market economy." Whether the egalitarian enemy was real or imagined, it was soon vanquished. No longer were the poor and middle class gaining ground against the rich, nor were they even holding their own. Instead, the old bugaboo of capitalist society had come back to haunt us: the rich were getting richer and the poor were getting poorer.

Another way of illustrating the widening gap between rich and poor is through the use of an index of income concentration known as the Gini ratio. This index, named after Italian economist Corrado Gini and now used by the U.S. Census Bureau, compares the actual distribution of income to an ideal arrangement of perfect equality; that is, a situation in which each quintile of families receives one-fifth of total income. That ideal is set at a value of zero, and the actual figures range upward to a theoretical maximum of 1—the value representing perfect inequality; that is, a situation in which all income is received by one family. Thus, the higher the index the greater the inequality.

From 1947 to 1967 the Gini ratio slowly made its way down from .376 to .348, the all-time low. Then the direction changed: thanks to a variety of economic trends and government policies, inequality was on the rise once again. In 1987 the index stood at .392, the highest level since the Census Bureau began making the calculations 40 years before.

The story is the same in the calculations of the revisionists. Estimates made by the House Ways and Means Committee, which got Republican hackles up in 1989, found that the average income of families in the poorest quintile fell nearly 10 percent from 1979 to 1987, while the richest quintile enjoyed a gain of more than 15 percent. Expressed otherwise, the share of total income received by the poorest quintile slipped from 5.2 to 4.3 percent during the period, while that of the richest quintile rose from 41.5 to 43.9 percent. The reversal was not limited to the poorest group. As in the Census figures, the combined share of all but the top fifth of families declined.

Frank Levy took the analysis further by estimating the effects of taxation and employee benefits as well as adjusting for family size. What he found was that "corrected" family income distribution did grow significantly more equal from 1949 to 1979, but after that there was a slide back toward polarization.

Evidence of severe imbalances in the distribution of income also emerges from estimates of what is called "discretionary income," that is, money available to be spent after taxes are paid and basic needs are met. A 1989 study conducted by the Census Bureau and the Conference Board concluded that only 29 percent of U.S. households had any discretionary income at all and that less than a fifth of all households controlled nearly 80 percent of the total of such income.

Trying to put a favorable spin on this information, the Census Bureau put out a press release hailing the fact that some 30 percent of American households "have income above that required for 'comfortable' living." In keeping with the warped thinking of the eighties, we were apparently not supposed to see what this wonderful news implied: that 70 percent of households had no discretionary income and thus had not attained a "comfortable" standard of living.

The Shrinking Middle

Increasing income concentration is not simply a matter of shifts of money from the poor to the rich; it is also a squeezing of the middle. One of the consequences of the trends described above is that the middle class, as prominent economist Lester Thurow put it, "is becoming an endangered species." In other words, society is increasingly being polarized into rich and poor.

The attempts to quantify the shrinking middle class have resulted in a heated battle of numbers among the econometricians, in large part because no one can agree on how to define this basic category of social science. The controversy about the Consumer Price Index also plays a role.

In 1988 conservatives were cheered by a study produced by two economists at the Bureau of Labor Statistics that acknowledged the evidence of a shrinking middle but claimed that this was happening only because middle-class families were moving into the upper class. Upward mobility, rather than polarization, was said to be the order of the day.

What was overlooked in the jubilation over these results was that the authors of the study, Michael Horrigan and Steven Haugen, had actually made two sets of calculations and that the second set had led to a very different conclusion.

The upward mobility result emerged when the middle class was defined in terms of a specific income range, namely $20,000 to $59,999 in 1986 dollars. Then when Horrigan and Haugen used the more appropriate technique of defining the middle class in relation to the median income, that is, as comprising those families whose income was between 68 and 190 percent of the median in each year, the result was polarization. From 1969 to 1986 the middle class declined from 60.2 to 53.0 percent of all families, while the ranks of those above and below expanded. This was nothing to cheer about.

The Incredible Shrinking Wage

After Rita Hamlet lost her $14-an-hour job as an inspector at Bethlehem Steel in 1986, the best new position she could find was that of a supermarket cashier. "They offered me $3.75 an hour," she said of her first new job after 13 years with the steelmaker. "My natural instinct was, that's a job for a child." But 42-year-old Hamlet, deciding she was not ready for the only other alternative—a life of crime—accepted the offer.

When General Tire & Rubber Co. demanded extensive concessions in wages and benefits from workers at its plant in Waco, Texas, the United Rubber Workers called a strike in 1982 that lasted for 119 days—to no avail. "I don't believe getting those concessions either makes or breaks General Tire," complained Carlos Gonzales, a forklift operator at the plant. "I feel the company is just doing this because other companies have done it and gotten away with it."

When labor shortages began to emerge in southern California in the late 1980s, personnel recruiters at Disneyland did not jack up starting wages to attract more applicants. Instead they counted on the supposed glamour of working alongside Mickey Mouse to keep 4,000 just-above-minimum-wage jobs filled. One Disney recruiter told a reporter: "Money isn't the answer."

Maybe for Disneyland it's not, but for workers in the real world the decline in the amount of money they were able to earn in the 1980s is the key to the present crisis in income levels and living standards. Earnings have been kept down by a variety of economic forces, government policies, and business strategies. Millions of workers like Rita Hamlet lost well-paying jobs in heavy industry and found themselves forced to take low-wage positions in the booming service sector. The minimum wage remained stuck at $3.35 from 1981 through the rest of the decade. Unionized workers faced a relentless campaign by employers to cut or freeze pay rates. Defying the traditional principles of labor economics, business resisted raising wages even when official unemployment rates sank and companies began to find it difficult to fill jobs.

By the late 1980s, publications that once thundered against excessive pay increases wondered why wage levels remained so moderate during the height of economic expansion. A bewildered *New York Times* published a series of articles with headlines like "Wages Sluggish in East Despite a Scarcity of Workers" and "The Wage Jump That Never Came." In one of the pieces the *Times* came dangerously close to sounding like a Marxist diatribe denouncing exploitation. "For the first time since World War II," announced the newspaper of record in 1987, "sustained and substantial productivity increases are not being shared with workers in the form of higher wages."

The dismal consequences of these trends are seen in the data on earnings compiled by the Bureau of Labor Statistics. The figures come in several forms. First are the hourly wage rates of nonsupervisory workers in private industry, which are derived from surveys of business establishments. In 1989 the average was $9.66, nominally the highest level ever. But once the numbers are adjusted for inflation, a very different picture emerges. Real hourly wages have been static since the early 1970s, and in constant dollars the 1989 figure was no higher than the wage rate in 1966.

An even greater degree of backsliding can be found in federal government data, compiled through household surveys, on the usual gross weekly earnings of nonsupervisory production workers. In 1989 the average was $335. But once the figure is deflated, someone earning that amount is transported back to 1960, the last time the average was so low. In other words, as far as wages are concerned, the typical worker has nothing to show for the past three decades. This is especially the case for black male workers, whose median earnings in 1989 were still less than three-quarters that of their white counterparts.

A broader data series compiled by the Bureau of Labor Statistics takes in all private sector earnings, including proprietors' incomes. By that measure there was also a sharp drop, after adjusting for inflation, during the 1970s. Yet unlike wages, this data series made a decent recovery during the 1980s, suggesting that Reaganism has not been all that bad for managers and small-business owners. It should be noted, however, that much of the improvement for salaried employees occurred among women, who have been striving to overcome discriminatory pay practices.

These statistics demonstrate that there is something very wrong with what has been hailed as the Great American Job Machine. It is true that a substantial number of jobs were created in the U.S. during the 1980s: total civilian employment rose from 99 million in 1979 to 117 million in 1989. Although this rate of growth was a bit slower than the U.S. record set in the two prior decades, it looked damned good to the rest of the capitalist world. Government officials in Europe, where employment growth was close to zero during the same period, marveled at the American performance and wondered what our secret is.

Despite this record, it should not be forgotten that the official rate of unemployment is seriously understated. An advocacy group called the National Committee for Full Employment calculates what it calls the "real rate" of joblessness by adding discouraged workers (those who have given up the search for work) and those working part-time involuntarily to the officially unemployed. This "real rate" stood at 9.7 percent in mid-1989, nearly double the standard Labor Department figure of 5.2 percent.

While it is true that joblessness is more serious than the federal government acknowledges—especially among blacks, for whom even official unemployment rates remained in double digits throughout the 1980s—the major issue now is the quality rather than the quantity of jobs. The honest response to the queries of the Europeans would be that the reason we have been able to add so many jobs is that many of the ones we have created are substandard. Instead of providing a moderate number of decent new positions, American business has been giving birth to huge numbers of jobs that are low-wage and often part-time, temporary, or otherwise precarious. At the same time, there has been a more modest expansion of high-paid technical, professional, and managerial positions. Those in between, the so-called middle-class jobs, are becoming increasingly scarce.

The result is a polarization of earnings that has helped to bring about the polarization of incomes. Since a "good job" is as slippery to define as "middle class," the efforts to quantify the trend in wages have brought about more conflicting statistical claims. Certain facts, however, are highly suggestive of polarization. First is the escalating level of inequality in annual wages and salaries. Economists Bennett Harrison and Barry Bluestone found that the index of inequality in earnings, determined by a statistical technique called *variance in the logarithm,* increased some 18 percent between 1975 and 1986, which pushed the index back to the level of 1966.

Additional evidence of earnings polarization was supplied in a report written by Robert Costrell for the Joint Economic Committee of Congress. Costrell analyzed by industry the jobs lost and jobs gained in the U.S. between 1981 and 1987. He found that industries with expanding shares of total employment paid an average of about $10,000 less in annual compensation than those whose employment shares were contracting. This gap between pay levels in shrinking industries and those in growing industries was wider during the eighties than at any other time in the postwar period. What this means is that the bulk of employment opportunities is increasingly to be found in the lower-paying sectors of the economy.

The strict proof of polarization of earnings, as with incomes, requires dividing wages into low, middle, and high groups. Then one needs to show that the middle group has been contracting while the extremes have been growing larger.

A study reaching just that conclusion was published by the Joint Economic Committee in late 1986. Subsequently, the authors of the report, Bluestone and Harrison, were criticized widely for having combined part-time and part-year workers with full-time/year-round ones, thus skewing the results. This and other methodological objections were used by conservative analysts to reject Bluestone and Harrison's argument that there had been a "great U-turn" in the movement toward wage equality. The Reagan-Bush administration kept repeating "good jobs at good wages"—a mantra meant to ward off the evidence of downward mobility. "The average American worker is better off now than at any time in the history of this country," asserted a propaganda sheet published by the White House in 1988.

While Bluestone and Harrison may have initially gone a bit astray, they later did new calculations which eliminated any grounds for regaining faith in the Job Machine. Limiting the study to full-time/year-round workers, Bluestone and Harrison made other methodological changes and extended the time frame, only to find that the great U-turn popped up again. The middle stratum of jobs, defined as those paying between 50 percent and 200 percent of the median annual earnings for all full-time/year-round workers, was cut in half from 1979 to 1986. At the same time, the other two groups expanded, the low-wage one by about a third and the high-wage one by a little more than 10 percent. The middle is indeed shrinking.

Spending What We Don't Have

"We consume today as if there were no tomorrow," exclaimed the Bush administration's budget director, Richard Darman, in a 1989 speech. "Like the spoiled '50s child in the recently revived commercial, we seem on the verge of a collective now-now scream: 'I want my Maypo; I want it nowwwwww!' "

If Darman had been talking only of the wealthy, then his statement would have made sense; but he was apparently referring to the entire population. In light of the stagnation of incomes and earnings, how is it possible for anyone to speak of an excess of consumption?

One of the paradoxes of the contemporary U.S. economy is that while many people are earning less, they seem to be spending more. Consumer expenditures kept rising throughout the post-recession 1980s, even when signs of a downturn started to appear at the end of the decade. What the Commerce Department's Bureau of Economic Analysis calls personal consumption expenditures per capita reached $13,131 in 1988. Some citizens met their quota with a single purchase. During a scare about a possible spending slowdown in 1989, the *Wall Street Journal* reassured its readers with the news that investment bankers were buying more $14,000 wristwatches, thus helping to prolong the recovery.

The first way to pop this balloon is to point out that the growth rate in per capita spending, adjusted for inflation, was slower from 1979 to 1988 than during the previous two decades. The same is true for per capita disposable (after-tax) personal income, which in real terms increased an average of only 1.7 percent a year from 1979 to 1988, compared with some 3 percent per annum over the preceding 20 years. While admitting that spending and disposable income have been decelerating, one might ask how it is possible for those variables to be rising at all during a time of stagnant earnings.

The explanation comes in two parts. First is the fact that labor income as a share of total income has been falling. Wages, salaries, and other compensation now account for less than 70 percent of overall personal income, compared with more than 76 percent in 1970. In other words, as earnings stall, families are depending to a greater degree on other forms of income—interest payments, dividends, rents, Social Security benefits, and so forth—to keep their heads above water. In fact, a look solely at the data on labor income (as calculated by the Bureau of Economic Analysis) per worker shows a paralysis similar to that of the Census Bureau's statistics on family income.

The other part of the solution to the puzzle is the fact that families are borrowing at record rates in order to go on buying the things they need. By late 1989 total consumer credit had soared to some $775 billion, equal to nearly one-fifth of total personal income, or roughly $3000 for every woman, man, and child in the country. "I'm really living beyond my means," a heavily indebted bank employee in Chicago told a reporter, "and it's all coming to a grinding halt. I'm making barely enough to get by."

Increasing numbers of Americans are not getting by. The number of personal bankruptcies surged in the late 1980s, reaching an annual total of nearly 500 thousand. Whereas bankruptcies usually decline in a time of expansion (and they did during the early part of the most recent recovery), the perverse economics of the day have taken hold once again.

Saddled with crushing debt, most families are in no position to put much away for a rainy day. Personal savings sank to about 4 percent of disposable income in the late 1980s, compared with more than 9 percent back in 1973. Baby boomers, whose adult lives have coincided with the slump in real earnings, find it almost impossible to save. Janet Cassidy, a vocational counselor in her late 30s, told a reporter she and her husband would like to be able to save enough for a down payment on a house, but that seemed far off. "Right now," she said, "we're saving to get out of debt."

Negative Net Worth

"There is no wealth but life," the nineteenth-century English essayist John Ruskin once wrote. He might have been talking about the majority of the American population. Most families, faced with stalled earnings, mounting debt, and shrinking savings, end up with little in the way of net assets.

However one assesses the degree of income inequality in the U.S., it is positively communistic compared to the distribution of wealth. That is probably why the federal government spends so little time investigating the latter. The main sources of information are the surveys of consumer finances conducted at irregular intervals by a group of agencies led by the Federal Reserve. The last such complete survey was done in 1983.

That survey found that financial assets were overwhelmingly concentrated among a tiny minority of families. The top 2 percent of families held 39 percent of corporate bonds, 50 percent of stocks, and 71 percent of nontaxable holdings such as municipal bonds. The median holdings of financial assets was only $2,300, while the average was more than $24,000—indicating how massive is the wealth at the top. In constant dollars, the median was down more than 24 percent since 1977.

When both assets and liabilities were taken into account, the top 2 percent of families held 28 percent of the total net worth, and the top 10 percent of families held 57 percent. This contrasted with an income distribution in which the top 2 percent had "only" 14 percent and the top 10 percent a third of the total income.

These results received little attention when they were published inconspicuously in the *Federal Reserve Bulletin* in 1984. The splash occurred a couple of years later when the Democratic staff of the Joint Economic Committee of Congress delved further into the data. In 1986 the Committee published a much-higher-profile report that drew attention to the increasing concentration of wealth. The Reagan administration, which was promoting the idea that supply-side policies were improving everyone's lot, was dismayed by the study. Most embarrassing was the finding that the share of total net assets held by what the report called the "super-rich" (the top one-half of 1 percent of families) had leaped from less than 15 percent in 1976 to more than 35 percent in 1983.

After the report revived charges about the unfairness of Reaganomics, the administration launched a subtle counterattack. The Treasury Department set out to find flaws in the study and held private meetings with researchers at the Fed and the Commerce Department. Within a few weeks someone at the Federal Reserve leaked to the *Wall Street Journal* the news that there had been a serious numerical error.

Supposedly, one of the very rich individuals in the sample, whose assets were recorded as $200 million, actually had only $2 million. Given the tiny number of the super-rich in the sample, that one change brought the 1983 share of the super-rich down to about 27 percent, which was considered politically acceptable, since it was only slightly above the 1963 figure. The Joint Economic Committee admitted the mistake to the press, and the Republicans gloated.

Yet it turned out that the purported error had been found not by questioning the person but by deducing it from his response in a 1986 follow-up interview, in which he listed his assets as $2.3 million (but did not indicate that his 1983 response had been incorrect). Since the individual's business assets were known to be in Texas oil and gas, a business that was in a severe slump in the mid-1980s, it is conceivable that he might have suffered a nearly 100 percent decline in the value of his assets. The decision to assume a mistake had been made was certainly questionable, and it is quite possible that the "correction" was made solely for political purposes.

While this controversy was raging, the Census Bureau came out with its first report on wealth and asset ownership, which covered 1984 and examined households rather than families. The people at Census played it safe by declining to provide detailed estimates of wealth shares for specific portions of the population. Instead they divided up households into four broad income groups and briefly noted how they compared. The result was that the top 12 percent of households owned 38 percent of total net worth, implying a distribution that was somewhat more balanced than the Federal Reserve figures.

Yet the Census figures also included some bad news in terms of the relative wealth position of the races. The median net worth of black households was a meager $3,397—less than a tenth of the figure for white households. Not all of the difference can be attributed to the relative number of female-headed households. Among married couples alone, blacks had a median only one-fourth that of whites. More than 30 percent of black households had zero or negative net worth, compared to 8.4 percent of white households.

In a broader sense "negative net worth" is a fitting description of the condition of black America. More than 20 years after the famous Kerner Commission Report on the causes of the ghetto riots of the 1960s, the U.S. is still "two societies, one black, one white—separate and unequal." A 1988 follow-up report concluded that there are now "quiet riots" going on in America's central cities, in the form of poverty, unemployment, housing and school deterioration, and other social ills. "These 'quiet riots,'" the report stated, "are not as alarming as the violent riots of 20 years ago or as noticeable to outsiders. But they are even more destructive of human life."

The Impossible Dream

"Let's talk about differences in living standards rather than wages," suggested a General Electric official a few years back. "What in the

Bible says we [Americans] should have a better living standard than others? We have to give back a bit of it."

Most of us have been doing just that. The economic, social, and political forces at work in the 1980s took a substantial bite out of the material well-being of all but the richest of Americans. Downward mobility, between and within generations, has been eating away at that broad social group called the middle class. The promise of social progress—especially for minorities—has been betrayed by a combination of corporate greed and cynical government policies.

"By comparison to us our parents were self-sufficient," Curtis Paltza, a 30-year-old white-collar worker in Los Angeles, told a reporter. "It was much easier to make ends meet back then," added his wife, Cynthia. "Our parents feel sorry for young people today—they know how hard it is for us." The traditional American middle-class goal of making a better life for one's children is heading for a dead end, and the younger generation is increasingly an object of pity rather than hope. The American Dream is becoming an impossible dream.

TWO

The Origins of Austerity

O N October 7, 1974 a little-known group called the Comptroller's Technical Debt Management Committee held its monthly meeting in New York City. The purpose of the Committee, whose membership included representatives of leading banks and brokerage houses, was to advise New York's financial officials concerning the market for the securities sold by the city to help finance the government operations of the nation's largest metropolis. The advice given to Comptroller Harrison J. Goldin and his aides was not what they expected. The gentlemen from Citibank, Morgan Guaranty, Salomon Brothers, Merrill Lynch, and other financial institutions said they were concerned about potential saturation of the market because of the magnitude of the city's projected borrowing. They hinted of possible difficulties with the next scheduled bond offering and warned that a point might soon be reached where the city would not be able to market its securities at all.

The ominous message conveyed to Goldin and his aides that autumn day in 1974 helped set in motion a series of events that became known as the New York fiscal crisis, which included a brush with bankruptcy for the city. Although New York was "saved," the steps taken to restore financial discipline had consequences far beyond the city's budget. In fact, the situation in New York was a turning point in the political economy of the entire country and a harbinger of the regressive national policies of the 1980s.

Shock Therapy

Several months after the meeting of the Goldin committee, the pressure from the financial institutions escalated. It was customary for representatives of the major banking syndicates that underwrote city securities to put sealed interest-rate bids in a small green tin box in the comptroller's office. On March 6, 1975 something very unusual occurred. When the box was opened, it was discovered to be empty. It was only after two days of intense talks that the city was able to arrange for the sale of its securities—at extremely high interest rates.

From there things went steadily downhill. The actions of the banks inflated the city's borrowing costs and turned a budget problem into a budget emergency. Mayor Abraham Beame was forced to plan for the elimination of tens of thousands of city jobs, wage cuts for those who remained, severe cutbacks in services ranging from public hospitals to garbage collection, and increases in the transit fare and tuition at the City University. Announcing a budget plan that he said amounted to "shock therapy," Beame charged that "those who control the money or have the power to raise the money . . . were involved in a concerted effort to make this city an object lesson and to force us to reach a balanced budget only through crippling cutbacks."

Despite Beame's complaints about the financial institutions, the private sector succeeded in gaining unprecedented power over the city's affairs. In May 1975 Governor Hugh Carey named a "blue ribbon" panel of corporate leaders to study the city's cash flow crisis. Within a few weeks Beame was being pressured to allow a group of "nonpolitical trustees" to take over the city's finances. This was soon accomplished through the creation of the Municipal Assistance Corporation and the Emergency Financial Control Board.

The key figure in both of these bodies was Felix Rohatyn of the investment banking firm Lazard Frères. Known to his dismay as Felix the Fixer, Rohatyn had made a name for himself helping the conglomerate ITT gobble up companies like Avis and Hartford Fire and Casualty, and putting together a plan that prevented the bankruptcy of many Wall Street brokerage houses during the slump of the early 1970s. As the new fiscal czar of New York, Rohatyn effectively had veto power over all city expenditures and labor contracts. He used this position to see to it that New York's finances were put back in order, by continuing to shrink the city's payroll, keeping a lid on wage levels, tapping public employee pension funds, and cutting more services. Somehow the concept of sacrifices never seemed to apply to Rohatyn's friends on Wall Street and in the banks, which continued to profit from selling the city's securities.

The lopsided imposition of austerity also characterized the terms demanded by the federal government when the Ford administration finally dropped its opposition to a bailout for New York. The loan plan was to be administered by Treasury Secretary William Simon, who made his position on sacrifices quite clear: "I have to have a complete assurance that wages are not going to be increased, or I'm not going to advance the money."

Although it was customary at the time to see these shifts in power as necessary to rescue the city from financial ruin, in retrospect it is clear that what happened was a fiscal coup d'état. Within a short period of time, the private sector and the federal government had managed to seize control of the nation's largest city and totally reorient its budgetary priorities. The fact that New York was a pacesetter in wages and benefits for municipal employees and in the services offered to its entire population was an extravagance that the city's new rulers were determined to end. Although the specific ideologies of these chieftains varied—Rohatyn was an advocate of business-government planning, Simon an apostle of laissez-faire—they agreed on one basic point: the poor and working people of New York had to be given a dose of fiscal discipline.

The Eroding Social Contract

The decision of business and government to crack the whip in New York in the mid-1970s was not arbitrary. It was a reaction to a vexing problem: the previous 10 years had been a time of great social upheaval, and New York had been at the center of it.

At the heart of this turbulence was growing unrest among those who had been excluded from the mass prosperity of the 1950s. Despite the hype about the affluent society, significant improvements in living standards were enjoyed mainly by white male production workers and the growing professional-managerial class. This occurred as many large companies abandoned their resistance to unionization and recognized that healthy profits were not necessarily incompatible with higher wages. The result was a postwar social contract between big business and organized labor by which pay levels were allowed to rise steadily as long as there were commensurate increases in productivity—and as long as unions did not seriously interfere with decision making in the workplace. The latter responsibility and related functions were the domain of a rapidly expanding cadre of relatively well paid middle managers and professionals.

The productivity deal between business and the better-situated white workers was in large measure made possible because there were poorly paid blacks doing the dirty work of industry and the service sector. Blacks and other minorities found themselves in a secondary labor market and limited to a second-rate standard of living. In 1959 the typical nonwhite male worker earned less than half that of his Caucasian counterpart. In some rural areas whites were also impoverished. This was the "other America" exposed by Michael Harrington in 1962.

The civil rights movement of the 1950s awakened expectations that intensified after John Kennedy took office. It is rarely recalled that in his famous "I Have a Dream" speech in 1963, Martin Luther King, Jr. alluded to economic as well as social demands. "In a sense we have come to our nation's Capital to cash a check," he declared, "a check that will give us upon demand the riches of freedom and the security of justice."

Faced with such demands, the liberal planners of Kennedy's Camelot and the Johnson administration realized they had to bring the excluded population closer to the mainstream of economic life. The result was a "human capital" strategy that sought to channel the frustrations of the poor in a vocational direction; hence, the Manpower Development and Training Act of 1962, the Vocational Rehabilitation Act of 1963, and, the crowning glory, the 1964 Economic Opportunity Act— Johnson's frontal assault in the War on Poverty.

Yet, from the very beginning, there were signs that the intended participants would not be satisfied with slow and far-from-certain integration into the system. Just before the Economic Opportunity Act became law, the first of the major ghetto riots of the sixties erupted in New York, beginning in Harlem and spreading in the July heat to Bedford-Stuyvesant and elsewhere. This social explosion, followed by another in the Watts section of Los Angeles in 1965 and dozens of other places over the next few years, put society on notice that the poor had their own agenda for social change.

In addition to ghetto riots, which are usually unfocused acts growing out of intense frustration, the urban poor also began to take action that was more targeted and productive. In New York, for instance, tenants in the rundown tenements of slum neighborhoods embarked on a rent strike movement, which at its height in 1964 involved more than 500 buildings. Disgusted with the condition of their apartments, rent strikers brought rodents caught in their homes to court proceedings and organized a Rats to Rockefeller action, in which hundreds of toy rodents were mailed to the office of Governor Nelson Rockefeller to protest the state's lack of action on housing problems.

The riots and rent strikes served as a prelude to a larger and more powerful struggle: the welfare rights movement. The movement, growing out of the discontent of recipients (mainly single women with young children) with the miserable standard of living on the dole, grew rapidly after the Poverty Rights Action Center organized a series of demonstrations of welfare mothers around the country in 1966. The National Welfare Rights Organization was founded that same year and expanded to a membership of 100 thousand at its height a few years later. Altering the words of a civil rights movement song—"We're gonna lay down our shufflin' shoes/Down by the welfare door/'Cause we ain't gonna shuffle anymore"—welfare protesters pushed the system to its limits, to highlight its inadequacies and to force changes.

The birth of militancy among welfare "clients" spawned a similar spirit of resistance among the public employees who were supposed to serve them (or control them, depending on one's point of view). The first major step in the transformation of meek and underpaid civil servants into angry and demanding workers was the 1965 strike of the Social Service Employees Union in New York.

The large wage increases and workload reductions won by the welfare workers opened the door to an avalanche of demands by other employees of state and local governments. Again the lead was taken by New York, where transit workers, sanitation workers, firefighters, even police officers staged strikes or wildcat actions in defiance of state laws and court injunctions. By 1968 a leading business magazine was noting with horror that public employees "increasingly look upon unions as a lever to pry loose more money." Two years later the "disease" spread to federal post office workers, who staged a nationwide wildcat walkout.

The Circulation of Struggle

While public employees and clients were making their material demands felt by the state, many other segments of society were also challenging the status quo in one way or another. The new spirit of defiance spread from those on the margins of society to those who enjoyed many of its privileges.

The civil rights movement continued, and some activists branched out in more militant directions. Prisoners became politicized and staged rebellions like the Attica uprising in 1971. A feminist movement arose to challenge the subjugation of women in the home, the workplace, and all other institutions. Gays began to fight back against discrimination and police harassment. Native Americans emerged from their isolation and cried out against broken promises. Environmental and consumer activists launched assaults on corporate irresponsibility. Several CIA agents and high-level military analysts leaked sensitive documents and became outspoken critics of U.S. foreign policy. Members of the military were also resisting the war in Vietnam and challenging the tradition of blind obedience to orders.

Perhaps the greatest degree of radicalization occurred on the campuses. Large numbers of students rejected their designated career paths and instead devoted their energies to fighting the war and other injustices. Among the targets was big business. Protests against individual companies like Dow Chemical, which manufactured the napalm used by U.S. troops in Vietnam, evolved into a general disdain for the corporate world. Pollster Daniel Yankelovich noted that "some of the demands arising directly or indirectly out of the student revolution include a desire to regulate business more closely, to curb its power and influence, to restrict its overseas investments, and to prevent it from growing through increased use of technology."

In 1969 the business magazine *Fortune* felt compelled to devote a special issue to the rebellion of youth—who, one editor wrote, were "challenging the institutions . . . in which the democratic capitalist order is rooted." A poll commissioned by the magazine found that nearly 50 percent of young people agreed with the statement that the U.S. was a "sick" society.

Part of that sickness was the degree of waste and what might be called mis-consumption. While welfare recipients and public workers were pushing the traditional (though in their cases, overdue) demand for more money, the student rebels and other movements were questioning the qualitative rather than quantitative aspects of U.S. living standards. The American definition of "the good life"—later to be ridiculed by singer Tracy Chapman as "mountains o' things"—was found to be bankrupt: unfair to the poor at home and in the third world, and ultimately oppressive even to its beneficiaries. As two New Left theorists wrote in 1971:

> The major objection to the capitalist class and the capitalist system is not the "things" possessed by a few, but the fact that capitalism is a

power over our lives which forces us to do wasteful and meaningless things when we want to do something radically different and marvelously new.

The Blue-Collar Blues

By the early seventies the extent of rebellion was nearly complete. After the outbursts of anger among those who had been excluded from the new affluence, the radicalization of public employees, and the spread of the ferment to virtually all parts of the population, including the upper-middle-class students who were supposed to be getting ready to join the professional-managerial class which controls business and government, there seemed to be one holdout: the blue-collar workers who had been among the prime beneficiaries of "mass" prosperity.

For quite a while it was assumed that the traditional working class was outside of—and hostile to—the maelstrom. These workers were celebrated by conservative politicians as the "silent majority" who rejected the chorus of demands for change. The views of blue-collar America were said to be symbolized by the "hard hat" assault on anti-war demonstrators outside the New York Stock Exchange in May 1970.

It is true that blue-collar workers were somewhat slow catching up with the zeitgeist, especially on foreign policy. Yet by the late 1960s upheaval was beginning to appear in the workplace, and when it came to fighting oppressive conditions on the job, workers were anything but silent.

The initial glimmerings of a new labor militancy came in two areas. The first was in the coalfields. Frustrated with the limited benefits of a labor-management truce orchestrated by United Mine Workers president John L. Lewis in the 1950s, miners, like the poor, entered the 1960s with pent-up desires. The new decade saw a growing wave of wildcat strikes that culminated in a struggle that succeeded in forcing Congress to enact a national compensation program for victims of black lung disease. Similar pressures helped bring about the passage of the Occupational Safety and Health Act of 1970.

The other crucible was among the young black workers who had made their way into the auto factories of Detroit. New organizations like the Dodge Revolutionary Union Movement and the League of Revolutionary Black Workers sprang up in the late 1960s to challenge what they saw as the racism of the United Auto Workers as well as that of management. Wildcat strikes organized by these groups unnerved auto managers who had become accustomed to an orderly relationship with the UAW. The challenges by black workers helped their white counterparts voice their own anger. Union officials in the auto industry were worried enough by the unrest that they tried to use a 1970 strike as, in the words of the *Wall Street Journal*, "an escape valve for the frustrations of workers bitter about what they consider intolerable working conditions."

Autoworker unrest, enflamed by frustration over long hours and assembly line speedups, was not so easily extinguished. Sometimes the outbursts were unorganized, as in the rising rate of absenteeism or individual acts of violence. In 1970 a black worker who had been suspended from his job returned with a rifle to the axle plant where he worked and fatally shot his foreman. A jury later found the worker not guilty by reason of temporary insanity brought on by workplace conditions.

In other cases the resistance was collective. The most famous labor rebellion of the era took place in the General Motors showcase factory in Lordstown, Ohio, in 1972. Lordstown was intended as an experiment by GM in the intensification and speeding up of the labor process; it ended up becoming a national symbol of worker unrest, or what the press called the "blue-collar blues." It also helped to color the pessimistic conclusions of the federal government's special report, *Work in America*, which found that "absenteeism, wildcat strikes, turnover, and industrial sabotage [have] become an increasingly significant part of the cost of doing business."

This statement, made in the even tones of a government report, amounted to an obituary notice for the productivity deal between labor and management. Workers were no longer willing to cede all control over workplace conditions to management in exchange for regular wage increases. The wage itself became political—not something to be determined by rising efficiency but instead by the power of workers to demand more.

An Excess of Democracy?

The late sixties and early seventies were a remarkable period in U.S. history. Just about every facet of American life was being challenged, criticized, subverted, turned inside out. Authority was questioned, dirty secrets were exposed, customs were overturned, taboos were broken, values were rejected, alternatives were sought, "revolution" became part of everyday vocabulary. A 1975 report by the elite Trilateral Commission complained that the U.S. was suffering from "an excess of democracy."

The turbulence of this period undermined the foundation on which postwar prosperity had been built. Once those who were deliberately excluded from the deal made it clear they wanted in, and many of the intended participants were challenging the terms of the "contract," the arrangement ceased to be viable. The combined force of business and government was not able or willing to provide prosperity that was truly mass in nature, nor was it able to accommodate the demands for radical qualitative changes in working and social conditions. Instead, the response of those holding the reins of economic and political power was to apply a dose of hard times to bring the population back in line.

The role of economic downturns in taming labor (by raising unemployment levels and lowering wages) had long been recognized. In 1943 the Polish economist Michal Kalecki noted that although boom periods were more profitable for employers, they dreaded these periods of low joblessness because workers became emboldened. " 'Discipline in the factories' and 'political stability,' " Kalecki wrote, "are more appreciated by the business leaders than profits." In the past, however, the dynamics of the business cycle had been largely outside the control of business and government. Employers benefited from the effects of recession on workers, yet they also risked financial ruin themselves. In the postwar period, the federal government began exercising a much greater degree of control over the nation's economy, but the aim was to keep stoking the engine of growth.

The early 1970s saw the application of these new macroeconomic powers for the opposite purpose. The Nixon administration used restrictive monetary and fiscal policies to end the boom of the 1960s and bring about the engineered recession of 1970. The next step was the announcement in August 1971 of Nixon's New Economic Policy, which instituted a 90-day freeze on wages and prices. Of course, wages were frozen a lot more solid than prices, and the pattern was repeated in the various mandatory and quasi-voluntary controls that followed.

After the expiration of the controls, Nixon's economic planners and then those of the Ford administration continued pursuing policies that promoted economic contraction. By the middle of the decade unemployment was higher than it had ever been since the Great Depression of the 1930s. At the same time the purchasing power of those who held onto their jobs was being eroded by record rates of inflation.

There were, of course, changes in the international scene that helped put the U.S. into this new economic condition. The collapse of the dollar-dominated world monetary system, the rise in energy prices, and the heightened competitive challenge from Europe and Japan served to undermine America's financial stability. Yet the real drama of the 1970s was the transformation of the domestic order.

While the corporate world publicly bemoaned the economic down-turn, insisting it had been caused entirely by external factors like the "oil shock," many leading businessmen privately welcomed this new state of affairs. "We need a sharp recession," said one executive at a mid-1970s conference of corporate leaders. "This recession," another said, "will bring about the healthy respect for economic values that the Depression did."

This prescription for discipline was also implied in an article by Felix Rohatyn that drew parallels between the situation of New York and that of the entire country: "A big part of the problem is simply that we don't work as hard as we used to. Our trade deficit with Japan, a country whose energy problem is far more severe and serious than our own, can really be called a balance-of-work-ethic deficit."

What was to workers an economic disaster—widespread joblessness and accelerating prices—was to business a chance to regain its control of the system. This difference in perspective is behind the confusion of interpretations of the word "crisis." In everyday speech and in journal-ism, a crisis is seen as a catastrophe. Yet, to be precise, a crisis is a turning point; in medicine, it is a decisive change in a serious disease, leading either to death or recovery. The economic troubles of the 1970s were precisely such a process. The snowballing unrest and re-bellion among the poor, public employees, students, blue-collar work-ers, and many other parts of the population constituted, from the point of view of business, a threatening disease. The cure was a radical change in the economic environment.

A group of left-wing economists who wrote *Beyond the Waste Land* have called this sharp turn in policy the Great Repression:

> With no swift and decisive victory for business in sight, the macroeco-nomic decision makers prepared for a prolonged period of programmed economic stagnation, hoping at least that high levels of unemployment in the long run would bring labor to heel. The trench-warfare strategy involved a waiting game: douse the economy in cold water long enough, and labor will succumb.

Succumb it did. Throughout the rest of the 1970s workers were bombarded with the message that hard times had arrived. The "limits to growth" became the catchphrase of the day. All the institutions of society seemed to be preoccupied with cutbacks, austerity, and the "politics of less."

At the federal level, restrictive economic policies continued—in fact, intensified—after the Democrats regained the White House in 1976. Problems with energy prices and general inflation were resolved in a most unprogressive manner. Budget and tax policies were oriented to the agenda of business ideologues rather than the social demands of the sixties.

The imposition of austerity on New York served as the most unambiguous signal of the change in climate. It showed that business leaders and conservative politicians were prepared to assume extraordinary powers in order to reorient fiscal policies and squeeze labor. If workers and the poor could be tamed in New York, then such an act of repression could be accomplished anywhere. As the publisher of the journal *New York Affairs* put it in 1976: "Whether or not the promises of social and economic entitlements of the 1960s can be rolled back to a lower order of magnitude without social upheaval is what is being tested in New York City."

The Rise of Regulation

Tightening up the economic climate through a period of recession was not sufficient for business in undoing the damage of the late sixties and early seventies. Corporate America also needed to reassert itself in the ideological and policy arenas. For within a short period of time the student, environmental, and consumer movements had succeeded in getting Congress to take a much tougher position on the regulation of business activities.

Ralph Nader's 1965 book, *Unsafe at Any Speed*, on the hazards of American-made automobiles, was a key event in the emergence of this new mood. Actually, the book itself did not make much of a splash when it was released. But when General Motors, whose Chevrolet Corvair was the main subject of the exposé, admitted that it had hired private detectives to spy on Nader in order to find out something to discredit him, the consumer advocate became an instant celebrity and his volume a best-seller. Within this climate it did not take Congress long to pass the National Traffic and Motor Vehicle Safety Act of 1966, which for the first time set federal safety standards for the production of America's favorite vehicles.

This was followed by the Fair Packaging and Labeling Act, the Federal Hazardous Substances Act, the Federal Meat Inspection Act, the National Gas Pipeline Safety Act, the Truth in Lending Act, the Flammable Fabrics Act, and the Child Protection Act. According to business historian David Vogel, "Such an outpouring of consumer legislation by the federal government was unprecedented in the history of business-government relations in the United States." It was also remarkable, Vogel added, that the proposed laws "were often strengthened, rather than weakened, as they made their way through Congress."

Federal lawmakers, following public opinion and receiving cooperation from the Nixon administration, brought about another wave of regulation beginning in 1969. Three new government agencies—the Environmental Protection Agency, the Occupational Safety and Health Administration, and the Consumer Products Safety Commission—were created as a result of laws that dramatically expanded the role of government in controlling the harmful effects of products and the production process on workers, consumers, and the general public. Perhaps even more daunting to the private sector were the Clean Air Act Amendments of 1970, which set strict timetables for reducing airborne pollution. Additional laws covering pesticides and water pollution were passed in 1972.

The arrival of the economic slump in 1973 quickly curbed the enthusiasm of Congress for regulating business. Over the next few years, construction of the Alaska pipeline was approved, strip-mining legislation was defeated, OSHA was weakened, an effort to establish a federal consumer protection agency was turned back, and calls amid the energy crisis to break up the integrated oil companies came to naught.

Corporate America was not yet out of the woods—and it was their own fault. As part of their effort to regain influence in Washington, a number of large companies had made secret and illegal contributions to Richard Nixon's 1972 reelection campaign. Early revelations regarding Associated Milk Producers and ITT led to the discovery by Watergate prosecutors of a pattern of illicit corporate contributions. Among the companies that ended up pleading guilty to this offense were American Airlines, Carnation, Goodyear Tire & Rubber, Greyhound, Gulf Oil, Northrop, Phillips Petroleum, and 3-M.

Watergate investigators also came upon evidence that a number of large companies were maintaining secret slush funds out of which bribes were being paid to obtain business abroad. The dimensions of the scandal that emerged went far beyond anyone's expectations. Responding to pressures from the Securities and Exchange Commission, more than 150 major corporations admitted making illegal or questionable payments. The aerospace company Lockheed was especially generous in this regard. It admitted to having paid out some $25 million from 1970 to 1975 to officials not only in the baksheesh-ridden Middle East but also in Japan, Italy, and the Netherlands.

Business Fights Back

By the middle of the seventies, American business found itself at a crossroads. The atmosphere of economic crisis had succeeded in dampening the social turbulence of the previous dozen years, and Congress was slowly being wooed back from the consumer and environmental movements. Yet the revelations about corruption and public suspicions over the true origins of the oil crisis made it clear that corporate America still had far to go in regaining the cooperation and trust of the population. Moreover, the fact that Congress was seriously considering the Humphrey-Hawkins bill, which would have required the federal government to promote full employment, showed that the labor problem had not been completely put to rest.

Business leaders could have waited for the storms to blow over and the gentle winds of favorable public opinion to drift back their way. But they didn't. Instead of mourning their loss of influence, top corporate executives followed the lead of Rohatyn & Co. in New York and began seeking a more direct role in shaping national policy.

At the center of this new offensive was the Business Roundtable, an organization consisting of the chief executives of nearly 200 of the largest and most powerful companies in the land. Formed quietly in 1972, the Roundtable began to assume a much more conspicuous and aggressive posture in 1976. Within two years the group, Roundtable, headed by Irving Shapiro of Du Pont, was in high gear, its members personally calling and visiting members of Congress and federal bureaucrats to push the interests of business on a wide range of issues. The Roundtable was instrumental, for instance, in turning the proposed federal consumer protection agency into, as *Fortune* gleefully put it, "a ghostly heap of rubble—a war memorial to the new firepower of business on Capitol Hill."

Before long, business and its allies were adopting some of the rhetoric of social movements, including that of presenting the corporate sector as an oppressed minority. Mobil stepped up the level of ideological confrontation by running a series of advertisements on newspaper op-ed pages depicting business executives as "radicals" and government regulators as "reactionaries." Conservative economist Herbert Stein wrote a column in the *Wall Street Journal* headlined "Businessmen of the World, Unite!" that urged executives to be bolder in opposing unfavorable federal policies. "Businessmen need to demonstrate in Washington as the civil rights activists have demonstrated," Stein declared. "We need a businessmen's liberation movement. . . . We need a few businessmen to chain themselves to the White House fence."

Civil disobedience did not catch on in the corporate set, but business did keep up the pressure and got results. Conservative foundations like Smith Richardson, Olin, and Scaife poured millions of dollars into think tanks that spewed out free-market positions on a wide range of policy issues. Right-wing legal foundations used the Nader model to help business fight government regulation through the courts. Groups like Accuracy in Media railed against a supposed anti-business bias in the press. Journals like *Commentary*, *Public Interest*, and *Regulation* churned out endless articles challenging liberal principles and promoting laissez-faire policies. And when ideology was not enough, there was always cash. Campaign contributions from wealthy individuals and corporate political action committees flowed freely to members of Congress. As Justin Dart, chairman of Dart Industries, bluntly told a reporter in 1978, talking to politicians is "a fine thing, but with a little money they hear you better."

As a result of this stampede of conservative initiatives, most of the populist projects of the Carter administration fell by the wayside, as did various efforts of public interest groups and organized labor. The latter was stunned at the massive lobbying effort mounted by business groups in 1978 to defeat a reform of federal labor law meant to encourage organizing and deter union-busting. The new climate was captured by Philip Shabecoff in a 1979 *New York Times Magazine* article: "Although the Republican Party, the traditional bulwark of business, is out of power, public policy has become increasingly responsive to the needs and desires of industry."

The Capital Gains Offensive

Those needs and desires were not limited to regulatory issues. The second front in the corporate offensive had to do with the other major area of contention between business and government: taxes.

In the early 1970s there emerged in the business world the idea that amid scarcities of fuels and other natural resources there was another shortage not getting its due. This was a supposed shortage of capital. The notion, promoted by figures like William Simon during his tenure as Secretary of the Treasury, was that corporations were finding it increasingly difficult to find money for investment from either internal sources, because of faltering profit rates, or external ones, because governments raising money for social programs were supposedly "crowding out" private borrowers. The salvation of capitalism, so it was claimed, required reduced social spending and changes in the tax code to make more money available for "capital formation."

While the overall theory of capital shortage was not universally embraced in the corporate world, there was great enthusiasm over the call for tax relief in the name of promoting investment. Seeing the success that Howard Jarvis and his Proposition 13 movement were having in fighting property taxes in California, business decided to embark on a tax revolt of its own.

This took the form of a forceful lobbying effort in 1978 in support of reductions in the capital gains tax. For decades business interests had promoted preferential tax treatment of capital gains income, arguing that this encouraged wealthy people to invest their money in job-creating ventures. Tax reformers, seeing this as a giveaway to the rich, sought to treat capital gains more like ordinary income, and the loophole was tightened in 1969 and 1976. Now business was determined to tip the balance of power back in its direction.

Leading the charge was a group called the American Council on Capital Formation, which was headed by former Treasury official Charls Walker and whose membership included the corporate elite, including the Business Roundtable. Walker put his mighty resources behind a bill introduced by Rep. William Steiger of Wisconsin while financing a study by Chase Econometrics, which concluded, as one observer put it, "that a capital gains cut would do everything but cure dandruff." Walker's efforts were a success. Congress cut the tax rate on capital gains and increased the portion of gains that were exempt from taxation.

Walker had taken a special interest of direct benefit to only a small segment of the population and turned it into a burning issue for politicians of both parties. "Within a relatively short period of time," he later boasted, "capital formation has entered the lexicon of 'good' words—not quite equal to Home and Mother, but still a public policy goal few would disagree with."

Fusion on the Right

As the 1970s were drawing to a close, the position of business was radically different from that at the beginning of the decade. Corporate executives had gone from being pariahs in the eyes of much of the population to being touted as the new heroes. College students were idolizing Steven Jobs rather than Che Guevera. Government regulation, previously regarded as a noble effort to control the ravages of industry, was now depicted as a form of oppression. The logic of investment incentives, of helping business in the hope that new jobs would be created, replaced the idea that direct social spending was the cure for poverty and inequality. The creed of capitalism—self-interest, competition, profit—was restored to its role as America's state religion.

To the extent that modern U.S. history has consisted of pendulum movements between corporate supremacy and populist insurgency, the developments of the 1970s might have amounted to nothing more than a temporary swing in the direction of business. And the arrival of the new decade would probably have shown signs that the momentum was shifting back to the progressive side.

Yet the normal ebb and flow was disrupted by an unusual confluence of conservative political forces. In the past there had been a great gulf between corporate Republicans and those who used the conservative label. In fact, the latter group was dominated by right-wingers of the *National Review* variety, who were on the fringes of mainstream politics and seen by many as just a few steps away from the Ku Klux Klan. During the late 1970s, as the political center of gravity veered to the Right, anti-government views started to become the new orthodoxy. It was suddenly socially acceptable for corporate leaders to espouse views once dismissed as ravings akin to those of the crackpots who want to abolish paper money and end fluoridation of water supplies.

In 1980 Ronald Reagan stepped in to solidify and exploit this new fusion on the Right. He brought together everyone from chief executives of the Fortune 500 to idiosyncratic economists like Arthur Laffer and religious fundamentalists like Jerry Falwell behind a program meant to take the conservative initiatives of the 1970s far beyond what anyone thought possible. No longer content with merely pushing the pendulum back to the Right, Reagan intended nothing less than a revolution in the role of the federal government.

After taking office, this was exactly the course he set for his administration. Regulation of business was put on the path to oblivion by free-marketeers who were appointed to head the regulatory agencies. Policies aimed at promoting environmental protection were replaced with efforts to open up federal lands to mining and development. Dubious business practices were given a green light with indications that antitrust enforcement would be eased and the administration would seek relaxation of the 1977 law outlawing bribery of foreign officials.

Fiscal policy was also transformed. Budget Director David Stockman declared war on the idea of government entitlements and set out to slash a wide range of social programs. Congress put up some resistance on the budget cuts, but were totally swept up in Reagan's tax plan, which was dressed up in populist terms but was in reality primarily of benefit to business and the wealthy.

Reagan also took steps to ensure that the political upheaval of the past did not return. One of his early acts was to pardon two FBI officials who had been convicted of authorizing illegal break-ins at the homes of antiwar activists in the early 1970s. Then he established a policy of domestic surveillance that led to widespread spying and harassment of opponents of the Administration's policies in Central America. Those who might try to keep track of government misdeeds were discouraged by a tightening of secrecy rules and a weakening of the Freedom of Information Act.

The new climate of repression also extended to unions. The Reagan administration set the tone for labor relations in the 1980s by smashing the air traffic controllers' strike and literally destroying the union involved. Free-market ideologues appointed to the National Labor Relations Board tilted the agency sharply toward management and gave comfort to union-busters.

The Age of Greed

In short, what emerged in the early 1980s was an unprecedented alliance of business, the federal government, and the Right, all dedicated to a radical restructuring of the U.S. political economy. What started as a reassertion of corporate and conservative values in the previous decade turned into a virtual coup d'état. As in New York, business interests stepped in to exercise much more direct control over public affairs. But what made things worse at the federal level was that the power now resided not with corporate liberals like Rohatyn who still saw the need to maintain some degree of social equilibrium, but rather with right-wing crusaders who were prepared to pursue their agenda regardless of the consequences.

The fundamental objective of the new conservative juggernaut can be summed up in a single word: greed. The forces of the Right were no longer satisfied with regaining the ground lost in the late sixties and early seventies; now they wanted it all. Reagan encouraged them to think that the country could be transported back to the supposed golden age before the New Deal. The Right's dream was that the concessions the Roosevelt administration had made to workers and the poor so that capitalism would survive the crisis of the 1930s could now be withdrawn. Unions would no longer have the protection of federal law in organizing and representing workers. Those same workers would no longer be cushioned from the effects of the business cycle by unemployment compensation. The poor would no longer have a call on a significant portion of federal outlays. Environmentalists and consumer advocates would no longer be interfering in the affairs of business. Antitrust laws would not inhibit the concentration of economic power. Tax and budget policies would no longer redistribute income downward. Government would return to its original functions: protecting property and fighting wars.

As it turned out, the country was not ready for a complete return to the laws of the jungle. Nevertheless, big business and the Right managed to inflict a fair amount of damage in their campaign. The following chapters analyze the setbacks experienced by workers and the poor in a number of major areas.

Reagan got elected in 1980 by asking people whether they were better off than they were four years earlier. Most voters answered no and were led to believe that Reagan would make a difference. He did, but the difference turned out to be that the deterioration was accelerated. Poverty rates rose, real wages sank, and the distribution of income grew more unequal. Yet through most of the 1980s the truth got lost in the torrent of hype and obfuscation flowing from the White House. Perhaps the Reagan administration's greatest achievement was to promote the impoverishment of the working population while riveting public attention on the enhanced prosperity of the few. What was once called voodoo economics also had a strong dose of hypnosis in it.

Now that the Great Communicator has returned to his reward in California, it is easier to see the harm wrought by the policies of greed. George Bush's inferior skill at public relations makes it possible to pierce the bogus optimism that characterized the preceding administration. Another advantage is that a flood of belated revelations—about scandals involving the Department of Housing and Urban Development, the Food and Drug Administration, military contracting, and so forth—have demonstrated that Reaganism was corrupt as well as unfair.

Yet as far as economic policy is concerned, the ideology of trickle-down remains stubbornly alive. The fact that an administration can simultaneously seek a substantial cut in the capital gains tax and a massive bailout of the crooked savings and loan industry (to be paid for by taxpayers), while opposing a decent increase in the minimum wage, is a sign that we have a long way to go in returning to some semblance of a humane economy.

THREE

Robin Hood in Reverse:
Fiscal Policies in the 1980s

"THE prosperity of the middle and lower classes depends on the good fortune and light taxes of the rich." These words were written in 1924 by Andrew Mellon, the tycoon who took pains to reduce levies on his fellow millionaires while serving as Secretary of the Treasury. Yet the sentiment just as accurately describes the credo of trickle-down economics that took hold of America in the early 1980s and quickly became the dominant ideology of a wide spectrum of politicians and policymakers.

Whether called supply-side economics, Reaganomics, or "voodoo economics," as George Bush denigrated it during one of his earlier incarnations, it amounted to the same thing: the federal government was reoriented to the task of using spending and tax policies to redistribute income upward to the highest strata of the social hierarchy. The welfare state, never very extensive in the U.S. to begin with, was scaled back, forcing workers and the poor to depend more on the tyranny of the market.

Ronald Reagan suggested to blacks in 1981 that his cutbacks would liberate them from the "bondage" of federal programs. What the self-styled Great Emancipator of our day did not say was that his underground railroad led not to freedom but to lower living standards for blacks as well as much of the rest of the population.

"P.T. Barnum, Move Over"

The fiscal revolution was plotted by a coterie of obscure economists, pamphleteers, right-wing populist politicians, and editorial writers for the *Wall Street Journal*. This eclectic group of outsiders boldly stepped in to fill the void left by the disarray conventional economics had fallen into as a result of the stagflation of the 1970s. Declaring Keynesian demand-oriented approaches bankrupt, this new group proclaimed themselves "supply-siders." They concerned themselves with not how much people had to spend but rather what incentives there were for people to produce.

The greatest disincentive, they maintained, was the supposedly crushing weight of federal taxes. Alleviate this burden, they said, and the economy would enter a perpetual boom as people felt free to produce and invest at a feverish pitch, knowing that the fruits of their labors would not be devoured by the revenuers in Washington.

The magic of tax cuts was not an original idea with the supply-siders. In fact, it was one of the main tools used by Keynesians to stimulate aggregate demand, as in the famous tax cut proposed by President Kennedy in 1963 and enacted the following year. The difference was that the Kennedy cut was aimed at all taxpayers, while Reagan & Company were acting in the earlier tradition of Andrew Mellon in concerning themselves most with providing relief to the rich.

There was also a dissimilarity at the macroeconomic level. Whereas the Keynesians argued that squeezing federal tax revenues directly served to stimulate gross national product, the supply-siders claimed, using a simple graph called the Laffer Curve, that in a tax reduction even the government would come out ahead, since the revenues, albeit at lower rates, from an expanded volume of economic activity would be higher.

It was this kind of Pollyanna-like theorizing that kept many established economists highly skeptical of supply-side claims. Walter Heller, who served as Kennedy's chief economic adviser, dismissed them with a wave of sarcasm: "Sound the trumpets and hear the heralds: There is, after all, such a thing as a free lunch! And it's not soft-headed liberals but hard-headed conservatives that bear the glad tidings. . . . Lunch is not only free, we get a bonus for eating it. P.T. Barnum, move over."

What was merely an economics fad in the late 1970s became the state religion in 1981 with the inauguration of Ronald Reagan. The B-actor turned conservative idol embraced this new ideological package and wasted no time using the Presidency to pursue the supply-side agenda. While some orthodox supply-siders downplayed the importance of budget cuts, Reagan inextricably linked a huge tax reduction to his old passion for cutting social spending.

Congress was enchanted by the supply-side promises, and in 1981 the Reagan program sailed through the legislature. Yet fate was initially not so kind to the practitioners of this new economics. Instead of the anticipated boom, the enactment of the new fiscal program was followed by a severe recession that propelled the unemployment rate up into double digits. The budget deficit began ballooning, and the great investment boom never occurred.

The economy did subsequently enter into a relatively strong recovery, though as we have seen, that has not stopped the erosion of living standards. Moreover, despite the stream of propaganda from the White House, the upturn was due not to supply-side initiatives but instead to unacknowledged demand-side ones. Without admitting it, Reagan was pursuing a kind of Keynesianism—the military variety. Instead of pumping up demand through social spending, he was doing it by feeding the Pentagon and the defense contractors, while promoting tax cuts that mainly helped the rich.

As the *Economist* magazine of London candidly put it in 1984: "America is booming today thanks to an anti-inflationary Federal Reserve, over which Mr. Reagan has little control, and to a demand-led recovery based on a huge federal budget deficit, for which he can take full credit. The name for this is turbo-charged Keynesianism."

The Right's Trojan Horse

What was so insidious about the supply-siders was that they took a genuine dissatisfaction with the tax system felt by virtually the entire population and channeled it into a program designed primarily to aid the few. The populist discontent, expressed by the Proposition 13 property tax revolt and Jimmy Carter's attack on the tax-deductible three-martini lunch, got corrupted into an assault on progressive taxation (i.e., the principle that those with higher incomes should pay higher rates).

The anti-tax passion was so intense that crucial facts got swept away in the tidal wave of anti-government zeal—a sentiment that quite remarkably was expressed by the head of government himself, Ronald Reagan. The first piece of ignored information was that the tax burden in the U.S., rather than being in the prohibitive range detected by the supply-siders, was light compared to most other advanced capitalist countries. In 1980 total tax revenue in the U.S. was only 30.7 percent of gross domestic product—a rate that was lower than 17 other countries in the Organization for Economic Cooperation and Development. The average for countries in the European Community alone was more than 39 percent.

Another flight from reality by the supply-siders was the claim that their constituency—wealthy individuals and corporations—were facing such high levels of taxation that they had little incentive to invest. Many tears were shed over the supposed confiscatory effects of the top federal income tax rate of 70 percent. The problem was that the supply-siders conveniently ignored the difference between statutory and effective tax rates.

Very few rich people paid that 70 percent rate (which in any event applied not to all their income but only that above $215,000). Thanks to all manner of tax shelters and other forms of legal tax avoidance, many members of the upper class rarely had to make out checks to the Internal Revenue Service.

The result was that even before the supply-siders got to work, the tax system had lost much of its progressive character. In 1980, according to analysis by Brookings Institution tax expert Joseph Pechman, effective rates of combined federal, state, and local taxes were essentially flat across the income spectrum. Depending on the assumptions made about where the ultimate burden falls for corporate income and payroll taxes, Pechman showed how effective rates could be seen as actually *dropping* from more than 30 percent at the lowest income level to 22 percent at the top; at best, the rates rose from about 20 percent among the low-income population to only 27 percent among the country club set.

Corporations also had little reason to complain. Throughout the 1960s and 1970s the tax code was frequently revised to provide incentives for business. Aside from the breaks given to specific industries, the statutory rate for corporations was reduced from 52 percent in 1960 to 46 percent in 1980. Thanks to the ingenuity of high-priced tax lawyers, the effective rate came down even faster, sinking from 38.9 to 22.5 percent in the same period.

With all of these annoying details safely under wraps, the supply-siders who took over the reins of power with the advent of Reagan persuaded Congress in 1981 to enact one of the most outrageous pieces of tax legislation in U.S. history. The Economic Recovery Tax Act was billed as a boon for the entire population, but the federal beneficence was skewed heavily toward the affluent. This was so for several reasons:

- The use of across-the-board cuts in rates (5 percent the first year and 10 percent in each of the next two years) was, rather than being equitable, a way of giving much larger absolute amounts of relief to those with higher incomes.
- Unlike earlier tax cuts, personal exemptions and the standard deduction—provisions that do the most to help lower-income taxpayers—were not increased.
- The degree of progressivity was further diminished by substantial decreases in the capital gains tax and estate taxes—two measures that went a long way in preserving America's lopsided distribution of wealth.

In case there were any lingering illusions about a populist tinge to the tax act, they were shattered once and for all by Reagan budget director David Stockman in his candid comments to journalist William Greider. "The hard part of the supply-side tax cut," Stockman admitted, "is dropping the top rate from 70 to 50 percent—the rest of it is a secondary matter. . . . In order to make this palatable as a political matter, you had to bring down all the brackets. But, I mean, Kemp-Roth [the original tax cut bill] was always a Trojan horse to bring down the top rate."

The 1981 tax act was also a Trojan horse for virtually dismantling the corporate income tax. Conservatives have long argued that taxing corporate profits should be abolished, saying out of one side of their mouth that it inhibits investment and out of the other that the tax is passed on to consumers and workers in the form of higher prices and lower wages, making it counterproductive. Although most politicians were loath to adopt a position such as this, which smacked of a giveaway to business at the expense of the bulk of individual taxpayers, the 1981 law went a long way toward reaching essentially the same goal.

This was accomplished, first of all, by the creation of an incredibly liberal system of depreciation. The Accelerated Cost Recovery System ended the practice of linking depreciation schedules to the useful life of assets, thus allowing corporations to recover their capital expenses much more quickly. Another bonanza was the "safe-harbor leasing" provision that allowed companies to buy and sell unused tax credits and depreciation deductions.

Just how great was this embarrassment of riches for corporate America was made clear in reports issued by Citizens for Tax Justice, a public interest group based in Washington. CTJ found that as a result of the 1981 law dozens of major companies ended up paying little or no federal income tax, despite their many millions of dollars in profit. High on the list was Ronald Reagan's old employer, General Electric, which in the period from 1981 to 1983 not only managed to avoid paying anything to the Feds on its $6.5 billion in profits but actually got refunds totaling $283 million.

In aggregate terms, the share of federal budget receipts represented by corporate levies, once about a third of the total, plummeted from 12.5 percent in 1980 to 6.2 percent in 1983. The corporate income tax did not have to be abolished; it was rapidly disappearing.

While corporations were paying less, most individual taxpayers were shelling out more. This was true not only in terms of relative shares but also in absolute amounts. The reason is that while federal income taxes were being reduced, federal payroll taxes continued their relentless rise. These taxes consist of the payments employees and employers must make to finance the Social Security system, which includes not only retirement benefits but also disability payments, Medicare hospitalization coverage, and unemployment compensation.

The Social Security tax rate climbed from 5.85 percent in 1977 to 7.05 percent in 1985. At the same time, the maximum earnings subject to the tax rose from $16,500 to $39,600, which meant that the maximum payment jumped from about $1,650 to more than $5,500.

Contributions to these federal insurance programs are certainly a socially desirable way of shoring up the living standards of the elderly and disabled. What is much less tolerable is that the method of financing is quite regressive. By setting a flat tax rate and a ceiling on taxable earnings, the system is forcing lower-wage workers to assume a burden that is proportionally much greater than their well-to-do counterparts. In fact, many people at the bottom of the income ladder pay more in social insurance contributions than they do in federal income tax.

Overall, the tax changes of the early 1980s were no boon for the working poor. An Urban Institute study found that from 1980 to 1984 the total federal tax bite faced by the lowest income quintile of families increased while the highest quintile experienced a slight decline.

Reform and Bamboozlement

It was not long after the enactment of the 1981 tax bill that the supply-side spell began to wear off. The equity issues were not addressed, but Congress began to worry about the impact of the tax giveaways on the federal deficit. New legislation in 1982 and 1984 tinkered with the code to raise modest amounts of revenue. Still there remained a strong public belief that the system was in need of more fundamental repair. The Reagan administration and Congress tapped that sentiment in enacting legislation that represented the most far-reaching alteration of the tax code in decades. The Tax Reform Act of 1986 swept away the 14-bracket system of tax rates and replaced it with merely two—15 and 28 percent. While bringing the top rate down so low, the bill restricted many provisions that had been used by middle-class and affluent people to shelter large portions of their income from taxation. The theory was that the lower rates would lure the moneyed class from their tax shelters and better-paid workers from their off-the-books moonlighting in the underground economy.

On the plus side, the legislation did help lower-wage workers by increasing the standard deduction, the earned income tax credit, and the personal exemption (while phasing out the latter for the affluent). This served to bring the threshold at which poor families had to begin paying income tax back above the poverty line; it had fallen far below that level as a result of the regressive features of the 1981 law. In this way the law removed millions of poor families from the income tax rolls.

At the same time, businesses were subjected to stricter minimum-tax rules, which sharply reduced the number of corporate freeloaders paying little or nothing to the IRS. The law did reduce the statutory corporate rate from 46 to 34 percent, but depreciation schedules were stretched out and the investment tax credit was repealed. The upshot was that corporations were supposed to pay an additional $120 billion in taxes from 1987 to 1991, while individuals were supposed to enjoy a reduction of the same amount. Citizens for Tax Justice found that among a sample of 250 large corporations the average effective tax rate in 1988 was 26.5 percent. This was still below the statutory rate but well above the 14.3 percent average effective rate from 1981 to 1985.

On the negative side, the law all but abolished the progressive income tax—which Ed Meese once labeled "immoral"—and replaced it with a system in which middle-income workers are lumped in the same bracket with the likes of David Rockefeller and Rupert Murdoch. Apologists for the law say that it is better to have the upper class paying 28 percent than maintaining loopholes that permit many of them to pay zero percent. Yet many lower-income taxpayers justifiably feel they have been bamboozled.

That perception is reinforced by the results of a study by the Congressional Budget Office on changes in the distribution of the tax burden. The CBO found that from 1977 to 1988, in spite of various legislative reforms, effective tax rates for total federal levies were essentially unchanged for most income groups. However, families with the lowest incomes experienced a significant increase in their tax burden over the period, while the top 5 percent enjoyed a substantial decline.

The election of George Bush brought more of the same. One of Bush's preoccupations was to bring about a huge cut in the capital gains tax. In promoting this idea Bush was conveniently forgetting one of the major compromises of the 1986 Tax Reform Act: in exchange for lowering tax rates for the wealthy, capital gains would be taxed as ordinary income, bringing to an end the preferential treatment they had received since 1921. Bush's notion was that the rich should have it all—the lower rates and special treatment for the profits from their investments.

Bush recycled the old supply-side argument that the cut would actually increase tax revenues and stimulate job-producing investments. Such a cut would, he declared, "encourage the entrepreneurial spirit that is the source of so many new jobs in America." At the same time the president sought to divert attention away from estimates that nearly 90 percent of the benefits would go to the richest 5 percent of taxpayers.

As in 1981, many members of Congress, including Democrats, succumbed to the voodoo. The House voted to support a cut, but limited it to a two-year period. Restricting the duration of the cut is actually worse than enacting a permanent reduction. Having the bargain tax rates available for only a short time would provide incentives only for selling off appreciated assets, and not for making any long-term investments that might increase employment.

After the House vote, the Democratic leadership in Congress successfully maneuvered to slow down the movement toward the capital gains tax cut. In early 1990 Senator Daniel Patrick Moynihan, a New York Democrat, managed to make a tax proposal that threw both parties into a panic. While Bush was preoccupied with giving more tax breaks to the rich, Moynihan pointed out that it was the working population that needed relief—from escalating Social Security taxes.

Noting that these rising payroll levies were generating a surplus that the Bush administration was using to reduce the budget deficit, Moynihan called for a repeal of the increase that took effect at the start of the year and the one scheduled for the beginning of 1991. Caught off guard, President Bush was forced to make the rather strained assertion that the Moynihan plan was "an effort to get me to raise taxes on the American people by the charade of cutting them." *Charade,* in fact, was the right word to describe the claim that the 1980s were a time of tax relief for the majority of the population.

The Moynihan proposal turned out to be too hot for even his own party to handle. Yet if nothing else, the New York senator's initiative made it quite clear that for a disturbingly large number of our politicians, the spirit of Andrew Mellon lives on.

It also lives on among the moneyed classes. The attitude of the rich toward the tax system was never more clearly expressed than in a statement attributed to self-styled hotel queen Leona Helmsley during her 1989 trial on tax evasion charges. "We don't pay taxes," Leona's former housekeeper quoted her as saying, "the little people pay taxes."

Shrinking the Social Wage

Along with giving to the rich, the Reagan administration, of course, busied itself with taking from the poor. The 1980s were one long assault on social spending.

Right-wingers like Reagan had never accepted the proposition that the government should take steps to protect people from the worst ravages of the market. Theirs is a tradition that sees Social Security as a giant step toward communism and unemployment insurance as an invitation to idleness.

For much of the period since the 1930s these ideas were far from the mainstream. The dominant view was that the government activism of Roosevelt's New Deal was essential in bringing the country out of the Depression, and a limited degree of intervention was tolerated even in the conservative climate of the early postwar period. By the 1960s social engineering was high on the federal agenda as Washington sought to enhance the quantity and quality of the labor force through the War on Poverty and other forms of "human capital" development.

To the dismay of the planners, many of the recipients of this federal largesse did not show the proper degree of gratitude; in fact, they began to regard government benefits as a right. Poor people organized themselves in groups like the National Welfare Rights Movement to assert their claims and to try to end the stigma that had always been attached to any government assistance. Starting in the late 1960s, demands on the state began growing at a rapid pace. Federal outlays for income security programs soared from $9.7 billion in 1966 to $86.5 billion in 1980.

Faced with this situation, many policymakers, especially at the state level, began pulling in the reins on social programs. By the early 1970s social welfare administrators were erecting barriers to eligibility for programs like Aid to Families with Dependent Children (commonly known as welfare) and trying to stem the growth of benefit levels. The total benefits available to a typical AFDC family declined from 88 percent of the official poverty line in 1970 to 71 percent in 1981.

After mainstream politicians spent the better part of a decade taking potshots at the welfare state, the election of Ronald Reagan provided an opportunity for the Right to come in for the kill. Budget Director David Stockman—one of whose qualifications for the job was having written a 1978 article calling for the abolition of welfare programs—served as the point man in this drive to put the poor back in their place. Only weeks after the inauguration in 1981 he began challenging the very notion of an entitlement program, insisting that no one had a right to any kind of economic assistance from the state.

The rhetoric flowing from Reagan himself was a bit more diplomatic. He insisted that there was no intention to dismantle the entire social welfare system; the "safety net" would remain in place, he promised, for the "truly needy" (formerly known as the "deserving poor").

That pledge seemed quite empty once the Reaganauts went to work on the budget. In the same way that the new administration railroaded Congress on the tax bill, the legislature was persuaded to take a meat cleaver to a variety of social programs, though it did not chop quite as deeply as the White House wished.

Among the programs that did feel the blade were: Social Security benefits for new retirees, black lung compensation, unemployment insurance, disability benefits, food stamps, child nutrition programs, energy and housing subsidies, discretionary grants to state and local governments, and, of course, AFDC.

After the uproar over the first round of cuts—which took place while military spending was being jacked up—Congress was more resistant to calls for further reductions. By the end of its first term the Reagan administration had sought a total reduction of about 17 percent in social spending, while Congress enacted changes equal to about half of that. A 1984 report by the Congressional Research Service found that even at those lower levels, the budget cuts had put at least 557,000 additional people into poverty.

When a group of doctors working with the Physician Task Force on Hunger in America set out to understand why food stamp participation rates were declining, they got the message loud and clear. "You doctors shouldn't be so naive," the food stamp director of a southern state told the delegation. "You act puzzled that the food stamp program is serving fewer people. Well don't be puzzled. It's doing what they (federal officials) want it to do. You're looking at success. They are deliberately trying to kill the program, and so far they are succeeding."

The retreat from the War on Poverty continued for the rest of the 1980s. For the most part, the assault on social spending was less brazen than in the early part of the decade, but occasionally the misanthropy came shining through. In late 1987, for instance, word leaked out that the Department of Health and Human Services was planning to reduce welfare benefits for elderly, blind, and disabled people who received free food, clothing, or shelter from churches and charities. That was a bit much, even for the ruthless 1980s, so the administration backed off after the plan was reported on the front page of the *New York Times*.

Yet the incident was an apt symbol of the federal government's new posture of doing as little as possible to assist the poor. One quantitative measure of this can be found in a set of annual calculations done by the Center on Budget and Policy Priorities on the effectiveness of federal benefit programs in removing families from poverty. The Center found a sharp drop in that effectiveness during the 1980s. Since the first Reagan cuts took effect, the portion of poor families with children that have been lifted from poverty by cash benefit programs has remained below 12 percent, compared to 19 percent in 1979. This means that in 1987 there were more than 500 thousand poor families that would not have been poor if cash benefit programs had been as effective as they were toward the end of the pre-Reagan era.

Charity instead of Empowerment

There were repeated charges in the 1980s that Reagan had replaced the War on Poverty with a war on the poor; the president was portrayed as "Reagan Hood," robbing from the poor to give to the rich. While the administration certainly deserved all the abuse heaped on it, there was something to Reagan's talk of exempting the "truly needy" from his fiscal wrath. The biggest victims of his policies were not those unable to work and totally dependent on government aid; rather they were the working poor. These are the people who do waged work at least part of the time but who remain below the poverty line. The ranks of the working poor increased markedly during the 1980s, including the most disturbing category: those who worked full-time throughout the year but whose meager earnings kept them poor. In 1988 there were nearly two million workers in that situation.

What seemed to get the goat of Reagan and his people was the idea that someone able to work was on the dole. This resentment was fueled by the Right's paranoia about the supposed hordes of able-bodied welfare recipients living lavishly at public expense. George Gilder, a right-wing guru whose book *Wealth and Poverty* was the bible of the first Reagan term, fulminated against government assistance that provided economic independence for single mothers. To Gilder such programs eroded "male confidence and authority" and led to social breakdown. Visions of "welfare queens" driving Cadillacs—whether in Reagan's anecdotal or Gilder's pseudo-philosophical version—so haunted the Reaganauts that they could not see the truth about recipients of income security programs.

Many AFDC mothers, for instance, were working outside the home, because benefit levels were simply too low for survival, and because the government pressured them to do so. Yet the jobs they were able to find paid so little that they had to stay on the welfare rolls to supplement those earnings and to maintain their eligibility for Medicaid, since their employers tended not to offer health insurance. Previous administrations had generally encouraged these women to remain in the labor market by allowing them to continue collecting benefits until they found better jobs.

For all its talk about work and incentives, the Reagan administration pursued policies that made things much tougher for people who were trying to free themselves from federal dependency. Hundreds of thousands of working AFDC recipients were forced off the rolls when Congress accepted the administration's call for repealing the "30 and a third" formula under which eligibility for AFDC was determined apart from the first $30 in monthly earnings of an applicant plus one-third of the rest. Also, the amount of disregarded earnings was reduced in the food stamp program, snatching benefits from some one million people.

One of the victims of the new AFDC policy was Beatrice Harris, a Chicago mother of six who was abandoned by her husband. When Reagan took office Harris was earning $260 a month in a part-time job and receiving $380 a month in AFDC benefits. Those benefits were cut to $118 a month by the new policy on earnings. It took Harris almost three years to find a full-time job to get off welfare. During that time, she told a reporter, "I was really hurting. It was hard for me to live. You can just get broke the first day and never catch up the whole month."

The more restrictive treatment of earnings was a strange policy for an administration concerned about high tax rates. The earnings disregard was a way of encouraging recipients to begin earning money without suddenly losing all benefits; abolishing it was in effect imposing an extremely high marginal "tax" on earnings.

The confiscatory policy also applied to assets. Many applicants for AFDC or food stamps were made ineligible by the fact that they had managed to hold onto a car considered too expensive for someone on the dole to own. In 1987 a 35-year-old farm wife and mother of five in Iowa told the Physician Task Force on Hunger in America: "We finally broke down and decided to apply for food stamps. When the welfare worker found we drove a '64 Chevy, she tried to disqualify us because you can't have an antique car. The thing hardly runs."

That the Reagan administration refused to acknowledge the high-tax nature of the earnings policy was a clear indication of the Right's view that the motivations of the poor and the rich are totally different. For the latter, the Reagan (and Bush) prescription consists of incentives: Taxes have to be cut and government intervention has to be reduced to encourage corporations and the wealthy to produce and invest.

Those lower down on the social ladder, by contrast, have to be treated with a firm hand; they require not incentives but discipline. Frances Fox Piven and Richard Cloward, who depicted Reagan's policies as part of "a new class war," have aptly described this attitude as a return to classic capitalist ideology. According to this view, they have written, "Working people respond only to punishment—to the economic insecurity that will result from reductions in the income support programs. It was just such a theory that 19th Century British political economists relied upon to justify the accumulation of riches by the few and accumulation of misery by the many."

The nineteenth-century reference is apropos. For what the Right is trying to accomplish with the assault on government benefits for the working poor is a return to that period's tendency to create pools of cheap labor totally at the mercy of the market.

Charles Murray, court philosopher of the second Reagan term, went so far as to suggest "scrapping the entire federal welfare and income-support structure for working-aged persons, including AFDC, Medicaid, Food Stamps, Unemployment Insurance, Worker's Compensation, subsidized housing, disability insurance, and the rest. It would leave the working-aged person with no recourse whatsoever except the job market, family members, friends, and public or private locally funded services.'' In other words, it's either the market or charity.

The greatest sin of the New Deal and Great Society initiatives, according to the likes of Murray, was that they gave working people a greater degree of independence in the labor market. Rather than taking the first lousy position that came along, and rather than being so mortified by the thought of getting fired that they put up with any kind of abuse from an employer, low-income workers were able to depend on government benefits to ward off starvation when things went sour on the job.

The ability of low-wage workers to stand up to their bosses was not part of the Right's vision for a revitalized America. A weak and vulnerable labor force is what was considered fit for the restructured, increasingly service based economy. The traditional notion that the government should help people cope with the dislocations arising during a time of transition was alien to the Reaganauts. Not only did the administration planners show no desire to smooth the passage of workers into the restructured economy, they seemed to recognize that the new model of accumulation was to a great degree based on an impotent labor force.

The success of the drive to make living conditions for poor and working people more precarious can be seen most clearly with regard to unemployment insurance and AFDC.

As a result of changes in eligibility standards (often made at the state level) and cuts in the duration of benefits, fewer and fewer jobless people collect unemployment compensation. The official rate of unemployment was relatively low in the late 1980s, but the impact of losing a job was more intense. The percentage of jobless workers receiving compensation declined sharply during the Reagan years. Whereas in 1975 three-quarters of the unemployed were receiving benefits, by 1988 the figure was down to 32 percent.

While workers were being made to feel the sting of unemployment more sharply, the poor were being taught not to expect to live decently on public assistance. Benefit levels were allowed to stagnate during the Reagan years as they did in the 1970s. A single mother in Boston confessed to a reporter that the meager level of AFDC payments she received forced her to shoplift food to be sure her son had enough to eat. "You just pray you're not going to get caught."

In 1988 the median of state maximum benefits for a single parent with two children (that being the average family size for AFDC recipients, despite conservative propaganda about excessive childbearing rates by welfare mothers) was merely $360 a month. In only a handful of states did the maximum AFDC benefit plus food stamps reach the poverty line. Such were the benefits that were supposedly destroying the will to work.

The Supply-Side Legacy

The standard response to the criticism of Reagan's repressive fiscal policies was that the losses some people experienced from budget cuts were more than balanced by the gains from tax cuts. Unfortunately, like many of the pronouncements from that administration, this simply was not true.

A 1989 study of after-tax family income by the House Ways and Means Committee made this clear. The report, which adjusted Census Bureau figures to account for inflation and differences in family size and included estimates of food and housing benefits as well as cash payments, found strikingly different trends at the opposite ends of the income spectrum. Families in the bottom quintile experienced a drop of more than 9 percent in their average income from 1979 to 1987. Families in the top quintile had an average gain of nearly 19 percent. Rather than helping lower-income Americans cope with wrenching changes brought about by economic restructuring, a decade of repressive fiscal policies served to make the gap between rich and poor even wider.

What was so cruel about Reaganism was that it took the high level of popular economic discontent that existed in 1980 and used it as a mandate for pushing through some of the most retrograde fiscal policies of modern times. A tax system that was not very progressive to begin with was made even more inequitable. Budget cuts did not abolish but seriously weakened benefit programs designed to keep families out of poverty and to cushion the blows from an unpredictable private economy. The talk of "getting government off our back" served as a smokescreen for a dramatic redistribution of income from the working poor to the working and nonworking rich.

And there is every indication that the Bush administration will continue on the same path. Hundreds of billions of dollars are being found to bail out the largely corrupt savings and loan industry, most of it coming out of the pockets of taxpayers, yet the "kinder, gentler" administration remains stingy when it comes to social needs. Bush's first budget contained a few token increases in programs like Head Start, but these were more than offset by proposed reductions in such areas as Medicare, child nutrition, and food stamps. Even the $500 million Head Start increase was illusory, since the budget proposed eliminating nearly $400 million in community services block grants, which help fund agencies that run Head Start programs. At the same time, despite the transformation of the Soviet bloc and the hopes for a peace dividend, Bush proposed an increase in military spending.

If any politician dared to repeat today Reagan's 1980 question as to whether we are better off than we were a decade ago, the answer for most Americans would still be a resounding *no*. But now, in addition to the mysteries of the economy, we also have the supply-side legacy to blame.

· FOUR ·

Left in the Dust: Workers and Industrial Restructuring

IN November 1956 a smiling Ronald Reagan, then a goodwill ambassador for General Electric, visited the company's flatiron plant in Ontario, California, to celebrate the production of the 50-millionth iron, which was gold-plated for the occasion. A quarter of a century later, not long after the plant attained a production record of five million irons a year, and as Reagan was about to enter the White House, workers in Ontario began to feel something was wrong.

GE's managers were neglecting to repair machinery and were letting inventories of spare parts run down; the product line was scaled back, and overtime was reduced. In July 1981 the workers' fears were confirmed: GE announced that Ontario would end its 80-year reign as the flatiron capital of the world. The plant was to be closed, and GE's iron production was to be transferred to factories in Mexico, Brazil, and Singapore, where workers earned less than a quarter of the wage rate in the Ontario plant.

The episode in Ontario helped give General Electric's chief executive, John Welch, his nickname: "Neutron Jack." Like a neutron bomb, he eliminates workers while letting the buildings stand. Since 1981, the jobs of more than 100,000 GE employees have been annihilated.

While the Ontario plant had been under GE ownership for some time, Morse Cutting Tool in New Bedford, Massachusetts, was an independent, locally owned firm for more than a century after its founding in 1864. In the late 1960s, however, specialized operations like Morse became attractive to conglomerates seeking to cash in on the lucrative military contracts being awarded by the Pentagon during the Vietnam

War. Morse was swept up in the buying binge and in 1968 found itself owned by giant Gulf+Western Industries. One of the more ravenous of the conglomerates—it took over some 80 companies from 1965 to 1970 alone—G+W was the model for the greedy corporation called Engulf & Devour in the Mel Brooks film *Silent Movie*.

Perhaps because G+W was busy digesting its many other purchases, things at Morse remained stable for a few years after its acquisition. The apparent honeymoon came to an end in 1982, when G+W told the union at Morse, the United Electrical Workers (UE), that unless steep contract concessions were granted, the company would simply pack up its machines and move them elsewhere.

Instead of panicking, UE officers brought in the Industrial Cooperative Association to investigate their suspicion that G+W's policies were at the root of Morse's problems. That hunch turned out to be right on the money. The ICA was able to document that G+W had been using Morse as a "cash cow," an operation exploited by a parent company for its earnings but which does not receive the investment funds needed to remain a viable business. G+W was running Morse into the ground for the sake of short-term profits.

Armed with that knowledge, UE conducted a successful strike and public campaign against the company in 1982. Two years later, however, G+W decided to sell the plant, and the Morse workers had to carry on the fight under new ownership, then bankruptcy, and then another takeover.

Industrial Decline in America

These two experiences—the quick demise at Ontario and the never-ending battle at Morse—are emblematic of the upheaval in American industry since the late 1970s. The manufacturing sector, once the backbone of the U.S. economy, has been subjected to a bewildering process of shrinkage, restructuring, transfer to foreign ownership, and outright dismantlement.

Announcements of plant closings have become commonplace features of everyday life, and by now the press bothers to report only the largest ones. Huge industrial complexes sit empty, abandoned and deteriorating, giving parts of the country the look of Germany after the war. The heavy industries traditionally seen as the defining characteristics of a developed economy are in disarray. Those operations that survive do so at great cost to their employees: great swaths of the labor force are sliced off, and the workers who remain find their compensation squeezed and their working conditions downgraded.

Probably the greatest impact has been felt in the once-proud steel industry. Starting in 1977 huge portions of the country's steel-making capacity were eliminated with the announcements of mill shutdowns affecting thousands of workers. In December 1983 U.S. Steel probably set a record by announcing the shutdown of three major plants and parts of a dozen others—a step that obliterated more than 15,000 jobs in one blow. Five years later the same company, which had taken the deliberately nondescript name USX, provided another stark symbol of industrial decline when it announced plans to sell one of its steel mills to the government of Iraq, which intended to dismantle the facility and reassemble it in its own country.

Countless communities have been thrown into crisis by the disappearance of institutions that provided livelihoods for their citizens, sales for their retailers, and tax revenues for their coffers. Millions of workers have been wrenched out of well-paying jobs and thrown into a labor market that has little need for their skills. One-time "labor aristocrats" have been reduced to scrounging for minimum-wage work and worrying if they can hold onto their homes.

The total U.S. manufacturing sector had a net loss of 1.4 million jobs between 1979 and 1989—a period during which overall employment increased by more than 18 million. This brought manufacturing's share of total employment down from 23.4 to 18.1 percent. The Bureau of Labor Statistics has identified more than 20 industries that have been declining, in terms of both employment and output, since the late 1960s. Among them are steel, tires, metal containers, and transportation equipment. From 1979 to 1989 the total number of employees of firms on the Fortune 500 list of the largest industrial companies decreased by more than a fifth. In merely a decade, this elite club of large corporations eliminated some 3.7 million jobs. By contrast, in the 25 years following the creation of the list in 1954, "500" employment rose 100 percent.

Some of this transformation is due to simple changes in international economic conditions, especially the value of the dollar and the volume of imports and exports. But there is more going on than the usual ups and downs of the market; the basic shape of American industry is being recast. Economists Barry Bluestone and Bennett Harrison have given a name to this "systematic disinvestment in the nation's basic productive capacity": the deindustrialization of America.

The dizzying pace of change has unsettled the life of people like Pam Portwood. Between 1975 and 1987 she went through eight jobs in her search for steady work. She was laid off from an assembly job at a stereo factory in Decatur, Illinois, when the plant was closed in the face of Japanese competition. She lost sales jobs at smaller firms that failed during the recession of the early 1980s. Another factory job, in the garment industry, disappeared when the plant was shut down.

Portwood, a divorced mother of two, learned to live with uncertainty, but her teenage daughter Kim longed for security. "I'm going in the Army," Kim told a reporter. "The Army recruiter came to our school and said if you go in the military you'll have a definite future. That's what I want—a definite future."

The Changing Fortunes of the Sunbelt

When industrial metamorphosis first became evident in the late 1970s, it was perceived as a regional issue. Corporations, it was said, had grown weary of the Northeast and Midwest and were heading for the more pleasing business climate of the "Sunbelt"—that tier of states across the bottom of the country from the Carolinas to southern California.

The Sunbelt quickly became the new pacesetter in American life. Aided by soaring energy prices and great flows of federal money (especially from the Pentagon and NASA), places like Houston and Huntsville, Alabama, were enjoying modern-day gold rushes.

The South also benefited from the collapse in the Northeast and Midwest of the social contract between management and labor. Employers up in the "Frostbelt" realized that their most effective collective bargaining move was to pull up stakes and transfer operations to one of those friendly southern states with low wages and right-to-work laws that kept out unions. Although many companies publicly claimed that high taxes and transport costs were the reason for moving, the more candid business spokespeople admitted that the real aim was to undermine the power of labor. A vice president of the relocation consulting firm Fantus explained his clients' motivations plainly: "Labor costs are the big thing, far and away. Nine out of ten times you can hang it on labor costs and unionization."

Thanks to all this, Sunbelt industry began to take off. Total employment in the southern region of the country grew nearly 33 percent from 1968 to 1978, while in the Northeast it rose less than 11 percent.

By the latter year, the South had a larger share of total U.S. manufacturing employment, some 29 percent, than the chilly states of the Northeast.

The movement of capital brought with it a movement of people. Many of those factory workers frozen out of jobs in the Midwest and Northeast jumped in their cars and vans and headed for the sun. Around 1981 the newspapers were full of stories of unemployed workers jamming the hiring halls and personnel offices of the Sunbelt states. So numerous were these new incarnations of the Depression-era Okies that in 1982 the president of the Texas AFL-CIO publicly urged northern workers not to come to his state unless they had jobs lined up in advance.

The enchanted life of the Sunbelt did not last for long. The collapse of oil prices and the onset of the recession of the early 1980s showed that a warm climate did not make a region immune to economic misfortune. It turned out that even the dreaded Frostbelt disease of plant shutdowns could occur below the Mason-Dixon line.

Bluestone and Harrison estimated that some 11 million Sunbelt jobs were "destroyed" by plant closings and capital migration from 1969 to 1976 while 14 million were created; or, to put it otherwise, 28 percent of the large manufacturing establishments (more than 500 employees) in existence in the South at the beginning of that period were gone by 1976. Later estimates put the number of workers in the South who had been dislocated during the period from 1981 to 1985 at more than 1.7 million.

Disinvestment appeared even in the celebrated Silicon Valley. There were many red faces among the touts of the high-tech solution to America's ills—including the group known as Atari Democrats—when their namesake Atari Inc. announced in 1983 that it was eliminating 1,700 jobs in Silicon Valley and transferring that work to plants in Hong Kong and Taiwan. If there were any doubts left, it then became clear that deindustrialization was not a regional but a national phenomenon.

The Ravages of "Creative Destruction"

Believers in the market see the changes taking place not as a problem but as a glorious example of capitalism's penchant for "creative destruction." Conservative economist Richard McKenzie has made a career of propounding this view. He has even argued that displaced workers should not complain about their fate because, although they lose their jobs, they are "beneficiaries of the competitive process (involving closings and openings) in other markets, which yields higher quality goods at lower prices."

If the indefinitely laid off steelworker in Pittsburgh remains unconvinced, let him listen to the words of the business magazine *Forbes*: "It is precisely through the shrinking of old industries—learning to make more with less—that new industries become possible and with them a broadening of the horizon of life for most people. The decline of old industries is sad. But it is not a tragedy."

Leaving aside "most people" for the moment, it is clear that deindustrialization has done nothing to "broaden the horizon of life" for those displaced from their jobs in plant shutdowns. For them life has gotten narrower and poorer. They are among the prime victims of the erosion of American living standards.

One of these victims was Ray Woolaghan, who was laid off from his $12-an-hour job at U.S. Steel's Homestead, Pennsylvania, mill in the mid-1980s. When his job was eliminated Woolaghan was only 17 days away from qualifying for his pension. It took him almost two years to find steady work, which turned out to be a $5.23-an-hour custodial position at the University of Pittsburgh. "You have to cut out a lot of things you were used to," he told a reporter. "There's no getting a new car. No going on a trip. You don't eat a steak. You don't even think about it. . . . But I'm just gonna be glad I've got a job."

For a problem so serious, it took the federal bureaucracy a long time to get around to measuring the dimensions of worker displacement. It was not until January 1984 that government employment surveys addressed the issue with a set of queries added to the usual questionnaire on labor market status. A later survey showed that from 1983 to 1988 some 10 million workers lost jobs because of plant closings or economic cutbacks.

The Bureau of Labor Statistics decided to focus its attention on those who had been on the job three years or more when they were laid off; these were the dislocated workers considered to be a bona fide public policy problem. In the 1988 survey they amounted to about half of those who had lost jobs for economic reasons. Even with this limited definition, the impact of displacement is staggering. Some 14 percent of this group were still unemployed in 1988, and another 15 percent had dropped out of the labor force. Finding a new job did not necessarily make a dislocated worker whole again. Nearly a third of those who had new jobs had taken a cut of at least 20 percent in pay.

After Bill Baudendistel of Goshen, Ohio, was laid off from his $13-an-hour factory job with General Electric in 1988, the best work he could find was a position as a night maintenance man at a shopping mall. The pay: $5 an hour. His wife had to take a part-time job as a secretary in a hospital, though she preferred to stay at home with their three children. Nonetheless, the Baudendistels, finding it hard to keep up, began buying their clothes at garage sales and stopped purchasing "luxuries" like fresh fruit.

Income is not the only thing lost by dislocated workers; their health is also put in jeopardy. The Bureau of Labor Statistics found that a third of displaced workers who had health insurance in their old jobs no longer had coverage. A growing body of research has found significant increases in mental illness, alcoholism; divorce, and various physical ailments among workers thrown out of work by plant closings and corporate restructuring.

One worker dismissed when U.S. Steel shut down operations in Cleveland in 1984 was aware of the emotional strains ahead. He told a reporter that as soon as he got news of the shutdown, "I sat down with my wife and told her I'm going to apologize in advance for the next year. In a year I could be like too many of my laid-off friends, single and going to AA meetings every night." Few workers are able to deal with dislocation so calmly; most lash out at their families or at themselves. Several studies have found that suicide rates among displaced workers far exceed the national norm.

Rushing to Restructure

It is unfortunate that the term *deindustrialization* has become the buzzword for analysis of the changes taking place in the U.S. economy. To many ears it sounds like disaster and deterioration, and while it may be experienced just that way in parts of the country, the reality is somewhat more complex than the straw men erected by right-wing debunkers. American industry is not simply taking a dive; it is undergoing an elaborate and sometimes well-planned process of restructuring.

Virtually every major company has tried some form of restructuring, whether de-diversification, subcontracting, rearranging its capital structure, or going private through a leveraged buyout. The total value of mergers and acquisitions announced from 1984 to 1988 alone was nearly $900 billion. What was once exceptional has become standard operating procedure. As one management consultant put it, "If a chief executive officer isn't thinking of restructuring, he's not doing his job."

At the corporate level it is difficult to tell whether all this upheaval has been for the good. There are tales with both sad and happy endings. Revco D.S. Inc., a fast-growing chain of discount drugstores, underwent a leveraged buyout in 1986 only to go bankrupt 16 months later. Management miscalculations had been magnified by the heavy debt load the company assumed in going private. The dismantling of food giant Beatrice, once hailed as the deal of the century and one that was supposed to yield some $4 billion in profits for those who took it private, stalled when buyers could not be found for some of its units.

On the other hand, after Anglo-French raider James Goldsmith took over Diamond International in 1982, the forest products company was split up into a number of different firms that began to prosper on their own. In another instance, M.A. Hanna Co., founded by robber baron Mark Hanna, successfully shifted from the iron ore to the plastics business.

In other cases companies have gone through so much cosmetic surgery that they become unrecognizable. American Can transformed itself into a financial services company called Primerica, which was later acquired by another financial firm; meanwhile the packaging operations were sold twice, ending up in the possession of the French state-owned aluminum firm Pechiney.

One business publication declares that "restructuring really works" and that "it will prove a permanent revolution"; another cites concerns that by streamlining operations "U.S. companies are damaging their future vitality, and even viability, through reluctance to undertake long-term investments and new-product development." All this suggests a profound uncertainty as to whether the restructuring mania is good for American industry. Some of the changes taking place reflect no more than companies slavishly following the latest fashion in corporate strategy or giving in to the blandishments of the management consulting firms, which stand to gain fat fees when a client agrees to a makeover.

When it comes to changes in ownership, the primary motivation of top management is often not the health of the company but rather how much they can gain personally. Just about every top executive has a personal arrangement, known as a golden parachute, that provides lavish severance benefits in the event of a hostile takeover. In the case of American Can, the top 10 executives of successor company Primerica got total settlements worth nearly $100 million when the firm was sold to Commercial Credit Group—even though it was a friendly takeover.

The greed factor is even greater in leveraged buyouts. The apotheosis of self-dealing came in late 1988 during the maneuvering over the $25 billion buyout of tobacco and food behemoth RJR Nabisco. The firm's president, Ross Johnson, proposed a deal in which he personally could have earned $100 million. In the end a competing wheeler-dealer won the bidding war, but Johnson's actions were so egregious that even the usual defenders of corporate excess were moved to protest. *Time* magazine, for instance, complained: "The battle for RJR Nabisco seems to have crossed an invisible line that separates reasonable conduct from anarchy."

When executives become "anarchists," the "bombs" they throw are usually directed at workers. Regardless of who wins a takeover battle, the employees of the target company run the risk of losing their jobs or at least having to make substantial sacrifices to preserve them. In 1986 Owens-Corning Fiberglas beat back a raid by Wickes Corp. by taking on nearly $3 billion in debt. To meet the interest payments, Owens-Corning began closing, selling, or scaling back many of its operations. Some 1,000 workers lost their jobs, and thousands of others were adversely affected. Similar results occur in leveraged buyouts. After Safeway Stores went private in 1986, the company bailed out of the Dallas market, eliminating more than 6,000 jobs, and began pressuring its remaining employees to lower wages down toward the level of non-union supermarket workers.

Unions are beginning to intervene in the takeover and buyout process to protect their members. Several suits against raiders were filed by unions in 1988, and while these initiatives have not yet posed a major obstacle to merger mania, labor has begun to raise the right questions. As an official of the United Food and Commercial Workers Union said upon bringing one of the lawsuits: "Someone has to stop American employees being sacrificed on the altar of Wall Street greed."

The Hollow Corporation

For more than a decade, restructuring has been the subject of animated debate at the level of macroeconomics. Advocates of industrial policy have issued urgent warnings about the erosion of U.S. competitiveness. The American economy, we are told, is going to hell in a handbasket unless there is better planning for the future. "We are gambling recklessly with our destiny," exclaimed the final statement of a 1987 gathering of business, government, and academic leaders. "We cannot long continue on this path without profound consequences."

One of the most forthright statements came a few years ago from Sony Corp. chairman Akio Morita. "American companies," he observed, "have either shifted output to low-wage countries or come to buy parts and assembled products from countries like Japan that can make quality products at low prices. The result is a hollowing of American industry. The U.S. is abandoning its status as an industrial power."

Many household-name companies are becoming hollow corporations. Fortune 500 stalwarts like Kodak and Honeywell have cut back manufacturing and expanded their role as distributors. With such products as videocassette recorders and compact disc players, a "made in the USA" label is virtually nowhere to be found.

Among those companies that have not entirely abandoned the messy process of manufacturing for the green pastures of marketing and finance, many have subcontracted much of the production to foreign companies. A famed American product like the IBM PC actually consists of components made by a variety of smaller companies—many of them foreign—and merely brought together for final assembly in a facility owned by Big Blue. Liz Claiborne Inc., one of the country's largest apparel firms, owns no manufacturing plants; all that work is subcontracted, mostly overseas.

Manufacturers have also been hiring other firms to do many nonproduction functions. In fact, the boom in business services like cleaning, accounting, and catering can largely be traced to the increasing tendency by industrial companies to send out for help rather than doing it in-house. Half a century ago a manufacturer like Ford was as self-sufficient as possible, down to the raising of sheep for the wool used in auto upholstery. Today the watchwords are outsourcing and disaggregation, the motto "when in doubt, farm it out."

Not everyone finds these developments cause for concern. Conservative analysts inside and outside the federal government have continued to preach complacence. "The move from an industrial society toward a 'postindustrial' service economy," said a report of the U.S. Trade Representative, "has been one of the greatest changes to affect the developed world since the Industrial Revolution. The progression of an economy such as America's from agriculture to manufacturing to services is a natural change." A document prepared by the New York

Stock Exchange was blunter: "a strong manufacturing sector is not a requisite for a prosperous economy."

The industrial planners shoot back with the "manufacturing matters" salvo. In an influential book with that title, Stephen Cohen and John Zysman insist it is a delusion to think the U.S. can prosper on service activities alone, since competitiveness in high-end services is directly linked to hands-on experience in state-of-the-art production. "Manufacturing matters mightily to the wealth and power of the United States," they maintain, "and to our ability to sustain the kind of open society we have come to take for granted."

The laissez-faire crowd have tended to parry that argument with references to Commerce Department figures showing that during the 1980s manufacturing's share of gross national product has remained in the same 20–22 percent range that characterized the previous two decades. These statistics allowed the 1988 *Economic Report of the President* to state smugly: "Except for business cycle movements, the shares of real manufacturing output and real final goods output have been remarkably stable for 25 years." Of course, even the Reagan administration had to admit that manufacturing's share of total employment has been declining in a big way, but that was lauded as a sign of elevated productivity.

The official numbers suggesting that manufacturing had held its own with regard to national output fell under increasing assault in the late 1980s. The coup de grâce came in a 1988 study by Lawrence Mishel of the Economic Policy Institute that raised a host of technical questions about the Commerce Department's figures. Mishel concluded that rather than remaining constant, the manufacturing share of GNP had fallen as much as 4½ percentage points since 1973. Federal statisticians, in other words, had been overestimating manufacturing output by tens of billions of dollars a year.

Several months after the publication of Mishel's study, the Commerce Department's Bureau of Economic Analysis, the source of the figures and the nation's GNP scorekeeper, began to admit that the criticisms had some merit. "There probably has been some overestimation," said Bureau director Allan Young matter-of-factly. It remains to be seen whether conservative economists revise their analyses accordingly.

Even if they admit the change in facts, the priests of the market are unlikely to abandon their contention that restructuring is a good thing. Yet it is not self-evident that the opposing view, that of the generally liberal advocates of industrial planning, is the one to adopt in the great manufacturing-versus-services debate. The liberal concern about man-ufacturing is rooted in the tradition of identifying a nation's power with its industrial capacity. The book by Cohen and Zysman, which had the imprimatur of the Council on Foreign Relations, made it clear from the beginning that the authors' concern was that the U.S. "stayed on top" through industrial superiority. The insistence that "manufacturing mat-ters" is often inseparable from the fretting over the decline of U.S. power that became popular in the late 1980s. Given that modern capi-talism and the leading countries practicing it grew hand in hand with the development of manufacturing, it is difficult for many analysts to imagine a superpower that has to import essential goods.

Since the world would be a better place without superpowers, the hope of maintaining U.S. hegemony is not a satisfactory basis for choosing sides in the restructuring debate. What is decisive is the im-pact of the shift to services on living standards. The likes of *Forbes* magazine may ultimately be correct in saying that the restructuring process is one of "healthy adaptability, not economic decay"—but for whom is it healthy?

At Your Service

Conservative economists are quick to state that it is the overall magni-tude not the composition of economic activity that makes the differ-ence. Output is output is output, they assure us; it matters not whether the product is an automobile, a sheet of steel, a Pet Rock, a legal brief, a completed tax return, or an emptied bedpan.

As long as we remain at the dark level of economic abstraction, where all statistical cats are black, this is true enough. The pulse of capitalism, after all, is profit—not the particular activity from which it arises. Yet once we look at specific groups of people, particularly those who work for a living, the ascent of the service economy starts to look more sinister. The reason is simple: On the whole, the jobs in the service sector are lousier than the ones in manufacturing.

It is true, as Republican politicians never tire of repeating, that the American economy churned out an extraordinary number of new posi-tions in the past few decades and that the overwhelming majority of these were in services. Of the 38 million jobs created from 1970 to 1989, nearly 80 percent were in financial services, wholesale and retail trade, and other kinds of services. From the point of view of living standards, however, the country might have been better off if many of those jobs had remained unborn.

Service sector jobs tend to be inferior in several ways. First, they tend to pay less. In 1989 the average hourly wage in manufacturing was $10.47, while the average for services was $9.40 and for retail trade $6.54. Because there tend to be more part-timers in the service sector, the gap in average weekly earnings was even greater: $429 in manufacturing versus $306 in services and $189 in retail trade. And this was at a time when manufacturing wages were still being held down by economic disarray and by employer demands for contract concessions from unions.

Aside from being generally lower, wages in the service sector are also less equitably distributed. Harrison and Bluestone have found that the shift of employment from manufacturing to services accounted for about one-fifth of the increase in overall wage inequality since the late 1970s.

Second, service jobs tend to show lower levels of productivity than those in manufacturing—which is part of the justification for low wages. Yet productivity is something of a fiction, especially with regard to services. How do you measure the productivity of a cashier or a security guard? Nonetheless, the BLS does attempt to measure something called output per hour for all employees. Those statistics show manufacturing rising faster than the rest of the economy, and the gap has been growing wider. The comparison is worse when you consider that the service figure is raised by a number of high-productivity areas like public utilities and telecommunications.

Third, the service sector has a lower level of unionization, which is another reason for the inferior wage rates. In 1989 only 13.5 percent of those in service occupations were members of unions, and even that figure was inflated by the high rate of membership among security guards. If those workers are put aside, the rate in the remainder of the sector was less than 10 percent. By contrast, among those in the blue-collar category of "machine operators, assemblers and inspectors" the membership rate was 29 percent.

Up to now we have been talking mainly in terms of averages and broad categories. It is undeniable that some service jobs are well-paid, just as it is indisputable that many manufacturing jobs provide lousy wages and working conditions. There is nothing about manufacturing or service jobs per se that is better or worse. But what restructuring has created is a situation in which superior manufacturing jobs are disappearing and inferior service jobs are appearing in overwhelming numbers. Emma Rothschild's observation in 1981 that the U.S. "is moving toward a structure of employment ever more dominated by jobs that are badly paid, unchanging, and unproductive," is disturbingly true even today.

And it probably will remain so. The Bureau of Labor Statistics has projected that the occupations that will grow the most by the end of the century are all in the service sector. Among those occupations expected to lead the pack are salespersons, janitors, and waiters.

The significance of the shift from an industrial to a service economy, from the point of view of workers, was captured in a *Wall Street Journal* portrait of the Gorol family in 1986. Bill Gorol, Sr. went to work at the Homestead, Pennsylvania, works of U.S. Steel straight out of high school and remained with the company for the rest of his working life. He made a good living and remained loyal to the company and to the union. His son, Bill Jr., worked briefly in the mill before it was shut down and was then thrown into the precarious world of the service sector labor market. He bounced between jobs as a car mechanic, gas station attendant, and shoe salesman before ending up as an automobile salesman. In the latter job he earned considerably less than he did as a novice machinist at U.S. Steel, and the position was somewhat lacking in job security: if he did not meet his quota two months in a row, he would be out on the street. "My father can't accept what I'm doing," Bill Jr. said. "He thinks I'm stupid."

Even some corporate figures question the wisdom of the shift to services. John F. McGillicuddy, chairman of Manufacturers Hanover Trust, has said: "We need to wonder whether we can really afford to become a nation of people solely engaged in selling Egg McMuffins and insurance to one another, treating each other's illnesses, or cutting each other's hedges or hair. Surely there must be a point of diminishing returns in all this. We may have reached it."

Whose "Healthy Adaptability"?

McGillicuddy's expression of concern is somewhat disingenuous. The use of the all-inclusive "we" makes it sound as if the process of restructuring is everyone's responsibility; as if it were a fad that had overcome the entire population and was getting out of control.

The fact that the word *restructuring* is used to describe the changes taking place, rather than traditional terms like *growth/contraction* or *expansion/recession,* indicates that what is afoot goes beyond the business cycle. The concept of restructuring implies a certain degree of planning, design, and purpose. Someone or something is changing the structure of the American economy in order to accomplish particular ends. The agents here are the large corporations, acting with the implicit or explicit encouragement of financial institutions and government.

Progressives usually interpret restructuring and deindustrialization in terms of the greedy and shortsighted policies of big business. Conglomerates like Gulf + Western, it is said, set unrealistically high profit requirements for each of the businesses they acquired, and when some poor plant did not measure up, it was summarily executed. This process is said to be a function of the overaccelerated mobility of capital, which, say Bluestone and Harrison, "has become so fast that people and communities are carelessly discarded to make room for new ones."

All of this is true, but it would be a mistake to see workers as no more than passive victims of this process. The wave of restructuring and disinvestment in the 1980s has to be seen in the context of the changing relations between labor and capital. It is no coincidence that the prime victims of economic change have been those members of the work force who had achieved the best wage deals for themselves on the job. And it is not by chance that the much-vaunted expansion of employment has been so heavily concentrated in low-wage, nonunion, dead-end jobs. While it is impossible to pinpoint a central intelligence behind this process, it is difficult to avoid the conclusion that the main objective of restructuring is to weaken the collective strength of workers. Dismantling heavy industry, slashing payrolls, cutting costs, subcontracting, shifting workers to lousy jobs in the service sector—all of these things not only reduce living standards immediately by cutting payments to workers, they also weaken workers' bargaining ability and tip the balance of power in favor of business over the longer term.

Attacks on unions, dispersal of labor into small workplaces with no history of struggle, and tight restraints on government social spending all serve to block the channels through which working people have fought to improve their material lot. Regardless of what the business ideologues tell us, improvements in living standards come from the bottom up, through popular struggle, rather than trickling down from a general growth in economic activity. This has perhaps never been clearer than during the past decade. Following the recession of 1982–

1983, the U.S. economy experienced one of the longest recoveries in modern history. Observers marveled as total output kept chugging along year after year, and corporate profits began reversing their long-term decline. It was this apparent prosperity that George Bush used to con the country into giving supply-side economics an extended run.

Yet it was during this celebrated economic expansion that the underlying erosion of living standards continued apace. As conservatives worshiped the supposed Reagan economic miracle, more communities were shattered by plant closings, more middle-aged workers were thrust into a hostile labor market through restructuring, more high school graduates were made to believe that success was a job at McDonald's, and more economically displaced persons found themselves among the ranks of the homeless.

It is true that external forces are also at work. International competition certainly is more intense, and the patterns of demand are more difficult to predict. Yet there is no reason why the response to these challenges has to involve a depression of American living standards. Large corporations have protected themselves by forming joint ventures and other cooperative arrangements with foreign producers. They have adopted new computer technologies to make production more flexible. Business has taken great pains to ensure itself a soft landing; why can't the same be done for labor?

Much of what is called restructuring is not a problem for business but rather its solution to its problems. Corporate America is indeed making itself "lean and mean" and more competitive; the scandal is that as part of that process, workers are having the life squeezed out of them.

· FIVE ·

No Strings Attached: America's Second-Class Labor Force

BACK in the early 1980s Arthur Ward felt he had it made. As a maintenance worker for Washington, D.C.'s Metropolitan Transit Authority he earned $11.40 an hour and enjoyed a full range of benefits. The bubble burst in 1986. He suffered a back injury that kept him out of work for nearly two years, and when he returned to the labor force the best he could get was a $4.25-an-hour half-time job cleaning office buildings for a maintenance contractor.

Besides the low pay, the job offered no health insurance, pension, or paid sick leave. To make ends meet, Ward took a second part-time job placing advertising inserts in newspapers at the *Washington Post*—another position without benefits. What he feared most, Ward told a congressional committee in 1988, was that he might get sick and be unable to work, preventing his teenage daughter from continuing her education.

Low pay and a lack of benefits was the prospect facing Nancy Packard when she became a part-time circulation aide in the Milwaukee public library system. Her position used to be filled by high school and college students working temporarily, but during the early 1980s it became the entry-level position for permanent employees. The regular library aides did essentially the same work as Packard but were paid nearly twice her $3.60-an-hour wage and got benefits. Addressing a congressional panel in 1988 Packard said: "Our country cannot afford the continuing growth of an underclass of temporary and part-time workers to erode the American Dream."

Unfortunately, such an underclass is very much on the rise; in fact, it was one of the most dramatic features of U.S. economic development in the 1980s. Behind all the hoopla about rapid American job growth is the sordid reality that much of the new employment is second class. In keeping with the general American flight to junk—junk bonds, junk food, junk mail, and junk fax—we now have a proliferation of junk jobs.

The employment opportunities being created are increasingly part-time, temporary, free-lance, or home-based. The pay is low, the benefits limited or nonexistent, the chances of union protection slim, and the possibilities for advancement less than dazzling. Participants in this contingent labor force, the polite term for the phenomenon, often are not sure what their employment status actually is. They may be given the dubious title of "independent contractor" or "consultant," or they may find that like a piece of equipment they are "owned" by one entity and leased out to another.

Beneath the legal ambiguity is a simple fact: most of these people are workers who have been devalued, degraded, and stripped of the guarantees associated with a decent job. A business magazine headlined its story on the subject: "The Disposable Employee Is Becoming a Fact of Corporate Life." Overwhelmingly female and nonwhite, these contingent workers are the vanguard of downward mobility. And a large vanguard it is: the size of this labor force has been estimated at roughly 30 million, or one out of every four workers.

Job Security and Insecurity

It has always been true that not all members of the labor force have enjoyed steady, full-time work at decent wages. Sporadic and irregular work has existed since the early days of capitalism. Historian Gareth Stedman Jones found that several dozen occupations in nineteenth-century London were characterized by a significant degree of "casual" labor. The trend was most pronounced among dock workers, but irregularity of employment was also prevalent in land transport, the building trades, and various other service and manufacturing occupations.

In the United States in the nineteenth and early twentieth century precarious employment was commonly found in farming, logging, and canning, while many members of the new immigrant labor force had to scramble for uncertain factory jobs offered by fly-by-night entrepreneurs. For many, a job was a one-day-at-a-time experience.

"We went to the doors of one big slaughter house," recalled Antanas Kaztauskis about job-hunting early this century:

There was a crowd of about 200 men waiting there for a job. They looked hungry and kept watching the door. At last a special policeman came out and began pointing to men, one by one. Each one jumped forward. Twenty-three were taken. Then they all went inside, and all the others turned their faces away and looked tired. I remember one boy sat down and cried, just next to me, on a pile of boards. Some policemen waved their clubs and we walked on.

After World War II, a stronger economy provided more predictable employment, and the market models of labor economics came to assume full-time, full-year employment as the norm. Behind this change of assumptions was a change in power relations: the rise of organized labor forced many large companies to offer a higher degree of job security to their workers. The traditional doctrines of employment at will and managerial prerogative no longer reigned supreme.

Yet these new protections were far from universal. Once the ghetto riots of the 1960s prompted a reexamination of the poor, social scientists realized that a significant part of the population was still not enjoying the blessings of a steady job. In the place of the confident assumption of orthodox economics that the labor market rewarded workers equitably, based on their marginal productivity, a group of analysts began speaking of dual labor markets. In addition to the commonly understood primary market, they said, there was a secondary market in which jobs were invariably irregular, poorly paid, and insecure. Elliot Liebow ably described the nature of this work in his book on "streetcorner men":

> With few exceptions, jobs filled by the streetcorner men are at the bottom of the employment ladder in every respect, from wage level to prestige. Typically, they are hard, dirty, uninteresting and underpaid. . . . [The worker] has little vested in such a job and learns to treat it with the same contempt held for it by the employer and society at large.

The analysis of the secondary labor market went in two directions. One was to focus on the marginalized workers themselves and argue the need to build their skills to enable them to break into the market for better jobs. Business and government concern over ghetto upheaval gave a certain urgency to this approach. Prompted by the Kerner Commission's conclusion that poor employment prospects for blacks contributed to the riots of the 1960s, the public and private sectors began pumping large sums of money into "manpower development" programs.

The other course involved looking at the structure of industry to see which kinds of businesses tended to offer lower-quality jobs because of the greater competitive pressures they faced. Dual labor markets were seen to mirror the existence of a dual industrial structure, divided between industries like auto and steel that were highly concentrated, and more fragmented ones like apparel and services in which the need to cut costs was a matter of life and death.

Some regarded the low wages and poor work conditions in the latter sector as simply inevitable, while others saw something more telling. Economist Sar Levitan has written:

> It is a curious irony of the free market system that those industries that are often the closest approximations of the mythical state of perfect competition are also the same sectors of the economy that contain high percentages of the working poor.

Whether ironic or not, it is undeniable that as the business system in the U.S. was restructured in the 1980s, the ranks of contingent workers expanded rapidly. Conditions that were once considered to have ended in the nineteenth century or to be limited to the ghetto or marginal industries are spreading to the most respectable sectors of the economy.

Labor as a Liquid Asset

Since the late 1970s the electronics firm Motorola has placed its employees in three categories: about 30 percent of them, those with 10 years or more of service, are guaranteed their jobs even during downturns in the economy; 40 percent are regular employees but have no such guarantees; and the remaining 30 percent are on six-month contracts which the company can terminate on 24 hours' notice.

Apple Computer laid off 20 percent of its work force in 1985 and began staffing more than 15 percent of its remaining labor needs with temps. Ten percent of Digital Equipment Corp.'s domestic manufacturing workers are hired on a temporary basis.

Low-paid part-timers called "adjunct lecturers" or "instructors" make up about a third of the teaching force at the country's institutions of higher education, with the figure rising to about 50 percent at community colleges. In addition, many of the full-timers are "gypsy scholars": teachers hired on short-term contracts who jump from school to school every few years seeking a tenure-track position.

A study of low-wage day labor pools found that among the users were companies like General Electric, IBM, Coca-Cola, and B.F. Goodrich.

These are but a few examples of how the use of contingent labor has become the rage among American employers. Large companies are beginning to abandon their role as providers of better, more secure jobs and are keeping more of their new hires in a peripheral status. At the same time, smaller companies, the traditional source of marginal jobs, have been expanding their share of total employment. While a precise measurement of contingent labor is difficult because of the elusive nature of the phenomenon, there is no doubt that it is spreading like a poisonous weed in American society.

To some eyes, of course, it is more like a fast-growing rose with a few unfortunate thorns. Former Labor Secretary Bill Brock, for instance, once gushed: "It's a phenomenal economic and social event. The leaning-down of American business over the last six years has been very substantial. . . . Tough on people, but we have more competitive companies as a result."

A leading management analyst of labor has noted approvingly: "As American industry tries to become more adaptive and responsive (that is, competitive), all employment relationships are going to become more fluid." What this suggests is that companies should be able to treat labor like a liquid asset—something that can be manipulated freely and discarded at will.

Like many management fads these days, the promotion of such fluidity was an import from Japan. As the U.S. marveled at the highly motivated, highly productive Japanese worker with guaranteed lifetime employment, Western observers were conveniently ignoring the fact that the glowing picture did not apply to the entire Japanese labor force.

The Japanese system works as well as it does because companies make use of a marginal work force that enjoys none of the advantages of the permanent employees. These precarious workers are often employees of small subcontractors that make possible the much-vaunted "just-in-time" inventory system and serve to absorb the blows of the Japanese business cycle. As one of the rare American accounts of the phenomenon put it, "It is this lower level of smaller plants that supports the entire structure. By forcing their subcontractors to do more for less, the exporting giants can keep their quality high and their prices low."

In many cases workers on the payroll of the subcontractors toil side by side with the core employees, the two distinguished only by the colors of their hardhats or uniforms. They can be brought in or shipped out at virtually a moment's notice, with no strings attached for the large firm. Japanese journalist Satoshi Kamata, who took a job as a contingent worker in a Toyota plant, was dazzled by the array of different uniforms worn by the various categories of workers. "There are so many ranks," he wrote, "that I can't memorize them all at once. It's as if we've joined the army."

A spokesman for Nippon Steel told a Western journalist that his company's contingent workers were "part of the family," but when pressed he admitted this was "an old sense of family"—one in which "the superior members think it natural that they are richer and more powerful than their lesser relatives."

This inegalitarian family structure is spreading rapidly among U.S. companies heeding the siren call of flexibility and labor cost reduction—not to mention union avoidance. The transient relationship contingent workers have with employers and the fact that many of them are isolated working in their homes make union organization extremely difficult. It is no surprise that the rate of unionization among part-time workers was only 6.7 percent in 1989, and among temps and contract workers it was close to nil.

Even where unions exist among the regular work force, companies have pushed for the right to make greater use of precarious labor. The Japanese auto company Mazda, for instance, successfully pressured the United Auto Workers to allow it to use short-term hires at its factory in Michigan. The temps have no guarantee of minimum hours—they can be called in and paid for only a few hours a day—and no seniority rights or protection under the grievance procedure. This dualism within its work force must make the Japanese company feel right at home.

Shortchanging Short-Timers

It is easier to get a sense of the dimensions of contingent labor by looking at its different forms. The first is part-time employment. The traditional view was that only certain categories of workers took part-time jobs and that they sought them for their own convenience. Married women looking to earn some pin money, students in need of pocket money, and retired people wanting to pick up a bit of extra cash: these were thought to constitute virtually the entire population interested in less than 35 hours of employment a week (the standard adopted by federal statisticians).

Employers providing these jobs were thought to be doing the workers a favor. During the 1970s articles in women's magazines implored employers to make more part-time work available to women with child care responsibilities. Control Data Corp. got reams of favorable press when it set up an operation staffed entirely by part-timers: a morning shift for women with school-age children and another in the afternoon for students.

The campaign was successful, and the army of the partly employed multiplied. Between 1954 (the first year for which data exist) and 1977, the number of part-time employees in nonagricultural industries increased at an average annual rate of 4 percent—more than double the rate of increase for full-timers. By that latter year nearly a third of all women in the labor force worked part-time.

During the 1980s the ranks of part-timers continued to expand, but for different reasons. While the earlier growth was primarily among so-called voluntary part-timers, the next wave consisted largely of those who had wanted full-time work but could only find a part-time job. There had always been a certain number of involuntary part-timers during recessionary periods, but in the mid-1980s this phenomenon continued to spread even when the recovery was in full swing. From 1979 to 1989 involuntary part-time jobs increased nearly twice as fast as voluntary ones, or full-time jobs for that matter. By the end of that period, during a widely hailed period of prosperity, some five million people were still working less than full time against their wishes—not including those who held two or more part-time jobs that added up to 35 or more hours.

Among those forced into this diminished status was Larry White, a worker at LymphoMed Inc., a small Chicago drug company that took great pains to restrict its full-time work force. White told a reporter in 1985: "You can't build a lifestyle around part-time work."

The trend was accelerating because many more employers had discovered the advantages of a part-time work force and began using short-timers for jobs that were previously held by people working a full week. The traditional sources of part-time work—retail trade and food service—continued to fuel the boom, but the growth was also seen in a wide range of white- and blue-collar jobs. In occupations like that of bank teller, full-time work became all but extinct. Even the federal government joined the bandwagon after a 1978 law allowed the expansion of part-time jobs within the civil service system.

In the most egregious cases, employers simply laid off regular workers and replaced them with part-timers. In 1985 many of the customer service representatives for People Express were told that they were being replaced by part-time college students. At the Spiegel Catalogue operation, part-timers were brought in to take over what had been full-time jobs. In 1986 Mellon Bank of Pittsburgh terminated its contract with a unionized cleaning company and arranged for the same 80 janitors to be rehired as part-time employees of a nonunion contractor.

A primary motivation in all this is cost. Employers feel justified paying most part-timers less per hour than full-time workers doing the same work—in part because women continue to make up two-thirds of the short-timers. In 1989 the median hourly wage for part-timers was $4.83—some 40 percent less than the $7.83 figure for full-time workers. Part-timers account for more than half of those workers earning the minimum wage.

Part-timers are also frequently denied fringe benefits. Less than 20 percent of them are covered by employer pension plans, and more than half get no medical coverage on the job. In some states, because of minimum earnings requirements, low-wage part-timers do not even qualify for unemployment insurance when they are laid off. One study summed up the conditions aptly: "The occasional ad for a part-time senior executive notwithstanding, the vast majority of part-timers hold the same types of positions they always have held—low-wage, dead-end jobs that offer few, if any, benefits or promotional opportunities."

The fact that most part-timers are in the "voluntary" category allows many observers to continue depicting the proliferation of short-time schedules as a largely benign trend. The problem is that the official categories do not distinguish between those unwilling to take full-time work and those unable to consider it, because of factors like the unavailability of affordable child care. All that the federal statisticians care about is whether one is available for full-time work, even if many of those who are not available are nonetheless in need of a full-time income.

Moreover, the fact that someone is working part-time voluntarily does not diminish the importance of those earnings to family well-being. Without the part-time earnings of a spouse, more than half a million additional families would become poor or near poor. In other words, that part-time work which many employers feel free to devalue is all that keeps many families from sinking into severe privation.

There is a certain irony in the whole part-time phenomenon. It was not long ago that the labor movement was still seeking a reduction in the workweek—a traditional quest which had stalled during the postwar period. Unions in Europe continue to push the demand, arguing that it would help reduce unemployment by forcing companies to expand their payrolls.

In a twisted way the goal has been achieved. Employers are offering shorter workweeks; the problem is that the weekly wage has shrunk along with the time on the job. Shorter hours, instead of being a process for improving the life of workers, has turned into another instrument of their depreciation.

The Throwaway Work Force

The second major component of contingent labor is temporary employment. As with part-time work, the growth of temp jobs has been portrayed as a boon to those people not available for a full-time, full-year work schedule. The traditional idea of temp work was an activity for housewives returning to the labor market, students working during summer vacations, actors picking up some cash between roles, and new workers looking to test out various kinds of jobs before settling down into one of them.

The only portion of this work force that has been accurately counted are those working through temporary help agencies. The temp agencies are the classic middlemen. Workers in need of temporary work register with them, are sent out to toil in the office or factory of another company, and are paid by the agency, which, of course, collects substantially more per hour from the company than is paid to the worker.

Originating in the late 1940s, the temp industry, led by companies like Manpower and Kelly Services, grew steadily but not dramatically until the early 1980s. Then something unusual happened. The ranks of agency temps, which had been in the vicinity of 300 to 400 thousand workers, started to climb sharply in 1983—this in the midst of economic recovery. As the 1980s progressed, the army of temps continued to expand, reaching the one million mark in 1987. In recent years temp services have been among the fastest growing industries in the U.S., and the sector's employment level is expected to increase more than 60 percent by the end of the century. These figures do not include the undetermined number of temps who are hired directly by employers. Their numbers have been estimated as high as 18 million. That may be greatly exaggerated, but there is no doubt that millions of American workers are employed in impermanent positions.

The sudden swelling of the temp work force was not the result of an outpouring of employer concern for all those who wanted short-term jobs. It was, instead, another symptom of the decision by business to convert more workers to precarious status. No longer were temps used simply to fill in for regular employees on vacation or maternity leave, or to work solely on special short-term projects.

In more and more companies temps are being used on an ongoing basis, permanently taking over work that was previously done by regular employees. The high tech companies of Silicon Valley have at times drawn up to 30 percent of their work force from temp agencies. Weyerhaeuser established a pool of 70 temps to handle secretarial and clerical jobs at its Tacoma, Washington, headquarters. Tektronix Inc. has a virtual phobia about hiring permanent employees. One of its executives told a reporter in 1988: "We'd rather have a distant relationship with that buffer work force than a close one because of our concerns about promising too much to someone."

One of the biggest users of temps is now the federal government. The practice was given a big push by the Reagan administration, and temporary employment (including those in the postal system) reached 300 thousand by 1988. Federal administrators obviously liked the cost savings and increased freedom to fire, for in the final months of the Reagan era, the Office of Personnel Management issued rules allowing managers for the first time to make use of temp services.

By 1985 a temp agency executive was able to gloat: "Our business has changed from a replacement and fill-in service to an effective tool for managing labor costs." As with part-timers, this was possible because temps are cheap labor. In 1987 their average hourly wage was $6.42, but that figure was skewed upward by the increasing number of professionals working as temps. The largest group of temps, general office clerks, earned an average of $5.11, and for construction laborers the figure was a meager $3.72.

Temps may cost business a bit more per hour than a part-timer, but that difference is more than made up for by the fact that no benefits have to be paid. In some cases temps will receive benefits from the agency they work for, but the eligibility requirements are usually stiff.

In 1987 only 24 percent of temps received health benefits and 37 percent got paid holidays. Some 74 percent received paid vacations, but they usually had to work 1,500 hours to qualify.

The near-universal absence of unions among temps helps keep these conditions dismal. Yet small groups of workers have fought back. In Auburn, New York, a group called WANT (Workers and No Temporaries) was formed to protest the increasing replacement of regular jobs with temporary positions. During a demonstration in which temps marched with paper bags over their heads to conceal their identity, one worker told a reporter: "The bottom line is that any time spent as a regular employee leaves you better off than being a temp."

The use of temps covers the entire gamut of occupations, from the lowest-paid and unskilled jobs to the most specialized and relatively well compensated. At the upper end of the scale are the growing numbers of professionals who have been "temporized." Accountants, engineers, and computer programmers are increasingly brought in as needed from agencies. There are special temp services for lawyers—a phenomenon that the American Bar Association finally gave its blessing to in late 1988 after years of handwringing over potential conflicts of interest and the traditional taboo against a lawyer sharing his fee with a nonlawyer. And if professionals can be temps, then why not the boss? Some temp agencies have gotten into the rent-a-boss business, supplying managers for small companies whose chief executives die or become seriously ill without designating a successor.

At the other end of the spectrum are the day labor pools that provide very short-term unskilled work for the most desperate members of the population. These pools function like union hiring halls without any protection for the workers, who are often homeless. The workers show up at the agency early in the morning and wait around for hours for assignments, which usually involve exhausting manual labor or unpleasant and dirty jobs like cleaning presses at a newspaper.

At Peakload Labor in Atlanta the job seekers arrive at 5:00 A.M. On a typical day in 1988 a worker named Johnny Tartt was one of those chosen to spend the day picking up trash and sweeping at the construction site of a Hewlett-Packard facility in the Buckhead section of the city. Compared to the jobs often provided by Peakload, this was a decent one: it was indoors and involved only light lifting. The next day, however, Tartt showed up at Peakload a bit late and the Hewlett-Packard slots had already been filled.

A study of these labor pools by the Southern Regional Council found that typical take-home pay for an eight-hour job was $20–25, after deductions taken by the agencies for transportation, work gloves, and whatever other charges they could fabricate. The agencies also arrange things so that it is almost impossible for the day laborers to qualify for unemployment insurance or disability payments. One of the few black owners of a day labor pool put it candidly: "To be honest, temporary service ain't nothing but a tossover from slavery. It's flesh peddling. They modify it and dress it up some. But it's slavery."

Unpadding the Payroll

If it makes sense for an employer to keep some workers off the regular payroll, then why not all of them? This stroke of capitalist genius occurred in the 1970s in the minds of some California entrepreneurs who saw that doctors and other professionals in private practice resented the trouble involved in keeping their assistants on a payroll.

Financial consultant Marvin Selter claims to have invented the arrangement that became known as employee leasing in 1972 when three ear, nose, and throat specialists approached him for advice on how to squirrel away large sums for their own retirement without doing the same for their employees. Whether or not Selter was first, he did help inspire the growth of a sizable employee leasing industry.

Following the model of the sale/leaseback arrangements used for equipment and airplanes, the leasing companies provided a service to small businesses under which they would fire all their employees and allow them to be rehired by the leasing company. The workers would continue to do exactly what they did before and in the same place, but they would now be paid by the leasing company, which received payments from the "subscriber" equal to the wage bill plus a markup of 5–10 percent.

Limited forms of employee leasing had existed for decades, including the leasing of security guards and truck drivers. But it took the contingent-labor mentality of the 1980s to permit a boom in arrangements in which a company's entire work force was put in this unorthodox arrangement.

There was also an element of personal greed. One of the prime incentives for small-business owners to use leasing was a provision in the 1982 federal tax act that allowed companies to avoid extending their pension plan to leased workers. This meant that entrepreneurs could set up lucrative plans for themselves alone and contribute large amounts of tax-free money into them. The juicy tax shelter was permissible as long as the leasing company contributed at least 7.5 percent of worker compensation into a pension plan for the leased employees.

The tax incentive was restricted by the 1986 tax law changes, but employee leasing continued to grow among business owners who still yearned to eliminate their payroll. In 1989 there were an estimated 500 thousand leased employees in the U.S., and the number was thought to be growing at an annual rate of 30 percent.

The advocates of leasing claim that it is a godsend for the employee as well as the employer. Leasing companies, it is said, can offer better benefits than most small employers, and there is usually no reduction in pay when workers are switched over to leased status. A brochure on the services provided by Employee Leasing of New York assures employers concerned about how their workers will respond to being leased: "Experience shows that they'll love it!"

The problem, however, is the change in status itself. Like temping, leasing puts workers in a position in which it is unclear who their employer is. There are specific legal problems—like the question of who is responsible for maintaining equal employment standards; but more generally, the ambiguity of the relationship weakens the power of the work force. Who does a worker negotiate with for a raise? Who has the power to discipline or fire a worker? What happens if the leasing company cannot meet its payroll or is unable to provide the promised fringe benefits?

The confusion also serves to deter union organizing. Don Henry, president of Los Angeles-based Wonder Industries, admitted to a reporter that this was a primary motivation for his move to leasing. "Union work rules would have devastated us," he said. "With Omnistaff as our employer, we have been able to keep out the union."

Exploitation Hits Home

Another form of contingent labor involves changing not the hours of work or the employment relationship, but the place of work. In the 1980s employers rediscovered one of the oldest production arrangements: home labor.

The practice of transferring work from the factory to the worker's home has long been characterized as one of the worst forms of capitalist exploitation. A century ago Marx described the miserable conditions of home laborers in Britain and left no doubt about their lack of autonomy. He described their activity as "an outside department of the factory" controlled "by means of invisible threads."

In early twentieth-century America abuses were rampant. A 1913 study of Italian immigrant women making artificial flowers at home contained the following account:

> In a tenement on Macdougal Street lives a family of seven—grandmother, father, mother, and four children aged four years, three years, two years and one month respectively. All excepting the father and the two babies make violets. The three-year-old girl picks apart the petals; her sister, aged four years, separates the stems, dipping an end of each into paste spread on a piece of board on the kitchen table and the mother and grandmother slip the petals up the stems.

After decades of such reports the federal government finally realized that it could not enforce labor standards in homework, and in the 1940s Washington outlawed the practice in seven industries that were the worst offenders. After that the practice seemed to decline, largely forgotten except for the occasional exposé about an unscrupulous garment subcontractor.

This changed in the 1980s. Suddenly newspapers in cities like New York and Los Angeles were again running stories about desperate workers, usually immigrant women, doing tedious and sub-minimum-wage work at their kitchen table. Often these same workers toiled long hours in a sweatshop—another supposedly antiquated work arrangement that was enjoying a resurgence—and then took additional work to perform at home.

One of the women pulled into this new labor market was Isabel Magriz. After a kidney ailment made it too difficult for her to work in a factory, she began sewing dresses for a garment contractor in her South Bronx apartment. She earned only $1.30 per dress, and the contractor took various phony deductions from her pay. "It's not for Social Security," she told a reporter, "They take out 6 percent for giving me the privilege of working off the books."

While many of the employers of home labor are anonymous middlemen, several big-name designers—including Nancy Reagan's favorite, Adolfo—have been accused of engaging in the practice. In 1987 the International Ladies Garment Workers Union launched a campaign against Norma Kamali, charging her with using homeworkers paid $2 an hour. The union found one Kamali seamstress who worked two whole days on a full-length velour coat and was paid $45. The coat retailed for $950.

The new homework is not limited to the cities. Companies like General Motors have literally begun to farm out subassembly work to rural workers in the Midwest. In Iowa farm wives like Sarah Johnson put together front-end suspension components for GM cars, earning piecework wages that often amount to only a few dollars an hour. "The worst part," Johnson told a reporter, "is that the work is always there waiting for you. On Sundays. On holidays. It's there when you get up in the morning. And after you're through farming at night. There's just no turning it off. I'm sure they're taking advantage of us. I mean, *somebody* was getting paid a lot of money to do this in Detroit."

Electronic Sweatshops

In addition to the industries traditionally associated with home labor, the practice began to appear, of all places, in Silicon Valley. Semiconductor companies saw an opportunity to cut their costs on labor-intensive operations like stuffing (attaching integrated circuits to printed circuit boards) by having it done by pieceworkers toiling at home. An investigation by the *San Jose Mercury-News* concluded that "thousands of people and millions of dollars are involved." Many of the workers involved were found to be Indochinese refugees and immigrants from countries like the Philippines, some of whom had been doing similar work at American-owned factories in their native land.

Although performing semiconductor work at home is not itself illegal, the practice usually ran afoul of the law by violating labor regulations and operating off the books. Another horror is the health aspect. The work often exposed homeworkers and their families to dangerous fumes from soldering and toxic solvents that had to be heated on the kitchen stove.

Precise figures on the numbers of homeworkers are impossible to assemble, for obvious reasons. A 1981 study estimated that there were more than 50 thousand illegal homeworkers in New York City alone. The director of the study told a reporter: "The enormity of industrial homework in New York went beyond surprise. It's almost like a typhus epidemic. You think it's stamped out, eradicated and brought under control, but there it is, massive and spreading."

It was in the middle of this epidemic that the Reagan administration decided to act. But rather than taking steps to control the plague,

Reagan made it easier for the disease to spread: in 1981 his administration began a relentless campaign to lift the ban on homework in the seven industries where it had been outlawed. The prohibition, it was said, represented an unwarranted government encroachment on the right of people to decide where they wanted to work.

This position was encouraged by analysts of the New Right who argued that homework was a desirable way of reconciling the need of many women to earn an income and their "proper" role as housewives. At the conservatives' 1982 Family Forum in Washington, for instance, one speaker at a panel on cottage industry declared: "Nothing is more important than helping women stay at home with their children." Pay was obviously one of those secondary considerations, for the same speaker happily announced: "If you work at home, you only need to earn a third as much money."

The Reagan crusade to allow workers in all industries to be exploited in their homes was blocked a number of times in the courts. Yet the champions of the right to work did not give up. The last major act of the Reagan Labor Department was to lift the ban once again, but opponents from organized labor vowed to continue the fight.

The 1980s also saw the emergence of an entirely new form of home labor, made possible by advances in technology. Dubbed "telecommuting," it involved shifting clerical work from offices to workers toiling at home on computer terminals linked by phone lines to the office. As with other kinds of contingent labor, the introduction of computer homework was depicted as an act of kindness for mothers of young children and others who could not leave home but needed an income.

It certainly was a boon for the disabled, but for others there was a high price to pay for the privilege of being able to work in the privacy of their own home. As with part-time and temp labor, most employers who began experimenting with clerical homework felt perfectly justified paying people substandard wages, denying them benefits, and offering no job security. While the employer saved on overhead, many homeworkers had to pay a rental charge for the equipment they used. One of the most controversial telecommuting programs was the one started by Blue Cross-Blue Shield of South Carolina. Workers like Ann Blackwell were required to process hundreds of claims a day at a rate of 16 cents each—minus equipment rental charges paid to Blue Cross. Blackwell ended up working some 50 hours a week, with no paid vacation time, no paid sick leave, and no other fringe benefits.

The advantages of not having to travel to an office are overshadowed by the pressures of toiling on a piecework basis and having one's productivity, down to the keystroke, monitored by the computer. Electronic homework can also be used as a testing ground for methods of intensifying work in the office. For these reasons the AFL-CIO in 1983 called for a ban on the practice.

If for the boss electronic homework means higher profits, for the worker the arrangement means isolation and an end to the socializing and informal cooperation that are often the only things that make a job bearable. In an advertisement for Lanier Business Products' Telestaff System, the supplier of homework equipment praised the virtues of a physically dispersed labor force: "The Telestaff Station. It brings work to your office. Not people."

Telecommuting has not been growing as fast as some enthusiastic proponents—including futurologist Alvin Toffler, who hailed the arrival of the "electronic cottage"—were predicting in the early 1980s. Various analysts have suggested that there may be millions of telecommuters in the U.S., but most of them are people, like workaholic executives, with regular jobs who do extra work on their computer at home. The number of full-time electronic home clerical workers is probably less than 20 thousand. The future growth of that number was put into question by a 1986 lawsuit brought by a group of eight electronic homeworkers employed by a California insurance company. They charged that the homework program was a "subterfuge" to avoid paying them benefits and that they were forced to work under extreme pressure up to 14 hours a day to meet their quotas. The case, which was settled out of court, has caused many employers to think twice about joining the telecommuting trend.

Dispersing the Factory

While business apologists depict the increasing use of various forms of contingent labor as merely a pragmatic measure to reduce costs, there is actually something more significant taking place. With arrangements like temps, leased employees, and homeworkers, business is transforming the employment relationship and in a sense dissolving it. As a result some workers cease to be workers and are metamorphosed into pseudo-capitalists. Known as free-lancers, consultants, project workers, or independent contractors, these are people who are not technically employees and who are paid a fee rather than a wage.

There are, of course, some truly autonomous free-lancers and consultants who work for a variety of clients and who exercise a great deal of control over their work. Yet a larger number are simply contingent workers who should be employees but who are forced into "independent" status by companies solely to deny them benefits and job security. No one knows how many people may fall into this category, but even the Internal Revenue Service recognizes it is a scam. The IRS has been investigating the independent contractor arrangement and has found irregularities in nearly all the companies examined. The freelance status also provides the worker with enhanced opportunities for tax avoidance, or if the situation is off the books, outright evasion; but the employer has much more to gain.

The conversion of employees into supposedly independent suppliers of services is part of a larger process in which companies are reducing the amount of work done by people on their regular payrolls. In addition to bringing contingent labor in, this phenomenon involves sending work out. Sometimes it is sent out to individuals, as in the use of homeworkers, but much more common is the practice of contracting out portions of production to smaller enterprises.

Subcontracting in certainly not new. In industries like apparel it has always been the way things were done. Yet the 1980s saw an increasing urge among companies of all sorts to engage in this method of reducing costs. Industrial giants like the big automakers have gotten the bug; at Chrysler, for instance, some 70 percent of the value of its U.S.-produced cars comes from subcontractors. The practice has also become rampant in the steel industry, and it was one of the main points of contention in the 1986 labor dispute at USX. The semiconductor industry is also fond of "outsourcing," either to the homeworkers mentioned earlier or to tiny workshops. The federal government is in effect doing the same thing under the guise of privatization.

The rise of subcontracting has been in part inspired by the Japanese model, but it is also patterned after a process that has been underway in Italy since the early 1970s. Italian business responded to the intense worker militancy of the late 1960s by shifting large portions of production from large factories, where the upheaval had been greatest, to small, dispersed enterprises that were often off the books. This decentralization of production served to weaken the labor movement by dispersing many workers into situations where unions did not exist and wages and working conditions were inferior.

Some sectors of the "fabbrica diffusa" (dispersed factory) were outright sweatshops, such as the basement operations in Naples in which child laborers were exposed to toxic fumes. Others were more artisan and avoided the worst forms of exploitation. Yet both represented a step backward from the social wage that workers were trying to achieve with their struggles in the industrial centers.

This background should be kept in mind when listening to the advocates of "flexible specialization" as the solution to America's competitive problems. The proponents of the Italian model envision a system in which highly adaptable small firms take the place of moribund large corporations and prosper in the ever-changing conditions of the world economy. Michael Piore and Charles Sabel have championed the system as part of a process of constructing a "yeoman democracy."

Putting aside the question of whether such small firms are as magically efficient as their apologists would have us believe, the decentralization of production does not bode well for those who depend on a wage to survive. The reason is that in general small business is not good for workers, even when they are regular employees rather than contingent ones.

A 1983 Census Bureau survey, the most recent available, found that 40 percent of workers in firms with fewer than 100 employees earned less than $5 an hour, compared with 21 percent in firms with payrolls of 100 or more. In 1986 only 16 percent of employees in small firms (under 100 workers) had pension coverage, compared to 69 percent in larger ones; for health insurance the figures were 55 percent versus 98 percent. The variations were due in part to the degree of unionization, which is inversely correlated with the size of firms.

Even the federal government's Small Business Administration, a tireless cheerleader for smaller enterprise, had to admit in one of its reports: "Compared to large businesses, small businesses hire more young workers, pay lower salaries to a larger proportion of workers, hire more workers on a part-time basis, and hire more 'secondary workers,' i.e. second wage earners in a family with two or more workers." In other words, they crank out lousy jobs.

Flexibility for Whom?

The proliferation of contingent labor, subcontracting, and decentralized production is praised by business analysts under the banner of flexibility—the new religion of corporate America. What is puzzling about this is that rigidities in labor markets and other economic institutions used to be considered a problem faced by America's competitors.

When U.S.-based multinationals were invading Europe in the 1960s they were constantly grumbling about the severe restrictions they faced in their personnel policies. The United States, on the other hand, was portrayed as a bastion of business freedom. It was here that managers could hire and fire at will, and even in unionized situations companies were able to use layoffs and plant closings to control their costs. Wages may have been higher than in Europe, but unions did not encroach on management's turf.

By the late 1970s this was no longer enough for a business class that was seeking to respond to heightened international competition by putting the screws on workers. Along with the direct assault on organized labor, this has meant the transformation of hiring practices discussed here under the rubric of contingent labor. What is so pernicious about this trend is that it exploits the genuine desire and need of many workers for more flexible working situations. Yet it is the employer's quest for flexibility that dominates today's contingent labor, not the employee's. Whatever the worker can obtain in limited hours, short-term jobs and work at home is purchased at a scandalously high price.

The way business has set the rules, insecurity and privation are inseparable from flexibility. The old idea that an employer has obligations to a worker has been discarded and replaced with a phony ideology of self-reliance. One business consultant expressed this as "a complete reversal of the fundamental notion that we 'work' for someone else. Instead, it says we only work for ourselves—for our own futures." In other words, the boss owes you nothing. You and your boss are simply two equal entrepreneurs coming together for a brief moment in the marketplace.

For the time being, business has been able to shed its obligations to a large portion of the labor force without much social outcry. That could change suddenly with the end of official prosperity. Even a conservative magazine like the *Economist* of London has warned that the new type of employment "has put several million Americans on a limb, which may be sawn off at the onset of recession."

The contingent strategy could also backfire for business over the longer term. A report by the Congressional Office of Technology Assessment noted that "an economy that achieves flexibility largely through the use of 'disposable' workers, who accumulate little experience and have little loyalty to an individual employer, pays a considerable price." This lesson was overlooked even as the business world was moaning about growing shortages of qualified workers. Somehow it never dawns on the captains of industry that poor wages and working conditions might be the reason why there continued to be close to a million "discouraged workers"—those who have given up the search for work as hopeless—during a time of low official unemployment rates.

While American business cannot be expected to rise above its preoccupation with short-term gains, it is surprising that government policymakers have not paid more attention to the long-term consequences of having a widening section of the labor force in precarious conditions. As work becomes increasingly fragmented, the set of protections that used to be provided by individual employers will have to be made available to everyone at a social level. This means a universal program of health insurance, an improved Social Security system, and some form of guaranteed income. Until this occurs, the dream of achieving a decent living standard through the labor market will become an increasingly distant one for millions of Americans.

· SIX ·

Sticking It to the Union

"**W**HAT galls me," said Charles Wilt, "is that we were one of the best, if not the best mill in the Hammermill system. We set production records. We won all kinds of awards." International Paper ignored all this when they took over the company in late 1986, Wilt said, "and all they were interested in was getting concessions."

Wilt, who in late 1988 was not living up to his nickname "Smiley," spent 40 years in the paper mill in the central Pennsylvania town of Lock Haven and served for more than a decade as president of the local union. In 1987 he and 2,300 other members of the United Paperworkers International Union in Lock Haven, Jay, Maine, and De-Pere, Wisconsin, went on strike to resist wage cuts and changes in work rules demanded by the $8 billion International Paper Company—and to support 1,200 other workers who had been locked out by IP in Mobile, Alabama, after they voted against the givebacks. To William Meserve, president of the Jay local union since 1972, "accepting the concessions would have set us back 30 years."

The paperworkers put up an aggressive fight, but it was not enough. The strike collapsed in October 1988, and the union made an unconditional offer to return to work. Yet IP stood firm on its refusal to rehire all the strikers, whose jobs had been given by the company to what are politely called permanent replacements, more commonly known in the labor movement as scabs.

While the locked-out workers in Mobile were entitled to their jobs back after the union reached a settlement with management, those in the other three locations had to wait to be rehired in order of seniority as openings developed among the scab work force. As of the middle of 1989 only about 100 of the 2,300 strikers were back on the job.

"It's hard to see our people out of work," said Wilt. "We created those jobs; we built this company. What they did to us was unjust. It's affected the community, dividing people against one another—even among the children, in the Little League. It's going to take a long, long time to heal."

Dale Martin, another Lock Haven striker, feels there is something self-defeating about the efforts of profitable companies like International Paper to demand contract concessions. "If these companies keep driving down wages, there's going to be no middle class left. We'll be back in a situation where there are only the rich and the poor. Then who's going to buy the cars made in Detroit and other products? Corporations are being very short-sighted—they're only concerned with a fast buck and are not realizing that they could go down the tubes too."

The Corporate Iron Fist

Whether short-sighted or not, the corporate assault against union wage levels was one of the most alarming developments of the 1980s. Throughout American industry a wave of employer militancy not seen since the 1930s knocked the wind out of organized labor.

Companies used the threat of mass layoffs and plant shutdowns to wring extensive contract concessions from even the strongest unions. The postwar custom of regular wage increases was brazenly challenged by firms insisting that workers had to make sacrifices to help management deal with the increasingly competitive business climate.

When unions dared to defy the new logic of austerity by calling a walkout, business responded with an iron fist. Strike after strike was crushed as companies used whatever means were necessary—scabs, court injunctions, the National Guard—to continue operating. The result was that workers lost not only the contract dispute but often their jobs as well.

Even those workers who dared not strike were vulnerable. Business revived the lockout (barring union workers from the job when contract negotiations break down) as a tool of coercion, and in some instances companies made use of the bankruptcy laws to rid themselves of union contracts.

Labor law also became a tool of corporate control, thanks to a series of anti-union rulings by the Supreme Court and the promanagement members of the National Labor Relations Board appointed by the Reagan administration. In this climate, employers were able to continue their offensive, begun in the 1970s, against new organizing, using antiunion consultants and techniques of psychological manipulation as well as old-fashioned intimidation.

"This is the worst antiunion, antilabor period in my lifetime," said United Auto Workers vice president Donald Ephlin in 1983, "We are the only country in the free world where the labor movement is fighting for its life."

The prevailing sentiment in the business world is that the country would be better off if labor lost that battle and there were no longer annoying third parties interfering with the sacred right to manage. "Unions are on their way out," management consultant Richard Lyles cheerfully announced in an interview with a business journal. "Twenty-first century historians will look back on this time right now—let's say from about 1982 to the mid-1990s—and they will call it the Management Revolution."

Brightening prospects for a union-free society may make corporate hearts beat faster, but such a development would bring nothing but woe for the vast majority of working Americans. Though it is no longer fashionable to mention it, unions have done more than any other institution over the past century to raise the living standards of the average American. It is for this reason that the business austerity drive consists in large part of a drive to cripple the labor movement.

What Unions Do

In decades past, the greatest benefits of unionism have been enjoyed, of course, by union members themselves. During the period from the rise of U.S. industry until the federal government's sanctioning of collective bargaining in the 1930s, the life of the American worker was a harsh one. For the most part, employers in the U.S. followed the stony-hearted example of their British counterparts in keeping wages as low as possible, imposing inhuman work schedules, firing at will, making use of child labor, and disposing of older workers when their productivity declined. Many workers were forced to buy goods at inflated prices in company stores, and others had to rent overpriced housing in company towns. Insecurity and deprivation were the hallmarks of working life.

Between 1840 and 1890, for instance, average wage rates adjusted for inflation swung up and down along with the business cycle and other economic and political variables. As a result, real wages in 1864 were lower than in 1840, those in 1881 lower than in 1869, to take some random examples. Writing about the era preceding World War I, historian Norman Ware noted that while wages in manufacturing remained stagnant, this was "perhaps one of the longest periods of 'prosperity'—for the few—in American history."

Not only were workers unable to count on secure, adequate pay, but they often felt powerless on the job. In her account of entering the labor force early in the century, Rose Cohen painted a vivid picture of tyranny in the workplace:

> He paid me three dollars [a week] and for this he hurried me from early until late. He gave me only two coats at a time to do. When I took them over and as he handed me the new work he would say quickly and sharply, "Hurry!" And when he did not say it in words he looked at me and I seemed to hear even more plainly, "Hurry!" I hurried but he was never satisfied. . . . Late at night when the people would stand up and begin to fold their work away and I too would rise, feeling stiff in every limb and thinking with dread of our cold empty little room and the uncooked rice, he would come over with still another coat."

Skilled workers had a better time of it until late in the nineteenth-century, when a process of homogenization of labor—caused by greater mechanization and standardization of production—reduced their autonomy. The craft system gave way to the scientific management championed by Frederick Winslow Taylor, in which the labor process was broken down into discrete units of time and motion. Managers were encouraged to use this analysis to push their workers to the limits of human endurance.

It was mainly through unions that workers were able to pose a countervailing force to the power of capital, which was transforming the economy at a dizzying pace. As far as the labor process was concerned, the dominion of management was never fully challenged, but unions did seek to introduce a degree of regularity and security in the process. It was in the area of wages and benefits that most union leaders focused their energies. Samuel Gompers, founder of the American Federation of Labor, was fond of summarizing the goals of the union movement in a single word: *more.*

To gain more for their members, unions had to make collective bargaining a substitute for the market in setting the terms of employment;

in other words, wages had to be taken out of competition. The determination of pay by union strength rather than the laws of supply and demand is upsetting to economists, and even the liberals among them fret how this "monopoly power" leads to "misallocation of resources." Yet what may appear to the theorist as inefficiency is precisely the process that raised workers out of poverty.

Estimating the union wage effect has a long history. The early studies were based on simple comparisons of the different pay levels and degrees of unionization among industries. It was not until the 1970s that analysts were able to use more extensive data samples and advanced statistical techniques to come up with more sophisticated estimates.

In their book *What Do Unions Do?*—a survey of research on labor economics—Richard Freeman and James Medoff found that the premium paid to union workers generally ranges from 20 to 30 percent. Moreover, workers who switch from nonunion to union jobs experience, on average, a significant gain in pay, nearly 28 percent in one study. Similar gains are experienced by workers remaining in union jobs compared with those who move to nonunion positions.

Despite more than a decade of declining union power, in 1989 the median weekly earnings of unionized full-time wage and salary workers were 34 percent above that of their nonunion counterparts. For the occupational group "machine operators, assemblers and inspectors" the differential was 49 percent.

The greatest reward from unionization is enjoyed by workers who are younger, less educated, and less skilled. This could be termed the *democratic effect* of unions: they give a special boost to those who come to the labor market with the fewest advantages.

In fact, contrary to traditional thinking, Freeman and Medoff argue convincingly that unions, on balance, diminish wage inequality. The customary argument, made by Milton Friedman among others, is that unions promote inequality by reducing employment in the unionized sector of the economy (because wages are raised above the market equilibrium level)—thus increasing the number of people seeking jobs in the nonunion sector, which drives down wages in that sector.

Freeman and Medoff acknowledge that this process does occur, but show how it is outweighed by the role unions play in lowering inequality in three ways: reducing disparities within firms, promoting equal pay within industries, and narrowing the gap between the pay of white- and blue-collar workers. The tradition of equal pay for equal work is one of the main reasons unions are so distasteful to employers, who covet the ability to control workers by controlling individual wage rates.

The Broader Constituency

Conservatives like to depict unions as a special interest group—organizations concerned only with improving the lot of their members, everyone else be damned. While such parochialism—what the British call the "I'm all right, Jack" mentality—has often been a problem in the Anglo-American labor movement, it is simply not true that unions serve to benefit only their members.

First of all, within many firms, the terms of the contract settlement with the union are used by management to determine wage and benefit policies for nonunion employees. When, for example, the Newspaper Guild and Time Inc. were engaged in protracted contract talks in 1986, raises for exempt employees, including managers, were held up while the company waited to see how the negotiations would turn out.

What this suggests is that unions are in effect bargaining not only for their members but also for coworkers who are outside the bargaining unit. That additional constituency is sizable. Freeman and Medoff estimate that about 50 percent of the private-sector labor force is in establishments where a majority of either the production employees or the nonproduction employees is unionized.

Unions also indirectly help to raise wages and improve working conditions for employees of companies that are totally nonunion. In some cases this is simply a result of the fact that nonunion employers determine their compensation policies by using wage surveys (of the area or the industry) that include union pay rates. More significant is the fact that many nonunion firms, especially the larger ones, deliberately match or even surpass union standards in order to eliminate the incentive for their employees to listen to the siren call of the union organizer. The classic example is IBM, which has successfully used superior pay and benefits to discourage unionization. Even a dissident employee group called IBM Workers United had to admit to a reporter that "we consider IBM a good company" and justify the group's existence with the generality "you'll never get managers to represent workers' interests anywhere."

Unions, then, have an impact far beyond their membership in determining the conditions of labor in America. "Employers today are better employers," says Mark DeBernardo of the U.S. Chamber of Commerce, stretching the point. "And ironically, part of the reason for that is unions. The threat of unions has prompted better wages and benefit increases."

In an even wider sense, unions have risen above their own narrow concerns by supporting social legislation that benefits not only their members. Unions have traditionally been at the center of efforts to win improvements in Social Security, unemployment insurance, and the minimum wage, and they have pushed for national health insurance. Some of the more progressive unions also played a role in the civil rights movement. Idealistic labor leaders have insisted that unions should be vehicles for transforming all of society. Back in the 1960s Walter Reuther, president of the United Auto Workers, declared:

> The labor movement will become less of an economic movement and more of a social movement. It will be concerned with the economic factors, of course, but also with the moral, the spiritual, the intellectual, and the social nature of our society, and all of this in terms of the ultimate objective—the fulfillment of the complete human being.

Rolling Back Unionism

Whether carrying out its narrow role of raising the price of labor or a nobler mission, the union movement in the U.S. has had to contend with a high degree of opposition from the powers that be. No other major institution in American life has had such tenuous legitimacy or has so often seemed to be headed for oblivion.

The National Labor Relations Act, or Wagner Act, of 1935 made encouragement of collective bargaining the law of the land. But that meant little to the business community, much of which continued to fight any attempts by employees to unionize. It was only during World War II, when the War Labor Board imposed compulsory arbitration and got employers to accept union security provisions in exchange for no-strike pledges, that unions became more firmly established. And that status was weakened soon after the war by the provisions of the Taft-Hartley Act.

Although many companies accepted unions as a fact of life, some firms in the 1950s began to reassert managerial prerogative. One of the most audacious was General Electric, which developed a method of bargaining, named Boulwarism after the company's head of employee relations, that consisted of making an initial offer that was also its final one. Another tack was taken by U.S. Steel, which launched an assault on local work rules and endured a 116-day strike as part of its explicit intention of "rolling back unionism."

At the same time that companies were beginning to challenge existing unions, they were also planning to restrict their adversary's sphere of influence by opening many of their new plants as nonunion facilities. This was done in large part by shifting production to new geographic areas, principally in the South, where unions were weak or absent. GE, for instance, opened more than two dozen plants in what would later be called the Sunbelt. Newer companies like Texas Instruments, Motorola, and McDonald's worked hard to stay nonunion from the start.

Many of them did this by creating a climate of fear among the employees. Just how effective this could be in discouraging even thoughts of unionization was discovered in the late 1970s by *Wall Street Journal* reporter Beth Nissen, who took a production job incognito in a Texas Instruments factory in Austin, Texas.

Nissen found that the anti-union indoctrination began during the first hour of orientation. When she tried talking union to her coworkers they began shunning her. One told her: "Don't you mess with unions, girl. That's the one thing that'll put you out the door faster'n what you come in. If TI finds out you're even bendin' that way, well, you won't progress at TI. You'll be the first one laid off." Sure enough, Nissen was fired on a pretext after only a few weeks on the job.

The growth of the nonunion sector contributed to a steady decline in the share of the labor force represented by unions. National union membership as a percentage of the nonagricultural labor force peaked at 35.5 percent in 1945. It then dropped in the late 1940s and recovered in the early 1950s, peaking again at 34.7 percent in 1954. Since then there has been a steady decline, which would have been even steeper if not for the rise of public sector unionization in the 1960s. By the late 1970s fewer than one in four private sector workers was a member of a union.

The customary way to explain this decline in "union density" is to cite factors like the shift in employment from blue- to white-collar work, the decline in manufacturing and rise of services, the rapid entry of women (who are less likely to be unionized) into the labor force, and the movement of business to the South. All of these factors had an impact, but they were not decisive. Economist Henry Farber has estimated that these four trends explain at most 40 percent of the 10 percentage-point drop in the unionization rate from the mid-1950s to 1977.

Complacency on the part of the labor establishment also played a role. Many unions simply lost interest in organizing or made it a lower priority. Fewer workers, relative to the size of the labor force, were targeted, and less money per capita was spent on the effort. Big Labor, meaning the AFL-CIO, was satisfied that its membership remained fairly constant at about 13 million, even though that figure represented a steadily decreasing percentage of the labor force.

Amazingly, when AFL-CIO president George Meany was asked in a 1972 interview why labor's share was declining, he responded: "I don't know, I don't care. We have never had a large proportion of the work force in this country." And when he was asked whether he would like to have a larger proportion, he answered: "Not necessarily. We've done quite well without it. . . . Why should we worry about organizing groups of people who do not appear to want to be organized?"

Meany's shortsightedness is revealed in his reference to people who "do not appear to want" the help of a union. Many of them did indeed want to enjoy the benefits of collective bargaining, but they worked for employers who had other ideas. By far the most significant factor in the decline of union density has been the resistance of business to organizing drives.

Outlaw Employers

"I don't feel like it's fair, but I'm going to have to go along," said Douglas Boan in 1980. "A number of people have died, and they never got justice." Boan was referring to his vote on a plan to resolve a protracted labor dispute stemming from the closing of a textile mill in Darlington, South Carolina, shortly after the 556 employees voted overwhelmingly for union representation in 1956. The owner of the mill, textile giant Milliken & Co., was found to have acted illegally, but the company fought the decision for more than two decades, appealing all the way to the Supreme Court, before agreeing to a $5 million settlement.

The epic battle in Darlington was unusual in terms of duration, but it was only one of thousands of cases in which employers were willing to defy the law to avoid unionization. Just how frequently this occurred is seen in the volume of union allegations of illegal employer activity during organizing drives.

Harvard Law School professor Paul Weiler found that the number of such unfair labor practice charges filed with the National Labor Relations Board soared from 3,655 in 1957 to more than 31,000 in 1980 (during which time the fraction found meritorious remained fairly constant). During a period in which the number of certification elections increased only 54 percent, unfair labor practice charges against employers jumped more than 750 percent.

By far the largest number of these charges concerned firings of union activists to weaken organizing drives—which is in direct violation of section 8(a)(3) of the National Labor Relations Act. Weiler notes that the weapon of the discriminatory discharge was used heavily by employers in the years just after the passage of the NLRA. "One would have assumed, however," Weiler states, "that once the basic principle of workers' rights to self-organization had become woven into the social and legal fabric, employer noncompliance would naturally have declined."

So it did—until the late 1950s. Then it became socially acceptable in business circles to fight unions, and many employers decided that the penalties for firing activists (reinstatement—though usually not until after the representation election—and back pay) were a small price to pay for gaining a major advantage in the battle against unions. A new class war was in the making.

The New Pinkertons

"We will show you how to screw your employees (before they screw you)—how to keep them smiling on low pay—how to maneuver them into low-pay jobs they are afraid to walk away from—how to hire and fire so you always make money." These blunt words, which appeared in a publication put out by a management consulting firm in the late 1970s, show how far the tentative anti-unionism of the late 1950s had progressed in two decades.

Aside from the rise of conservative ideology, employers were motivated to fight unionization for one clear-cut economic reason: in a period of rising prices it was a lot more profitable to have a work force with no recourse to collective bargaining. Once inflation began to rage, it was only unionized workers, with their cost-of-living adjustment contract clauses, who were able to defend their real wage levels.

An estimate of this phenomenon was made by Richard Edwards and Michael Podgursky, who traced what they called the "productivity surplus" for production workers in manufacturing industries, that is, the percentage by which productivity growth exceeds real wage growth. During the 1960s the rate of surplus was roughly equal in the industries with above-average and below-average levels of unionization. In the 1970s the two groups began to diverge, with the largely nonunion industries showing a much higher rate of surplus. In other words, the employers were making a lot more money from the labor of the unorganized.

By the late 1970s the business world was willing to go to great lengths to keep that pool of the unorganized from expanding. But instead of the crude approach of Milliken in closing the Darlington mill, employers had discovered a new weapon: psychological manipulation.

A new breed of management consultants appeared on the scene. They would help an employer facing an organizing drive to persuade the workers to vote against the union, or else help prevent such a drive from developing in the first place. Firms like Modern Management Methods prescribed a subtle blend of cooptation and intimidation for their clients, ranging from Mom and Pop companies to denizens of the Fortune 500. The service sector was especially taken with these new techniques. Among employers reported to have used the consultants were Equitable Life Assurance, various Federal Reserve banks, Boston University, and numerous hospitals, including some operated by the Catholic Church. The AFL-CIO claimed in 1979 that more than 1,000 union-busting consultants with combined revenues of more than $500 million a year were in operation.

The New Pinkertons, as they have been called, enter a company quietly, and usually the employees do not know of their presence. Working behind the scenes, the consultants indoctrinate supervisors and use them as the main vehicle for carrying out the campaign. Supervisors are instructed to spread rumors about job eliminations and other nasty consequences if the union is voted in. They are also trained to mete out rewards and punishments depending on a worker's apparent attitude toward the union. During a consultant-led campaign against a unionizing effort at the Oster Corporation in Tennessee, a supervisor was told to reassign the leading activist to an unusual task: he was to spend all day sweeping an eight-square-foot area in the shipping department and was to continue doing so day after day until the painted lines on the floor were gone.

Employers do not have to bring consultants directly into the firm to take advantage of the "science" of union-busting. Access to that knowledge is available through hundreds of seminars held across the country each year by self-appointed experts in "union avoidance." Charging $700 or more per person, hustlers like Francis T. Coleman provide a union-busting version of an est training course: managers are made to "feel good" about denying their employees the right to collective bargaining.

The advice is not limited to helping companies avoid unions; it is also addressed to unionized companies seeking to rid themselves of that burden. Coleman is one of the leading lights of deunionizing. "The time is ripe," he declared in a session attended by a reporter, "for employers to examine what the procedures are for deunionization. . . . There is nothing illegal. Nothing to be ashamed of."

What Coleman meant is: "There's nothing to worry about." The reason is that a radical reorientation of labor law in favor of employers started to take place in the late 1970s. The new climate became clear in 1978, when an attempt by the AFL-CIO to push through a modest program of labor law reforms elicited an hysterical reaction from the Right. Corporate leaders, even those that supposedly accepted unions as partners in production, stood by silently and let the likes of Orrin Hatch bring down the plan.

The next blow came in 1981, when newly installed President Reagan nominated two fiercely anti-union individuals to fill vacancies on the National Labor Relations Board. John Van de Water, named to the chairman's spot, was a union-busting consultant in California. Robert Hunter was a member of Senator Hatch's staff who had helped plan the filibuster that defeated labor law reform.

Confirmation of Van de Water's nomination was blocked in the Senate; but Reagan's second choice, Donald Dotson, did manage to win congressional approval and turned out to be a nightmare for labor. Once Dotson was in office, it was revealed that he had written a number of anti-union articles, including one in which he said: "Collective bargaining frequently means labor monopoly, the destruction of individual freedom, and the destruction of the marketplace as the mechanism for determining the value of labor." This from a man who was supposed to uphold a federal law that affirmed the right of workers to self-organization.

The NLRB under Dotson took pains to restore that "individual freedom," especially for individuals who happened to be employers. In a series of bold decisions that reversed policies established in the 1970s, the Board ruled:

- that companies had the right to move operations to a nonunion facility to avoid the higher labor costs of a union contract;
- that companies need not bargain with a union when shifting work from one location to another in the course of restructuring;
- that individual employees are not protected when protesting working conditions on their own; and
- that the Board would no longer penalize companies that egregiously violate labor laws by ordering them to negotiate with a union even when the union has not won a representation election—a step that abandoned one of the few punitive tools available to the NLRB.

At the same time, the Board slowed its handling of unfair labor practice charges to the point that the agency's backlog reached a record high of more than 1,600 cases in early 1984. What this meant was that workers discharged for organizing had to wait longer than ever for justice. For example, in 1982 Jerry McColley, Sr. was fired by the Southwire Co. in Carrollton, Georgia, for union advocacy. It took 18 months for the NLRB to get around to ordering the reinstatement of the 62-year-old McColley, who by that time had depleted his bank account and was forced to live on early Social Security benefits.

The legal climate got so bad for unions that in 1984 AFL-CIO president Lane Kirkland declared federal labor laws a "dead letter" and suggested that workers might be "better off with the law of the jungle." Taking an uncharacteristically militant stance, Kirkland argued that the deregulation of labor relations—that is, the repeal of the Wagner Act— would leave workers free to fight more aggressively for representation. "Let us go mano a mano," he declared. Kirkland's idea got kicked around for a while, but then the traditional conservatism of the labor leadership took hold once again. Rather than combat hand to hand, the situation for unions was more than ever hand to mouth.

Conceding Defeat

"What's it all about if not to bring back the highest buck for our people?" Jimmy Hoffa, president of the International Brotherhood of Teamsters, is reputed to have said some time before his mysterious disappearance. In the early 1980s, Hoffa must have been turning over in his concrete grave, wherever it was. Rather than fighting for "more," according to the old Gompers prescription, unions increasingly found themselves compelled to settle for less. A new vocabulary crept into the discussions of collective bargaining: "givebacks," "takeaways," "union concessions."

The exact point at which unions shifted from forward into reverse is difficult to determine. Yet there are some significant milestones. The first was the fiscal crisis in New York City in the mid-1970s. A credit squeeze by the major banks forced the city to make major cuts in expenditures and led to the creation of two business-dominated entities, the Municipal Assistance Corporation and the Emergency Financial Control Board, which essentially took over the city's finances and imposed austerity measures that included a wage freeze for municipal workers. When that was not enough, a federal bailout plan was devised to help the city avoid bankruptcy. But the bailout was for the budget (and the banks), not the workers; they had to make more sacrifices.

Another bailout that took its toll on workers occurred a few years later at Chrysler Corp. In 1979 the United Auto Workers agreed to give more than $200 million in concessions to the ailing company, but Congress insisted that in order for the $1.2 billion loan-guarantee plan to go through, union workers had to make concessions totaling $462 million.

The workers reluctantly agreed, but the following year Chrysler chairman Lee Iacocca, with the backing of the federal agency overseeing the loan guarantees, was demanding another round of substantial cuts in pay. The UAW had to put the screws on an increasingly restive rank and file to get them to agree. One union official, sounding more like a member of management, told workers: "Those of you who don't want to take a wage cut, go out and find another job. No one's stopping you from leaving this organization."

Granting concessions to Chrysler may have been unavoidable, but the UAW soon found that in doing so it had opened a Pandora's box. Other employers, including manufacturers of auto supplies, began making their own demands for concessions. In 1981 General Motors and Ford joined the crowd. Claiming an intolerable competitive disadvantage with the Japanese in labor costs, the Big Two wanted the same consideration that was given to crippled Chrysler. Again, the UAW capitulated. In February 1982 the union agreed to a 31-month pact with Ford worth up to $1 billion in savings for the automaker. In exchange, the UAW got a profit-sharing plan and a commitment from Ford not to shut down any plants for two years through its shifting of work to subcontractors. A few weeks later the UAW granted essentially the same terms to GM, to whom they were worth some $2.5 billion in savings over the life of the contract. A new era had begun in Detroit.

Unhappily for the union movement, that new era was not limited to the auto industry. Concession fever swept through U.S. business amid the depressed economy of 1982–1983. Whether employers cited the recession or foreign competition or deregulation, the result was the same: unions were coerced into granting givebacks under the threat of mass layoffs.

Wage cuts or freezes were imposed in industries that included steel, meatpacking, rubber, trucking, airlines, and supermarkets. Cost-of-living adjustments were postponed or dropped entirely from countless contracts. Long-established industrywide contracts (known as pattern bargaining) began to crumble as individual companies seemed to compete against one another to see who could take back the most from unions. By 1983 one-third of all workers covered by new contracts were taking wage cuts. In the first quarter of that year, median wages in major pacts dropped 1.6 percent—the first decline since the Bureau of Labor Statistics began collecting such data in the late 1960s, and probably the first since the 1930s.

One particularly insidious type of giveback was the introduction of two-tier pay systems. Replacing the traditional union principle of equal pay for equal work, this new arrangement reduced starting pay for new hires while allowing existing workers to avoid concessions or suffer smaller ones. Some companies embraced two-tier as a religion; an executive of American Airlines, which won wage reductions of up to 50 percent, called it "the key element of our whole growth plan."

For new employees, the outcome of the plan was not growth but shrinkage—of living standards. B-scale flight attendants at American Airlines were paid so little that some of them qualified for food stamps. In New York as many as eight flight attendants had to share a one-bedroom apartment. "You can't get by on what we're making," said b-scaler L.D. Crumly. "I can fly to Los Angeles for $7 and to Europe for $30," he said, referring to the cheap travel available to airline employees, "but I can't afford to stay in a good hotel and have a couple of meals [when I get there]."

While unions and employers may have thought it safe to shift the burden of sacrifice onto those not yet hired (labeled the "unborn") and thus not yet eligible to vote on contract settlements, that sense of security did not last for long. Once on the job and aware of the situation, many workers on the bottom tier became resentful of coworkers, management, and often the union as well.

"It makes me mad," Chris Boschert, a package sorter and teamster member at United Parcel Service, told a reporter in 1985. "I get $9.68 an hour, and the guy working next to me makes $13.99 doing exactly the same job." Mark Bocchetti, a second-tier copy editor at the *Baltimore Sun*, said the fact that he and others in his group will never earn as much as coworkers hired earlier made them "very bitter toward the paper, and very bitter toward the union."

Something for Nothing

Throughout the early 1980s many union leaders argued that taking concessions was the prudent course of action to save jobs. In some cases that may have been true, but labor was not able to draw the line. Once some companies got concessions, others wanted them, whether or not they were really necessary. In a 1982 *Business Week* poll, 19 percent of the 400 executives surveyed admitted: "Although we don't need concessions, we are taking advantage of the bargaining climate to ask for them." A steel industry executive confided to the *Wall Street Journal*: "The whole posture of negotiating is changed. Basically we're asking for something we're not entitled to."

It also turned out that granting concessions did not ultimately protect jobs. U.S. Steel, General Tire & Rubber, Firestone, and United Technologies were among the companies that took givebacks and ended up closing plants or eliminating jobs anyway. A study by the United Food and Commercial Workers, which was faced with a torrent of concessionary demands by meatpacking companies, found that "the evidence is overwhelming that concessions do not prevent the closing of plants." A pair of labor observers concluded: "Concessions do not save jobs. They just prolong the agony of dying plants and finance runaway moves that the employers would have made anyway."

If unions required proof that much of the concessionary climate was the result of corporate opportunism rather than true need, the evidence came in 1984 and the following years. Although the economy was said to be rebounding nicely, employers kept up the pressure for permanent givebacks, and they were usually successful. As late as 1987 nearly three-quarters of all major contracts (those covering 1,000 or more workers) contained some concessions; in the manufacturing sector the portion was some 90 percent.

By the late 1980s pay increases did reappear, but they were less than generous and were often accompanied by nonwage concessions. Throughout the period of economic recovery, average annual wage changes in major contracts remained below 4 percent, less than half the average during the 1970s.

It is true that the level of inflation was significantly lower during the 1980s than it was during the previous decade; nevertheless, union wage settlements were often below that diminished rate of price increases. Union workers began to lose ground in terms of their real earnings. Among those workers who experienced a plunge in living standards were employees at Kroger Co.'s supermarkets in the Pittsburgh area. After union members refused to accept substantial pay and benefit cuts in 1983, the company sold the stores to another firm, which brought in a new, low-wage work force. "I made a good living," said Ernest Arzberger, one of the replaced workers, who had worked 37 years for Kroger and earned $12.37 an hour. "I bought my own house, sent my boy through college, and gave the girl a nice wedding. But it won't be that way for the younger people who get our jobs."

Striking Out

While Arzberger was willing to go quietly into early retirement, other union workers have tried to resist the concessionary juggernaut. The results have not been encouraging.

In July 1983 more than a dozen unions representing 2,400 copper miners at Phelps Dodge Corp. went on strike against management demands for major concessions. The company sat out the strike for a year, but then brought in scabs to resume production and got Governor Bruce Babbitt to suppress militant picketing. A drive to decertify the unions was initiated among the scab work force, which naturally voted against the union. The strikers lost their jobs and were thoroughly defeated.

In November 1983 some 12,700 members of the Amalgamated Transit Union working for Greyhound Corp. across the country walked off their jobs to protest a shocking set of demands by the profitable bus operator. Greyhound was seeking to cut wages nearly 10 percent, end company contributions to pension plans, reduce the number of holidays from ten to six, and set up a two-tier system with new hires being paid 20 percent less than the reduced pay rate for existing workers. The company quickly issued a call for scabs, and given the high levels of unemployment, many people were willing to apply. After seven weeks the union agreed to a settlement that still had sizable concessions but allowed the strikers to return to their jobs.

In August 1985 the 1,500 members of Local P-9 of the United Food and Commercial Workers struck the Geo. A. Hormel & Co. plant in Austin, Minnesota to demand the restoration of a 23 percent wage cut which had been imposed the year before. The local ended up fighting not only the company, which arranged to bring in the National Guard, but also the UFCW leadership, which regarded the militancy of P-9 as an impediment to their policy of "controlled retreat." The UFCW took over P-9 by putting it in trusteeship and negotiated a new contract on behalf of the scabs, who remained on the job in place of the strikers.

In 1986, after granting concessions to some of the smaller steel companies, the United Steelworkers union found itself confronted with demands for givebacks from industry leader U.S. Steel. After talks broke down at the beginning of August, the first national work stoppage—labeled a strike by the company, a lockout by the union—at Big Steel since 1959 was underway. Given the slump in the industry, the company, which had renamed itself USX, did not bother to try to keep production going. After 24 weeks the two sides reached a settlement in which the company got $2.45 an hour in labor cost concessions while making some job security commitments. Those promises turned out to be empty: only days after the rank and file approved the pact, USX chairman David Roderick announced a corporate restructuring that involved the elimination of thousands more jobs.

In 1989 two major strikes—by miners against Pittston Coal and by employees of Eastern Air Lines—continued the pattern. In both cases there were extraordinary demonstrations of solidarity. At Eastern, the pilots and flight attendants refused to cross a picket line set up by the machinists—a rare example of cooperation among the usually warring airline unions. Yet Eastern owner Frank Lorenzo refused to budge. After nearly nine months on strike, the pilots and flight attendants called off their sympathy strike, and the machinists were left to carry on what appeared to be a hopeless struggle. The Pittston workers were luckier. Whereas President Bush vetoed a bill that would have set up a special commission to investigate the Eastern strike, his Secretary of Labor, Elizabeth Dole, intervened in the Pittston dispute by appointing a special mediator and pressuring the two sides to settle. This action, reportedly prompted by threats from European dock unions to refuse to handle U.S. coal shipments, led to a settlement in early 1990. Although the UMW declared victory, the union had to make major concessions in areas like work rules to preserve health benefits.

What these experiences illustrate, first of all, is that the diminished power of unions in the 1980s to secure wage increases was matched by a decline in their ability to win strikes. The crushing of the air traffic controllers' walkout by the Reagan administration in 1981 set a tone for the rest of the decade that has only rarely been interrupted. (The 1987 victory of the workers at Watsonville Canning in California was a notable exception.)

In fact, many labor analysts have come to the conclusion that the strike is now more a weapon of management than labor. All too often a strike merely allows a company to replace union members with scabs, or even eliminate the union altogether.

This is possible because American labor law, while protecting the right to strike, at the same time gives employers the right to hire permanent replacements. Amid the labor market turmoil of the 1980s, these have been in plentiful supply. The scabs can then file a petition with the NLRB to decertify the union—a step that is invariably taken at the instigation of management. Once a walkout has gone on for 12 months the strikers lose their right to vote on the issue. During the 1980s some 200 thousand unionized workers were turned nonunion as a result of decerts.

As perilous as it is to strike, there are also risks for those who remain on the job. One danger is that the employer may decide to take refuge in the bankruptcy laws. In 1983 Wilson Foods used just that ploy to abrogate its union contract and unilaterally reduce wages up to 50 percent. "We are emphatically not going out of business," chief executive Kenneth Griggy assured investors. "Union leaders must understand we simply cannot continue under the existing competitive disadvantage." He did not mention that the union, the United Food and Commercial Workers, had already agreed to a four-year wage freeze.

The bankruptcy ploy, also used in 1983 by Frank Lorenzo after he took over Continental Airlines, was upheld by the Supreme Court in 1984. However, Congress then passed legislation making it more difficult for companies to nullify contracts. Nevertheless, in 1989 Lorenzo again turned to Chapter 11 to deal with the strike against Eastern Air Lines, and although he could not get rid of the contracts, the bankruptcy court did make it much easier for Lorenzo to endure the protracted dispute.

Another management tactic of the 1980s was the revival of the lockout, aided by a NLRB decision giving employers the right to hire temporary replacements after locking out permanent employees. In 1984 the U.S. subsidiary of German chemical giant BASF locked out 400 members of the Oil, Chemical and Atomic Workers in Louisiana. In 1986 Deere & Co. locked out 12,000 members of the UAW when the two sides reached a deadlock over company demands for contract concessions. That same year Iowa Beef Processors locked out 2,500 workers in Dakota City, Nebraska, and Lockheed locked out 700 workers at a shipyard in Seattle. Seven months after the latter dispute began, Lockheed put the shipyard up for sale. Seeing no future for themselves, two of the workers committed suicide. "I'm too old and too tired to start over," said one of them in a note to his family.

Paternalism and Feudalism

The same might be said of the labor movement. At the threshold of the 1990s, American unions remain in a precarious state. Management's concessionary thrust has become somewhat less intense, but unions are still having a hard time winning wage settlements that keep up with the rate of inflation. Two-tier wage systems are on the decline, but another anti-worker innovation—lump sum payments (bonuses) instead of increases in base pay—is on the rise. Average wage increases given to nonunion workers are running ahead of what is being won through collective bargaining. The unionized share of the work force fell to 16.4 percent in 1989. And unions continue to find it extremely difficult to win strikes.

Having forgotten the positive role played by collective bargaining in rationalizing labor relations, business seems enchanted with the prospect of a union-free America and has seduced a large number of workers into accepting that vision. Yet the relatively benign policies pursued by many nonunion companies could easily evaporate in the absence of a union threat. Today's corporate paternalism could degenerate into industrial feudalism. Even feudalism had its serf revolts, and it is likely that workers would eventually organize themselves once again. But until that happened, the once-proud American work force would continue its descent out of the middle class.

SEVEN

Backward Basics: The Crises in Health, Housing, and Higher Education

"A CHICKEN in every pot, a car in every garage": that was the Republican Party's concept of prosperity in 1928. Today it is a bit more difficult to determine what constitutes a decent, middle-class standard of living. Yet, in addition to a certain level of income and wealth, there are three elements that are essential: access to health care, affordable housing, and an ability to send one's children to college. The 1980s were a time of trouble in all three, as the cost of these services and goods rose at a rapid rate. A full explanation of medical, housing, and tuition inflation is beyond the scope of this book; instead, the focus is on the difficulties faced by Americans in meeting these costs.

Health Care: The Crazy Quilt of Coverage

The United States spends more than half a trillion dollars a year on health care, some 11 percent of the gross national product—well in excess of any other capitalist nation, even the social democratic countries of Scandinavia. For this reason, Americans like to think they enjoy the best care in the world. If best means the existence within our borders of the most advanced medical technology, the most prestigious hospitals, and the leading specialists, it may very well be true. But if the issue is access to good and affordable basic care for the broad mass of the population, then the U.S. is nowhere near the top of the heap.

"We have a goal," said Walt Seaver of his family, who live in Colusa, California. "We're not trying to finance a car. We're not trying to buy a house. We're trying to save our kid's life. . . . I don't need a lot of things. I just need Emma's health care paid for." Seaver told a public forum in 1989 that his quest to find a way to pay for the treatment needed by Emma, his five-year-old daughter who has leukemia, had turned into a nightmare.

The reason is that the Seavers are among the 31 million Americans who are without any form of health insurance and thus in most cases must pay for care out of their own pockets. When the illness is severe, like cancer, and the treatment expensive, the absence of insurance frequently means the absence of care. According to a survey by the Robert Wood Johnson Foundation, some 19 million persons face financial barriers to getting the health care they need.

This is the dilemma faced by the families who fall between the threads in the crazy quilt that is the American system of health coverage. The elderly have some protection through the Medicare system, and the very poor have Medicaid. Military employees and their dependents are covered by a plan called CHAMPUS, and veterans with a service-connected disability are provided with care in Veterans Administration facilities. The largest segment of the population, some 65 percent, are covered by employer health plans. After all these groups, plus those who buy their own plans from private insurance companies, are tallied up, there is still one American out of every eight with no coverage.

During the recession of the early 1980s, the main concern was the workers who lost their health insurance when they became unemployed—a problem addressed in part by Congress with its 1985 law on benefit continuation. Yet by the latter part of the decade the problem had shifted, from the unemployed to the employed. Thanks to the preponderance of low-wage, precarious jobs created by the Reagan recovery, more and more workers were finding that getting a job did not necessarily mean getting health benefits.

About 40 percent of those who work are not included in an employment-based health insurance plan. This includes some 24 percent of full-time, year-round workers and 75 percent of part-time, year-round workers—the latter being one of the fastest-growing segments of the labor force. Lower-wage workers are more likely to be denied health insurance than their better-paid counterparts. Some 37 percent of those earning $10,000 to $15,000 a year get no coverage, compared to about 12 percent of those making $30,000 to $50,000. Workers in the service sector and those employed by small firms—two other rapidly expanding groups—are also less likely to participate in a health plan on the job. Many workers in these precarious jobs receive coverage through a spouse's employment, but as the number of good jobs (i.e., those with decent wages and benefits) declines, the number of the uninsured will rise even faster.

The uninsured population is also increasing as a result of decisions by some health insurance companies to blacklist entire occupations. Among them are people in the arts, who are thought to be AIDs risks; restaurant employees, who supposedly have high rates of alcoholism; sanitation workers and lumberjacks, who experience frequent accidents and illnesses; and medical workers, because they tend to use health services a lot. In other words, insurers seem to want to restrict coverage to those least likely to make use of the benefits.

"Adverse Outcomes" for the Uninsured

The most vulnerable of the uninsured are children. Nearly one-fifth of all children in the U.S. are in families without coverage, and this can cause disaster, especially for infants. A study of newborn babies of uninsured parents found that they are significantly more likely to suffer an "adverse outcome" (prolonged hospital stay, transfer to another institution, or death) than babies of insured parents.

In older children the lack of insurance can stand in the way of normal social activities. Michael Dukakis scored one of his best points in the 1988 debates with George Bush when he told the story of an unemployed man in Texas who refused to let his children participate in sports because the family was uninsured and he was worried that if the kids injured themselves he would not be able to afford the medical costs.

Access to health care is a problem not only for the uninsured. Many of those who are insured do not have enough coverage for a serious illness. The House Select Committee on Aging has estimated that more than three-quarters of those participating in private health plans are "underinsured" for catastrophic acute or long-term illnesses.

Another kind of underinsurance results from the fact that plan participants must often pay a substantial portion of medical expenses themselves. Many costs—routine checkups, dental care, eyeglasses, and hearing aids are among the most frequent—are simply excluded from coverage, and the amount of reimbursement available in private plans is limited by deductibles, ceilings on allowable fees, and coinsurance (a deliberately obscure term that means further reductions in repayments).

All of this adds up to substantial out-of-pocket expenses for the insured. Some 15 percent of families pay in excess of 5 percent of their income for medical expenses, and 6 percent of families pay out more than 15 percent. These figures, unfortunately, do not separate out the uninsured from the insured, but one gets a sense of what the latter have to pay from the Hay/Huggins Benefits Report on private plans. According to the 1989 edition of the report compiled by Hay/Huggins, an employee benefits consulting firm, more than a third of the plans surveyed required participants to pay 20 percent or more of hospital costs, and more than half of the plans required such coinsurance for surgical expenses. In the case of a hypothetical family auto accident leading to $10,000 in expenses, almost a third of the plans required out-of-pocket expenses in excess of $1,000.

For seriously ill persons, the problem often goes beyond out-of-pocket costs. AIDS patients, in particular, are frequently the target of efforts by insurance companies to cancel coverage to avoid paying for the massive medical bills that come during the advanced stages of the disease. Brent Nance, an insurance counselor with the AIDS Project Los Angeles, told a reporter in 1989 that he receives at least 30 calls a day from AIDS patients having problems with their coverage. One caller said he was forced to drop his insurance after being hit with an increase in his premium from $200 to $1,500 a month. When another policyholder submitted claims for AIDS-related treatment, the insurance company combed through his medical records and found he had failed to disclose on his application form that he had been seeing a psychologist. Although that therapy had nothing to do with his present illness, the fact was used to cancel his coverage.

The Corporation as Doctor

Lorraine Andree of Muskegon, Michigan, had enough to worry about a few years ago when her doctor detected a lump in her breast and ordered a biopsy to see if it was malignant. Then she recalled that recent changes in her husband George's health insurance plan, provided by his employer, Dresser Industries, required prior approval before being hospitalized. Repeated calls to the insurance carrier by the doctor's assistant and Mr. Andree resulted in busy signals or no answer. The time came for the biopsy, and Mrs. Andree decided to proceed without authorization. As a result she and her husband were reimbursed at a lower rate, and the procedure ended up costing them $647.

What the Andrees had come up against was a new corporate assault on health benefit costs. Employers have been erecting an elaborate new web of regulations, euphemistically known as "managed care," relating to medical expenses. Along with prior approval for hospitalization, there are rules mandating second opinions on surgery, restricting the length of hospital stays, and encouraging outpatient procedures. The motivation for this is clear: during the latter half of the 1980s the average health insurance premium paid by employers nearly doubled, reaching more than $3,000 per worker in 1989, or 13.6 percent of total payroll costs.

While the desire for cost containment is understandable, the problem is that many employers are taking the easy way out. Rather than addressing the causes of the problem—the way doctors are paid and the inefficient way hospitals operate—companies are putting the squeeze on the most vulnerable party: the employee. Throughout the 1980s workers faced an onslaught of efforts by employers to shift the burden of skyrocketing health costs onto them. This meant, first of all, making employees pay a greater share of the escalating premiums. From 1980 to 1986 the portion of workers whose premiums for individual coverage were totally paid by their employers sank from 72 percent to 54 percent; for family coverage the drop was from 51 to 35 percent. According to the Hay/Huggins report, the average amount paid by employees for family coverage jumped nearly 600 percent from 1980 to 1989.

Companies are also taking steps to reduce the outlays of their insurance carriers and thus control the rise in premiums. This means raising the outlays of workers by hiking deductibles, raising coinsurance rates, and widening the range of uncovered expenses. In 1988 J.C. Penney eliminated coverage for spouses when the employee was not the principal wage earner in the family. First Interstate Bancorp lowered reimbursement rates for employees using doctors not on a list of recommended providers.

In the most audacious move, the Circle K chain of convenience stores announced in 1988 that it would cut off coverage for employees suffering from AIDS, alcoholism, drug abuse, and other health problems the company said resulted from "personal life style decisions." An uproar over the announcement caused the company to retract the proposal, but the fact that the attempt had been made illustrated the new attitude of business toward health benefits.

"This is a Rambo strategy," said Mark V. Pauly, a professor of health economics at the University of Pennsylvania, of these corporate policies. "It might work, but it really is pretty extreme. A major question is whether employees will tolerate being pushed around this much."

The Battle over Cost-Shifting

When the employees involved are nonunion, they have little choice but to accept management-initiated benefit cuts. Where workers are organized, attempts by companies to engage in wholesale cost-shifting have resulted in many bitter clashes with unions. The first major confrontation occurred in 1978, when coal miners across the country remained on strike for 110 days in an unsuccessful effort to resist a move by employers to gut the path-breaking free health plan for miners established in 1948.

For much of the 1980s other unions were successful in beating back the more draconian management proposals. By the end of the decade, however, employers had become more militant. Insistence by Pittston Coal on reductions in health benefits, among other concessionary demands, prompted a walkout by miners in April 1989. The company responded to the United Mine Workers' high-profile campaign against the firm by suspending the medical benefits of retired and disabled workers for the duration of the strike. Thanks to federal intervention, the strike was settled after nine months, but the UMW had to make concessions in other areas to protect the health benefits.

In 1989 there was also a walkout by some 60 thousand union members at NYNEX, the regional telephone holding company in the Northeast, in response to management efforts to shift health care costs. What was significant—and ominous—about the NYNEX position was that the company wanted the ability to put a ceiling on its share of health expenses, while requiring workers to pay everything above that. In other words, the company was trying not only to shift costs but to shift risks, forcing employees to suffer all the consequences of uncontrollable medical costs. The dispute was resolved after three months when the union accepted a smaller wage package in exchange for NYNEX's dropping of its health insurance demand.

The ability of unionized workers to resist the cost-shifting trend may very well determine the future of the health care system in the U.S. If companies are able to get their employees to absorb the full impact of runaway medical costs, there will be little incentive for corporate America to deal with the crisis. The end result could be a return to the ways things were before employers began offering health plans in the early postwar period. Paying for care will once again be the private problem of working Americans, and serious illness will all too often result in financial ruin.

Some leading corporate figures are betting that business will not be able to pull it off, and they are also concerned that business will end up being forced to subsidize coverage for the uninsured. So in the great tradition of American capitalism, they are proposing that a mess caused in the private sector be dumped in the lap of the federal government.

"I never thought I would be in favor of a government health policy," confessed Robert Mercer, retired chairman of Goodyear Tire & Rubber, "but there are things the government must do. We have to spread the burden." Robert Heckert, head of the traditionally laissez-faire National Association of Manufacturers, has stated: "No matter how the system is designed, we're all going to pay for it. Running these costs through industry and business is one of the dumbest things we can do if we want to be internationally competitive." Chrysler Corp. chairman Lee Iacocca, one of the leaders in this drive, pipes in: "How would you like to compete with this albatross around your neck called runaway health-care costs?"

It is amusing to see American business suddenly get religion on the issue of a national health plan, after spending decades resisting such proposals as a giant step on the road to communism. Today the U.S. shares with South Africa the dubious distinction of being the only Western capitalist countries without a universal health care program. The U.S. falls short not only on access and cost, but also on results. With regard to the two broadest measures of the quality of health care, America is falling behind: infant mortality rates are now higher and life expectancy lower than in countries like Britain, Canada, West Germany, Sweden, and Japan. For black Americans, life expectancy actually started declining in the mid-1980s.

It remains to be seen whether the new business crusade, even if successful, can address deteriorating U.S. health care performance. The prospect of a movement led by the likes of Lee Iacocca does not inspire confidence in the chances for a populist outcome. What is more likely is that business will resolve its health care crisis but not the nation's.

Housing: "You Can't Have Everything, I Guess"

At the close of the workday at the facilities of a certain defense contractor in the Los Angeles suburb of El Segundo, most of the employees are in a hurry to get home. Yet one worker who has nicknamed himself the Owl hangs around his office after everyone else has left. Several nights a week he eats a brown-bag dinner prepared by his wife, reads, relaxes, and then goes out to his car in the parking lot and curls up in a sleeping bag to spend the night.

The Owl is not homeless; he simply cannot bear the daily grind of driving the two hours in slow traffic it takes for him to reach his house, some 55 miles away in Yorba Linda, where he and his family ended up in their search for an affordable place to live.

Harold Gilbert, an aerospace worker in his 50s, gets up at 3:00 A.M. to begin the grueling 90-mile commute by car and van pool from his home in exurban Victorville, California, to his job in Long Beach. "It is a lot of time out of your life," Gilbert told a reporter, but moving that far away was the only way he was going to be able to afford to buy a house: "You can't have everything, I guess."

By the late 1980s Willie Totten, a 34-year-old assistant manager of a sporting goods shop in Greenwich, Connecticut, and his wife Cindy, 27, a buyer for a bookstore chain, had a combined income of $70,000. That put them well above the national median, but they were unable to enjoy a central element of their parents' standard of living: a private house of their own. Instead they lived in a rented apartment while they continued what appeared to be a futile search for something affordable. The Tottens were finding that even in areas far from their jobs a two bedroom house on a small lot was going for at least $140,000. "That means a down payment of at least $15,000 and then closing costs and points that will add up to another $7,000 or so," Willie told a reporter. "I don't know any of my friends who has $25,000 in the bank."

These are but a few examples of Americans striving to overcome the obstacles to achieving that badge of middle-class status: home ownership. As incomes have failed to keep pace with escalating real estate prices, more and more young families are unable to make the leap from renting to owning. And many of those who do perform that feat are able to do so only because they have moved to remote locations and subjected themselves to punishing commutes, or else they are devoting a dangerously high percentage of their total income to housing.

During the 1980s home ownership rates declined for the first time in the postwar period. At the beginning of the decade 65.6 percent of households were owners; by 1988 that figure had slipped to 63.9 percent. More dramatic was the drop among younger people. Among households headed by persons under the age of 25, the rate plunged from 21.3 to 15.5 percent. Substantial declines were also seen among those in their late 20s and their 30s.

The major barrier to home ownership is, of course, cost. For a typical young family, the required down payment for their first house jumped from 40 percent of their annual income in the late 1960s to about 60 percent in the early 1980s. In the following years, as interest rates came down from their record highs, the down payment burden eased a bit, but the 1988 figure was still close to 55 percent. Most young families trying to make that down payment through savings would be well into middle age before accumulating enough to satisfy the bank.

Those families lucky enough to obtain the down payment from a rich relative or a winning streak in Las Vegas are not necessarily home free. For the typical young family, the total cost (mortgage, property tax, insurance, fuel, utilities, and maintenance) of owning the median-priced home climbed from 14 percent of their income in 1973 to 33 percent in 1988.

Many people simply cannot keep up. During the recession year of 1982 more than 200 thousand homes were lost to foreclosure. Despite the official recovery of the economy, the rate of foreclosure and the rate of mortgage-loan delinquency remained lofty. In early 1985 the delinquency rate reached 6 percent, the highest level since the Mortgage Bankers Association began keeping records in the early 1950s. In mid-1989 nearly one homeowner out of every 20 was behind in mortgage payments.

The Boomerang Kids

Larry Carbone left his parents' home in the Howard Beach section of Queens in New York City at the age of 18 and spent seven years at Cornell University getting his undergraduate and law degrees. He then returned to the city and took a job as an attorney for Consolidated Edison, the local electric utility. But instead of doing what a young urban professional is supposed to do—buy a condo in a chic neighborhood, or at least rent a fancy apartment in a modern high-rise—he moved back in with his parents. "I don't have enough money for a house," Carbone told a reporter. "And I didn't want to waste money on an extremely expensive apartment."

By returning to his childhood home, Carbone was joining the growing ranks of what have been called the boomerang kids: adult children who cannot afford a place of their own and instead fall back on their parents' hospitality. A Census Bureau survey found that in 1988 there were some 18 million single adults between the ages of 18 and 34 living with parents, an increase of about one-third since 1974. "You

think you've done your bit and put them through college an
come," one exasperated parent said to the *New York Times.*

The predominant reason for this mock horror-film scenari
Return of the Offspring—is the frightening state of the housing ma
Just as young couples are struggling to buy a place of their own, you
singles confront overwhelming obstacles in the rental arena. In big
cities like New York, Boston, and Los Angeles this can mean studio
apartments going for $1,000 a month. Affording anything larger usually
requires doubling or tripling up with strangers; and it often involves a
move to a marginal neighborhood, where hapless young adults from
out of town are turned into shock troops for gentrification.

Thanks to rent regulation there are many moderate-priced apartments in New York. The problem is that they are almost never available. According to the most recent housing report of the city
government, the vacancy rate for apartments renting for less than $300
a month was below 1 percent, while the rate for units costing $1,000
or more was nearly 7 percent.

While New York is admittedly an extreme case, rental trends elsewhere in the country are not encouraging. During the first half of the
1980s there were sharp rises in average rents, especially in the West and
the Northeast. Rents then leveled off, but by 1988 the median rent in
the West had reached $427. This represented an increase of 24 percent,
in constant dollars, over the course of a decade, and this during a period
in which real incomes, especially for the young, were stagnant.

When rents outpace earnings the result is that people spend larger
shares of their income on shelter and have less left over for the other
things of life. The old real estate rule of thumb that housing costs
should equal no more than 25 percent of income is obsolete. In New
York nearly one household in four shells out *50 percent or more* of its
income to the landlord. Nationally, the median gross rent (including
utility costs) consumes nearly 30 percent of income, which means that
about half of the country's renters are forced to spend roughly a third
of their earnings on housing.

Unhousing the Poor

For the middle class, the disappearance of affordable housing means a
decline in the quality of life; for the poor it is a catastrophe. Two or three
decades ago when poverty officials spoke of the housing problem they
were generally referring to substandard and overcrowded dwellings. To-

there is simply no place for many low-income
ation of gentrification, abandonment, and ar-
ed the stock of inexpensive rental housing.
ficulties faced by young middle-class families
ng many of them in rental units that would
er-income people. In 1970 there were 9.7
nits and 7.3 million low-income renter
(the latest figures available), the number of inex-
housing units had declined to 7.9 million, while the number of
low-income households had expanded to 11.6 million.

In the worst cases the result of this shortfall is homelessness. The
1980s saw the rise of a social ill not experienced since the days of the
Great Depression: large numbers of people living on the streets and
panhandling or frequenting soup kitchens in order to survive. By the
end of the decade it was estimated that between 650 thousand and 4
million persons in the U.S. were homeless on any given night. A survey
by the U.S. Conference of Mayors found that, in most cities, emergency
shelter and food facilities were being overwhelmed by the rising number of homeless persons, many of whom had to be turned away.

For years the Reagan administration attempted to portray the homeless as an unfortunate side effect of the deinstitutionalization of mental
patients. Yet there has been a growing realization that material conditions have played a more important role. A 1989 survey of social service officials by the General Accounting Office found that shortages of
affordable housing—as well as unemployment and low wages—were
considered to be the main social factors causing homelessness.

Even those who get a break in the labor market have a hard time
getting over the housing hurdle. In 1989 Larry Fuller moved from Tioga,
West Virginia, to Washington, D.C., in search of work. Fuller, who was
25 at the time, had little difficulty landing an $8-an-hour job with the
local power company. Finding an affordable place to live was another
matter. Discouraged by the high rents in the nation's capital, Fuller
remained homeless, living out of a tent pitched in a suburban camping
ground. "I was stunned," Fuller told a reporter. "Back in Tioga I could
live in a palace and have money left over on what I make here."

The Assault on Subsidies

The shortage of inexpensive housing came about not only by market
conditions; the federal government also had a hand in it. When the

Reaganites came to town they made dismantling the housing subsidy system one of their prime objectives. Also on the agenda was a drive to pressure those localities with rent control laws to abolish what the Right considers to be an abomination against property. The latter aim was too much for Congress, even in the new conservative climate.

Housing assistance, on the other hand, was quietly strangled. Appropriations for the subsidy programs of the Department of Housing and Urban Development plummeted from a high of $32 billion in 1978 to less than $10 billion a decade later—a decline in constant dollars of more than 80 percent. The number of new HUD commitments for rental assistance, which had been running at an annual rate of about 300 thousand in the late 1970s, declined to an average of around 80 thousand during the Reagan years. At the same time, those already participating in the subsidy programs were compelled to fork over a larger share of their income for rent.

HUD benefits were more vulnerable to budget slashing than food stamps or Social Security, because housing subsidies do not, strictly speaking, constitute an entitlement program. Not everyone who is eligible for aid gets it. In fact, less than a third of renter households below the poverty line live in public housing or receive subsidies. The picture is likely to get substantially worse in the coming years. Many of those receiving subsidies live in privately owned buildings that were constructed by developers who received federal aid in exchange for a commitment to provide places for low-income tenants. These obligations were for limited periods of time, often only 15 to 20 years. Between 1990 and 1994 contracts covering more than 700 thousand units are scheduled to expire. Unless there is funding to renew these contracts, landlords will be free to raise rents to market levels or convert the units to condominiums. Many thousands of poor renters could be forced out of their apartments and into the ranks of the homeless.

What makes the Reagan-Bush assault on housing subsidies seem even more callous is that, as a series of revelations in 1989 brought to light, it was going on at the same time HUD was being turned into a honey pot for prominent Washington insiders. During the tenure of Samuel Pierce, leading lobbyists, political consultants, and GOP loyalists were able to collect millions of dollars in fees from developers seeking subsidies that were unabashedly awarded according to political criteria. One former HUD official told Congress it was common knowledge that "people who are politically well known had an absolute entree" to Republican appointees directing the subsidy programs. Although President Bush tried to distance his administration from the influence-peddling scandal, it came uncomfortably close to home. Among those named in the affair were President Bush's chief fund-raiser in the 1988 campaign and the consulting firm that advised current HUD secretary Jack Kemp during his presidential bid.

When the HUD revelations broke, there was some concern among advocates of low-income housing that the Bush administration would use the scandal either as a pretext for further cuts in the subsidy program or for replacing subsidies with housing vouchers, one of Kemp's pet projects. Vouchers are less expensive for the government and they do nothing to add to the stock of low-income housing; about half the low-income tenants who now receive vouchers return them unused because apartments are so scarce. As housing expert Peter Drier put it, "In cities with low rental vacancy rates, handing out vouchers is like providing food stamps when the grocery shelves are empty."

The fears about the administration's intentions were heightened when Bush announced his housing initiative in November 1989. The $7 billion proposal included mortgage assistance for lower-income families and tax breaks for first-time home buyers but no funding for building new public and low-income housing. The plan, dubbed Project HOPE (Home Ownership and Opportunity for People Everywhere), was concerned as much with the interests of business as with those of poor and working people seeking shelter. Included in the proposal were provisions for enterprise zones in which the capital gains tax would be eliminated.

Higher Education: Closing the Golden Door

"Education was not simply another part of American society. It was the key that opened the golden door. Parents who never finished high school scrimped and saved so that their children could go to college." For once Ronald Reagan, who spoke these words in a 1983 radio address, was right. Higher education has been essential to the process of intergenerational upward mobility; when working-class parents sent their children to college, they were also sending them up the social ladder.

Today a college degree is not necessarily a ticket to rapid social advancement, but without it one does not stand a chance of escaping the erosion of living standards. Being able to send one's children to college is one of the major preoccupations of that sprawling social category known as the middle class. Given the pricing policies of universities and the budget policies of the federal government, there is a lot to worry about.

Each spring a chill runs down the spines of millions of parents as they learn of the tuition increases planned for the coming academic year. The cost of sending a child to one of the elite private colleges seems to be headed for parity with median income levels. In 1989 the race was being led by Sarah Lawrence, which was asking close to $20,000 for a year's instruction and lodging. When a broader range of institutions are examined, the prices are a bit less exorbitant but still hefty. According to the College Board, the average charges for tuition, fees, room and board at four-year private colleges amounted to $12,635 in the 1989–1990 academic year. For the economy-minded there are the public institutions, where the average was $4,733.

In both categories the increases during the 1980s were formidable. The total cost of attendance at private colleges rose by about 50 percent, after adjusting for inflation, during the decade, while at public schools the financial burden went up by about a third. This was during a period in which real family incomes were going nowhere.

Raising the Debt Load

After the Soviets launched their Sputnik satellite in the late 1950s and forced the U.S. to consider the possibility of losing its global supremacy, education was in vogue. A variety of federal aid programs—including the candidly named National Defense Student Loans—were set up to allow more young people to attend college. They worked. Total enrollment in institutions of higher education increased from about 3 million in the late 1950s to about 10 million two decades later. The percentage of people in their late 20s who had completed four or more years of college rose from about 10 percent to more than 20 percent in the same period.

Congress stepped up its assistance in 1972 with the creation of Basic Educational Opportunity Grants (later renamed Pell Grants), which put money in the hands of the poorest students. When the economic pressures of the 1970s threatened to prevent families a bit higher on the social totem pole from sending their children to college, Congress came to the rescue of the middle class. The Middle Income Student Assistance Act of 1978 raised the family income ceiling for Pell Grants to about $27,000, opened the College Work Study program to students from families earning more than $16,000, and lifted the income restrictions on Guaranteed Student Loans.

In its crusade to dismantle social spending, the Reagan administration put student aid high up on its hit list. First to go was the $2 billion in aid paid through the Social Security system to children of deceased, retired, or disabled workers. Then the budget cutters went after the Pell Grants. Maximum awards were not even allowed to keep up with the rate of inflation, and more of the money was channeled to students in vocational rather than academic institutions. Income restrictions were restored for Guaranteed Student Loans. Overall, federal aid dropped, in constant 1988 dollars, from about $20 billion during the 1980–1981 academic year to $16 billion two years later. By the end of the 1980s the figure had been increased somewhat by Congress, but merely to the level at the beginning of the decade.

The stagnation of federal spending on college aid has had two major consequences. First, it has forced schools to pick up some of the slack. Institutionally awarded aid increased some 80 percent, after adjusting for inflation, from 1980 to 1988, reaching about $5 billion in the latter year. For some students this was a boon, but the need of colleges to dole out more in aid has been a leading contributor to escalating tuition levels, thus creating a burden for a much larger number of students.

The other effect has been to compel students and their parents to borrow larger sums of money to pay the tuition bills. When insufficient aid or no aid is available, parents may have to turn to commercial lenders. A good number of the home equity loans that have proliferated in recent years were taken out in order to meet college costs. Borrowing by students themselves has expanded rapidly because of both the federal cuts and the fact that more of the available assistance is in the form of loans rather than grants. From 1980 to 1988 the portion of total student aid coming from grants declined from some 56 to 49 percent, while the share coming in the form of loans moved up from about 40 to 49 percent, with work-study accounting for the rest.

Behind these figures is the dismal fact that large numbers of young people are leaving college weighed down by debts that are increasingly difficult to repay in a time of faltering real incomes. A 1986 study published by the Joint Economic Committee of Congress found that the volume of student borrowing had quintupled during the previous decade and had reached an annual volume of about $10 billion. "Not only do students borrow more than they used to," the report stated, "but more students take out educational loans. Real indebtedness levels, after adjusting for inflation, are higher than they were 10 or 15 years ago."

In its customary blame-the-victim fashion, the Reagan administration concerned itself not with relieving the burden but with cracking down on those borrowers who had been unable to keep up with their payments. The Reaganites, building on efforts initiated during the Carter years, intensified the campaign against defaulters by using private collection agencies and filing federal lawsuits against alleged deadbeats. The Internal Revenue Service was also enlisted in the crusade. IRS records began to be used to track down debtors, and the agency was asked to withhold tax refunds from defaulters. "Now we're playing the ultimate trump card, which is to use the IRS," gloated an official of the Department of Education.

Even more disturbing was a proposal put forth by Education Secretary William Bennett in 1987. In an approach that smacked of the Nazi practice of collective punishment, Bennett suggested that federal aid be denied to any school where previous borrowers had a default rate of 20 percent or more. Congress and the academic world expressed concern over the harshness of the proposal, and the plan was withdrawn. Yet essentially the same approach was adopted by the Bush administration in 1989. Under that plan, schools with default rates in excess of 60 percent can be suspended or terminated from participation in federal loan programs. This version received a warmer response since the higher figure focused the penalties on proprietary trade schools that admittedly often do con students into taking out loans for courses of dubious merit.

Repressive tactics are politically acceptable because defaulters have been portrayed as affluent professionals who are thumbing their nose at government programs that helped put them through school. Like the "welfare queens" Reagan liked to rave about, such cases may exist, but highlighting them serves to obscure the fact that many debtors are struggling to get by. One of these was Ann Calvin. In the late 1970s she borrowed $4,000 for graduate study at Morgan State University in Baltimore. After dropping out in 1981, all she could find was part-time, low-paid work, so she defaulted on the loan. She later got a slightly better position as a teacher's aide and resumed payments. But Calvin told a reporter in 1988 that she did not know how quickly she could pay off the debt: "I still have never found a job that pays more than $10,000." Officials in Pennsylvania found that 25 percent of its defaulters were unemployed and another 45 percent earned under

$8,000 a year. "They're not deadbeats," said Jerry Davis, head of research for the state's loan-guaranty agency. "They don't have the money."

Signs of Trouble

The greatest risk arising out of escalating tuition rates, stagnating federal aid levels, and growing indebtedness is that fewer high school graduates will be able to attend college, and the country's progress in educational attainment will be reversed. So far, the figures on college attendance for high school graduates in general do not show a significant decrease.

There are signs of trouble, however, and they concern young blacks. For them the enrollment rate declined from a peak of 34.2 percent in 1976 to 28.6 percent in 1988. The problem is most critical among black males. According to the Census Bureau, the enrollment rate for that group sank to 25.1 percent in 1988.

Black men are becoming especially scarce at the nation's four-year colleges. At such institutions there were fewer black male enrollees toward the end of the 1980s than there were at the beginning of the decade. The gap between the educational achievement of black males and females—not to mention that between blacks and whites—is a recipe for increasing social tension.

The crisis in black college participation is bad enough by itself; what would be worse is if it is a harbinger of things to come for the larger population. A precipitous drop in enrollment rates is unlikely, if only because employers these days require B.A.'s for virtually all white-collar jobs. Yet there is still the danger that in higher education, as in health care and housing, the ranks of the have-nots will continue to grow.

EIGHT

Women and Children Last

THE bottom fell out of Peg Tennant's life in 1985. After being abandoned by her husband, she was forced into a desperate search for work to support her infant son. Tennant exhausted her savings in the effort and ended up with a minimum-wage job at a day-care center in Des Moines. The cost of the baby-sitter taking care of her own child was nearly half her wage, so college-educated Tennant reluctantly turned to public assistance. "During this time I discovered some very disturbing things," she told a congressional committee in 1988. "I found out that despite common rhetoric and popular press to the contrary, our United States society does *not* really care about children."

At the same hearing Lynn Hudson, a single parent from Tyner, Kentucky, made a passionate plea: "Talk won't cut it anymore. It just won't cut it. We've asked nicely, we've got no results. Then we've lowered our pride and we've begged humbly and we got no results. . . . You know what the problems are. Now how far will you go for our children? Will you give them what they need?"

For the most part, the answer to that question has been an emphatic no. Neither Congress nor the executive branch has been willing to do what is necessary to address a growing national scandal: the rise of privation and poverty among millions of American women and children.

Goodbye to the Nuclear Family

The crisis in the living standards of women and children is inseparable from the crisis of the family. The transformation of American domestic life has been astounding; the following statistics attest to how in the course of only a few decades the family has been remade:

- The annual divorce rate has shot up from about 10 per 1,000 married women in the early 1960s to more than 20 per 1,000 today. Roughly half of all marriages end in divorce.
- The portion of births to unmarried women has jumped from 5.3 percent in 1960 to 10.7 percent in 1970 to 24.5 percent in 1987. For black women the rate in the latter year was more than 62 percent.
- These two trends have brought about a dramatic rise in the number of female-headed households. Back in 1960 only about one household in six was headed by a woman; today the figure is more than one in four. Among black households, some 45 percent are headed by women.
- As a result, the frequency of children living with one parent has been climbing. In 1988 some 24 percent of children lived with their mother only, up from less than 12 percent in 1970. More than half of black children live with their mother alone.
- More women than ever are in the paid work force. Female labor force participation rates have reached nearly 60 percent, compared with about 38 percent in the early 1960s. Even for married women with children below school age, the participation rate is more than 50 percent.
- The classic nuclear family—husband employed, wife at home taking care of kids—now accounts for only about 12 percent of American families.

Within the new conservative credo, these trends are the fruits of liberalism run rampant; George Gilder, for instance, has written of how "families break down under the pressure of taxes and welfare." America is supposedly in decline because too many boys are growing up without male authority figures in the home, and even where families are "intact," the large amount of time employed mothers spend out of the house is said to undermine the moral development of children.

Notions about the need for male authority may reek of chauvinism; still, those sympathetic to feminism will find it hard to avoid a certain ambivalence when evaluating alterations in the family. In one sense the trends are the results of challenges posed by the women's movement to male domination. It is a sign of progress that women can escape bad marriages, and there is nothing wrong with a female-headed household, much less women working for a wage. Yet this form of liberation can seem empty when it means a slide into hardship and perhaps poverty.

"The primary cause of economic insecurity in America used to be old age," says Professor David Ellwood of Harvard, an expert on poverty. "Today it is family break-up." Ellwood is right, up to a point. Changes in the family are indeed closely tied to the economic difficulties of women and children, but to call them causes is to give the misleading impression that it is inevitable that nonnuclear families will suffer hardship. The problem for women and children is not the fact that large numbers of them are outside traditional nuclear families, but rather that these "broken" families are much more vulnerable to the economic pressures afflicting all types of households today.

Not on a Par

The problems of women and children can be seen most clearly in the area of income. In 1988 the median income of female-headed families was only $15,346 compared to $36,389 for married-couple families. On a per capita basis, the median income of women was $8,889, or less than half the $18,908 figure among men.

Economist Randy Albelda has shown the fuller dimensions of this inequality by creating an index on Per Capita Access to Resources. What Albelda refers to as the PAR index measures all sources of income, including earnings, government transfer payments, family transfers, and property income. Albelda's calculations show both that women enjoy less access to total resources than men and that the gap has been widening. In 1967 women's share was 91.8 percent of men's; by 1985 the figure had sunk to 86.8 percent. Albelda blames "the continued undervaluing of women's work, the stagnation in the real value of wages, and the inadequacy of government or family child-support payments."

One of the most economically vulnerable groups of women consists of those who undergo a divorce. The breakup of a marriage almost certainly leads to economic hardship for a woman and her dependent children. A study by Greg Duncan and Saul Hoffman found that in the year following a divorce the income of women fell an average of 30 percent and remained at that level for at least five years. The income of divorced white women who had been in households with above-median income fell even further, dropping 39 percent in the first year.

In her book *The Divorce Revolution*, Lenore Weitzman reports on research concerning the income of divorced women and men in California in relation to needs. The study found that one year after divorce, men experienced a 42 percent improvement in their standard of living, while women experienced a 73 percent decline. Weitzman sees these results as proof that "divorce is a financial catastrophe for most women: in just one year they experience a dramatic decline in income and a calamitous drop in their standard of living."

"We ate macaroni and cheese five nights a week," one divorced woman told Weitzman. "There was a Safeway special for 39 cents a box. We could eat seven dinners for $3 a week. . . . I think that's all we ate for months." Another woman, formerly married to an engineer, said: "I didn't buy my daughter any clothes for a year—even when she graduated from high school we sewed together two old dresses to make an outfit."

The main reason for these stories of woe is the inadequacy of help from divorced men to their former wives who keep custody of the children. To begin with, alimony is awarded to only a small minority of divorced women. A Census Bureau survey found that less than 15 percent of divorced or separated women had been awarded alimony and that only 3 percent of the total were actually receiving payments.

Child support payments were more common, but there are problems here as well. The Census Bureau found that of the roughly 9 million women who were living with children under 21 whose fathers were not present, about 61 percent had been awarded child support. Yet only about a third of the total were actually receiving any payments, and a third of these women were not receiving all they were entitled to. Of those who were receiving some child support, the average payment was only $1,679 a year for one child and $2,597 for two children.

"I was awarded $55 a week for my two kids, which was the standard order in Nebraska," Geraldine Jensen told a reporter. "My husband had been a very good father, so when he left I never expected that he would stop paying. But he paid for six months—that's the national average—and then he stopped calling, he stopped visiting and he stopped making payments." As a result Jensen lost the family home, tried working two jobs to support her children, and finally ended up on welfare.

Stories such as these persuaded Congress to include stronger child support enforcement provisions in the Family Support Act, the 1988 legislation that overhauled the welfare system. However, many of the measures will not come into effect for a number of years, and it seems likely that many divorced men, faced with stagnant earnings, will continue to find ways to avoid their responsibilities. Women will go on paying a high price for the right to get away from failed marriages, and they will continue to be saddled with primary responsibility for raising children in a society that puts women at a disadvantage in the labor market. Weitzman warns that in light of these conditions, rising divorce rates "are sentencing a significant proportion of the current generation of American children to lives of financial impoverishment. . . . If current conditions continue unabated we may well arrive at a two-tier society with an underclass of women and children."

The Feminization of Poverty

The emergence of such an underclass can already be seen in the dramatic change in the composition of the poverty population. Whereas 20 years ago the dominant group among the destitute were the elderly, today it is women. About two out of three poor adults are women. More than a third of female-headed households are below the poverty line, and more than half the children in such households are poor. The upshot of these trends is what has been termed the feminization of poverty.

What is especially insidious about this kind of poverty is that it persists even when women are working for a wage. Nearly one-fourth of female householders in the labor force are below the poverty line. The poverty rate for black women who head households and who are in the labor force is about 32 percent. Even when women in this category worked full-time, some 15 percent of them remained below the poverty line.

This last, startling statistic explains a lot. Despite all the self-righteous rhetoric about the value of work in fighting indigence, many single mothers find that holding a paid job is not necessarily a ticket out of poverty. The core problem for such women is neither their family status nor their employment status. What keeps female householders—and many other women—down is that they get lousy wages.

The devaluing of female labor has a long history, as well as the authority of the Bible, which (in Leviticus 27:1–4) states that women's work is worth three-fifths that of men. In this regard modern American employers are inclined to act like religious fundamentalists: the average earnings of women have hovered around 60 percent of the figure for men at least since 1955, when the federal government began collecting data. In the 1970s the women's movement turned "59 cents" into a rallying cry to end pay discrimination on the job.

Countless social scientists have spent untold dollars in research money trying to explain why the earnings gap has persisted. Market-oriented economists, with their gospel that workers are always compensated according to marginal productivity, simply assume there are good reasons why women are paid less. In this Candide-like perspective, such discrepancies are always the result of perfectly rational economic facts, not something so crude as sex discrimination or the undervaluing of women's work.

Indeed, some of the pay gap can be explained by differences in job tenure, skill levels, education, and continuity of work experience; but careful research has shown that these factors do not tell the whole story. An analysis by Greg Duncan of data from the University of Michigan's ongoing Panel Study of Income Dynamics found that these factors explained only 35 percent of the wage gap between white women and white men, and only 28 percent of the gap between black women and white men.

Undaunted, conventional economists reply that this merely shows the need for better research to find the other economic variables. The Reagan administration's 1987 *Economic Report of the President,* for example, blithely attributed the remaining gap to "the failure to measure all of the gender differences that can affect market productivity." The report was thus able to conclude its examination of women's work singing the praises of the "adaptability" of free markets.

In reality, the source of the inferiority of women's earnings can be found in a tradition of male dominance that has used a variety of justifications for paying women less. In the nineteenth century, when industrial workers were often paid the least amount necessary for subsistence, employers could rationalize lower pay for women by saying that they ate less than men.

In this century the ideology shifted. As many women were pressured to leave the labor market and become full-time housewives, and as increasing union organization of male workers lifted their wages above subsistence levels, the compensation paid to men came to be depicted as a family wage. Proponents of the nuclear family, including social reformers who regarded the employment of women outside the home as an abomination, regarded it as a great social achievement that men were paid enough to support a family.

Higher wages for men were indeed a good thing, but it was far from true that women were no longer present in the labor market. Those who remained found themselves at a disadvantage. The rise of the family wage helped engender the notion that women were not serious workers. They were taking jobs simply to supplement their husband's pay or to earn "pin money" for special occasions. For younger women, the claim was that they were working only until they found a husband or, if married, only until they had a child.

All of this allowed employers to treat women as secondary workers and to pay them substandard wages. It was not until 1963, with the passage of the Equal Pay Act, that employers were barred from paying women less than men for doing the same work. Yet by that time it was too late for pay equity in the strict sense—equal pay for identical work—to do much to reduce the earnings gap. The reason is that employers had long since channeled women workers into low-paying occupations. Equal pay meant little in such pink-collar ghettoes as clerical and lower-level health care jobs, since the workers involved were paid pretty much equally—equally bad.

As women flooded into the labor market in the 1970s and 1980s, the process of occupational segregation continued. There was some progress by younger, well-educated women in entering traditionally male professions like law and medicine, as well as a bit of an increase in the access of women to better-paying blue-collar jobs. Yet most of the 25-million-person growth in the female labor force since 1970 has been centered on the lower-paid, nonunion service sector.

Apologists for business like to present this absorption of millions of additional workers as a great tribute to the resilience of American capitalism. In a limited sense this is true. The U.S. economy has been better able than other industrial countries to accommodate the desire and the need of women to participate in the paid labor force.

American employers were not, however, acting out of benevolence. By keeping most of the new female workers occupationally segregated, U.S. business was able to exploit these millions of women as a vast new supply of inexpensive labor. In fact, it is probably only because of this rise in female labor force participation that the service sector was able to blossom. As *Business Week* put it in 1985, "Just as the shift from high-labor-cost manufacturing to low-labor-cost services was gaining momentum, the influx of women provided a cheap pool of labor." The cruelty of this process is that women continued to be paid secondary wages at a time when more and more of them had primary responsibility for supporting their families. Now that large numbers of women needed it, the family wage had disappeared.

The persistence of substandard pay has also taken a heavy toll on married women. Since many of their husbands have seen their family wage disappear through industrial restructuring and corporate austerity, these women are more than ever compelled to work. Millions of "intact" families must now combine a diminished family wage earned by the husband and the wife's inferior wage in a mad scramble to survive. "Sometimes I feel it's just a waste," Linda Hankins, a factory worker in St. Joseph, Missouri, said of her job. "Half of my paycheck and sometimes all of it goes to the grocery store."

The rise of waged work among married women has not changed the fact that most of them remain stuck doing the lion's share of the housework. Working what amounts to double shifts has made leisure time a dim memory for many married women. "It's like 24 hours a day you're working," said Michelle Pisano, the superintendent of her building in Lodi, New Jersey, and a mother of two. "The women work all day and then work at home all night. At least that's what I do. My day never ends."

Redistributing Privation

Conservative economists have made much of the fact that the wage gap began to shrink in the late 1980s. This was great news to those who were seeking to blunt a rising movement to extend pay equity to encompass the principle of comparable worth: the idea that workers in female-dominated jobs should be paid wages equivalent to those received by workers in male-dominated jobs involving comparable levels of skill, training, and effort. In 1984 the chairman of the Reagan administration's Commission on Civil Rights called comparable worth "the looniest idea since Looney Tunes."

A report suggesting that the gap had been substantially reduced was released by the Census Bureau in 1987 and greeted by some degree of fanfare. The report stated that the female-to-male earnings ratio had risen to 69 percent and that it was even higher for younger women, suggesting that the gap would shrink even more in the future.

To the extent that the numbers represent real progress, they are to be welcomed. Yet it is a mistake to attribute the improvement to the magic of the marketplace. Much more to the point would be the increase in sex discrimination lawsuits and increased union activity among women workers, as seen, for instance, in the successful struggles concerning pay equity by unions representing staff members at Yale and Harvard.

At the same time, the Census figures served to overstate the degree of improvement. The numbers that were highlighted were earnings per hour, whereas the wage gap had traditionally been calculated on the basis of annual earnings of year-round workers, which is considered a more reliable measure because it covers more people and makes a more valid comparison. On that annual basis, the female-to-male ratio had risen only to 64.3 percent in 1986.

The other reason to limit the celebration was that a significant part of the improvement in the ratio was due to the poor showing of men's pay. An analysis of the Census Bureau study by the National Committee on Pay Equity pointed out that one-fourth of the reduction of the wage gap was due to the decline in the real earnings of men. Between 1973 and 1986 the annual earnings in constant dollars of year-round, full-time male high school graduates aged 25–34 *dropped* 16 percent; women in the same category experienced a 3 percent gain. Among college graduates in the same grouping, men faced a 1 percent loss, while women had a 12 percent rise.

It may provide some psychological comfort for women to see men slipping, but it doesn't necessarily do them any material good. A cartoon in the *Chicago Tribune* a few years back showed two coworkers, one male and one female, standing before their supervisor's desk. The boss is saying to the man: "[She] is right, Henry. She should be making as much as you are, so I'm cutting your salary in half."

When men are losing ground, women can improve their relative earnings without necessarily enjoying any absolute improvement in their own condition. During a time of eroding living standards, women may reach greater economic equality with men, but more equitable distribution of privation is no great social achievement.

Suffering at a Young Age

When women suffer financial hardships, it is immediately visited on their dependent children. The feminization of poverty during the 1980s was also a juvenilization of poverty. The number of poor children in the U.S. increased from 11.5 million in 1980 to more than 12.6 million in 1988; the child poverty rate in the latter year was close to 20 percent. During the Reagan era the rate had risen as high as 22.3

percent, in 1983. A study of eight industrial countries found the U.S. to have the highest level of child poverty, and the American rate remained the worst (except for Australia) even after government transfers and taxes were taken into account.

Marian Wright Edelman, president of the Children's Defense Fund, wrote in 1989: "All groups of children are poorer today than they were at the beginning of the decade—especially white children, whose poverty rates have increased by almost a third. . . . If we do not rise off our national rear end and mobilize to prevent and reduce child poverty, between now and the year 2000 *all* of the growth in our child population will consist of poor children."

There has been a remarkable complacence about the deteriorating economic environment so many American children are born into and in which they remain trapped. When poverty is more prevalent among the elderly (as it was until 1974), that is tragic, but at least there is the hope of improvement in the generations to come. When more and more children are born into poverty, that is a sign of national decline. As Senator Daniel Patrick Moynihan of New York has put it, "The U.S. today may be the first society in history where children are much worse off than adults."

Hardship among children is a matter of not only money but also physical survival. The impact of poverty is beginning to be seen in one of the basic indicators of the well-being of children, and, by extension, the general state of society: the infant mortality rate. In the U.S., as in other industrial countries, the number of children who die during their first year of life has steadily declined—from about 100 per 1,000 live births early in the century to 12.6 in 1980. In the 1980s, however, the pace of improvement in the U.S. slowed appreciably. By 1986 the rate had inched down to 10.4 per 1,000, but there were signs that a plateau may have been reached. Federal health officials admitted in 1988 that the U.S. would not reach the 1990 infant mortality goals set by the Surgeon General in 1979.

At the same time, the rate for some subgroups of the population remained at alarmingly high levels. Among black infants the rate was 18 deaths per thousand, and in the District of Columbia it was 21. One estimate put the rate for infants born to homeless persons living in shelters in New York City at 25 per thousand. While the U.S. has faltered, other countries have brought their infant mortality rates down below American levels. At last reckoning, the U.S. had slipped to 18th place—behind countries like Singapore, Spain, and Ireland. The rate

s weekends," he told a reporter. "I was serving people, cookir
ing the cash register, and cleaning. The job was a monster."

n though the Reagan plan ran into strong opposition, many er
s were inspired to seek underage workers when labor shortag
ed in the late 1980s. The General Accounting Office report
e number of minors found to be employed illegally more th
d from 1983 to 1989 reaching 22,500. Illegal child labor
hops is flourishing in many cities, especially among children
imented aliens. A newspaper exposé of conditions in New Yo
state inspectors as estimating that 75 thousand children we
g illegally in the New York metropolitan area alone.

years of neglect of the problem by the Reagan administratio
h Labor Department decided to act. In early 1990, Labor Secr
izabeth Dole announced a tougher enforcement policy ar
suit against the Burger King Corporation for child-labor viol
Nonetheless, the current penalties for violations—including
im fine of $1000—are weak deterrents.

ironic that the resurgence of child labor came at a time wh
older workers were still suffering the effects of persistent jo
. Throughout the late 1970s and early 1980s, social scientis
icymakers were wringing their hands over the problem of tee
mployment. Jobless youth, especially blacks, were depicted
cause of street crime and a variety of other social ills. A lot le
n was paid to the impact that long-term unemployment had c
hs themselves.

t, conservatives (and some liberals) kept insisting that t
the joblessness was the supposedly inflated minimum wag
eologues were unwavering in their argument that the greate
t could be done for teenagers was to allow employers to e
m even more. They found a conservative black economis
Villiams, who was willing to denounce the minimum wage
because it deprived black youths of the "right" to sell the
heaply as necessary. Ronald Reagan, of course, parroted the
aiming that "the minimum wage has caused more misery ar
yment than anything since the Great Depression."

to abolish the minimum wage entirely, the Right set its sigh
xt best thing: reducing it for young people. Throughout t
e-market "friends" of unemployed youths pushed for the cr
"teenwage"—a subminimum wage for workers under the a
1985 the Reagan administration embarked on a campaign

among black infants alone would have put the U.S. in 28th place—behind such countries as Cuba, Bulgaria, and Costa Rica.

The immediate cause of the slowdown of progress in the U.S. rate has been the lack of improvement in the proportion of infants born with low birth weights (less than 5.5 pounds), whose chances of survival are much less than their heavier counterparts. In 1985 the U.S. experienced the first increase in the low-birth-weight rate in 20 years. This trend, in turn, is the result of inadequate prenatal care for mothers. During the 1980s there was essentially no improvement in the rate of women receiving early care (during the first trimester), and among teenage mothers more than 12 percent still received late care (third trimester) or none at all.

For many lower-income women the lack of care is a matter of money. About one in six women of childbearing age has no health insurance, public or private, and when those with coverage that does not include maternity benefits are taken into account, some 25 percent are completely unprotected against the cost of prenatal care. Congress did act in 1987 to allow states to provide Medicaid coverage to all pregnant women and infants with family incomes less than 185 percent of the poverty line. But as of 1989 fewer than a dozen states had fully exercised this option. A report by the National Association of Children's Hospitals and Related Institutions estimated that almost half of all poor children do not have Medicaid coverage.

Health problems persist even among those poor children who survive their first year. Federal surveys found that in 1986 only about 40 percent of children in families with income below $10,000 were in excellent health, and more than one-fifth of children in such families had not seen a physician in the previous 12 months. The major reason, as with pregnant women, was the lack of health insurance. More than 30 percent of children in families with income below the poverty line—as well as those below twice the poverty line—have no coverage. What is disturbing is that the insurance gap is even higher for children in families with at least one working parent, since most low-wage workers are not offered family health coverage by their employers, and they are not eligible for Medicaid as long as they hold a job.

Poor children are also endangered by the slippage in immunization levels. In 1985 more than 30 percent of nonwhite children aged one to four in large cities had not received vaccines to protect against measles, mumps, or rubella. That same year more than 40 percent of nonwhite infants had not been fully immunized against polio. It is difficult to tell how much the problem worsened in the second half of the decade: no data were collected after 1985 because the Reagan administration discontinued the U.S. Immunization Survey.

Care and Not Caring

Working parents and their children have also suffered from the absence of a serious national commitment to child care. Only a small fraction of employers offer child-care assistance to their employees. With the annual cost of such care ranging up to $10,000 per child in some cities, many families are finding that child care is the largest outlay in their budget after food, housing, and taxes.

Even at inflated prices, good, reliable care is hard to find. Theresa Canada, a secretary living in Hillsborough, North Carolina, went back to work when her daughter, Elizabeth, was four weeks old. By the time Elizabeth was six months old she had been cared for in eight different facilities. "Each time, on a Friday, they'd tell me I had to find somewhere else for Monday," Canada told a reporter. "It made me miss a lot of work, and I was tearing my hair out."

For poor families the cost issue is especially acute. They pay an average of 22 percent of their income on child care, and many of them still cannot afford quality care. The result is that many children from low-income families end up in substandard facilities. When the rescue of young Jessica McClure, who fell into a dry well in Midland, Texas, caught the nation's attention in 1987, not much was said about the fact that she was in an unlicensed child-care facility at the time of her accident.

Retrenchment in federal spending on children has also contributed to the problem. The Reagan administration carried on the tradition of Richard Nixon, who vetoed a comprehensive child-care bill in 1971, saying that it would undermine the family. Title XX Social Services Block Grants, which provide child-care assistance for low-income families, dwindled during the 1980s, while enrollment of poor children in Head Start preschool programs dropped from more than 25 percent in 1978 to about 18 percent in 1987.

By the end of the Reagan years it was finally dawning on the federal government that the meager investment of public funds in the well-being of children was short-sighted. As George Bush took office, children were suddenly "in" again, and during 1989 Congress began considering a host of bills to aid the youngest Americans. The bills were

said to have a bipartisan head of steam, but resisting the more ambitious proposals—incl that all employers allow parental leave—and p the child-care tax-credit plan put forth by the E House and Senate passed compromise measure veto.

The political environment for children ha still an undercurrent of resistance to major fe As Barbara Ehrenreich and David Nasaw put time when the Reagan administration was try school lunches and have ketchup classified a ture dominated by laissez-faire ideology, chil precarious; to put it bluntly, children do no Rejected by the labor market, children subsis butions of their parents or, failing that, mak ings of the state."

This warning was echoed in a 1989 repor Californians about the deteriorating conditi state's eight million children. "California is human and capital resources," said Shirle Education in the Carter administration an called Children Now, that issued the repor thousands of children California is like livi

The Right to Be Ex

The status of young people can remain pr old enough to enter the labor market and on their parents. The first problem is tha drive in recent years to get youngsters to The Reagan administration, forgetting th scandals of the nineteenth and early twe sistent effort to ease restrictions on the e ers. Coming at a time when family incor initiative can be seen as an attempt to reduced living standards on to adolescer

Young workers are especially vulnerab year-old Christopher Kelly quit his job v a K mart store in Warwick, Rhode Islan unbearable. "I had to do several jobs a

establish a $2.50-an-hour teenwage, dubbing it, with characteristic obfuscation, a "youth opportunity wage." Organized labor and civil rights organizations pulled out the stops in their opposition to the plan, which they predicted would do little to impel teenagers up their career ladders while threatening the jobs of low-wage adults who could be replaced by cheap youths paid a subminimum wage.

The battle ended in a stalemate. The teenwage plan was derailed, but the price that was paid was an absence of increases in the minimum wage. The rate remained stuck at $3.35 an hour from 1981 through 1989, and the real value of that amount eroded 40 percent. Once equal to more than 50 percent of the average wage rate, the minimum rate was down to about 35 percent of that figure in 1989.

The stagnation of the minimum wage does not affect only teenagers; fewer than 40 percent of minimum-wage workers are in that age group. The failure of Congress to increase the minimum has been a bane for low-wage adults. Through most of the late 1960s and 1970s full-time, year-round minimum-wage earnings were enough to bring a family of three to just above the poverty line. In the 1980s this ceased to be the case, and by 1989 such earnings would have brought that family to only 70 percent of the poverty level.

By the time George Bush took office, the need to adjust the minimum wage was becoming apparent even to some of the most obdurate conservatives. Yet the old insistence on a two-tier arrangement reared its ugly head once again. While Democrats were pushing for an increase to $4.65 (which was still below the increase necessary to restore the purchasing power the minimum wage had lost), the Bush administration was holding the line at $4.25 (to be phased in over several years) and seeking to keep the $3.35 figure as a "training wage" for new workers.

Congress ended up passing legislation that would have raised the minimum to $4.55 over two years. Bush made good on his threats and cast the first veto of his administration against the bill. Congress capitulated and in late 1989 agreed to Bush's more modest plan, improving it only to the extent of accelerating the timetable for reaching the $4.25 figure and shortening the period during which the training wage, set at 85 percent of the minimum, could be paid.

Amid this political jousting two pertinent facts were usually forgotten. The first is that thanks to labor shortages, fewer and fewer workers are stuck at the minimum wage. In 1988 only 4.3 percent of hourly wage earners were receiving $3.35. This is not to say that raising the minimum is unimportant; the minimum level helps to determine pay rates for a large portion of lower-wage workers. Yet the willingness of conservatives to expend so much political energy on an issue directly affecting so few people is an indication of the intense ideological commitment to the principle of cheap labor.

The other unacknowledged fact is that for many years there has been a subminimum wage for numerous categories of workers exempted from the minimum pay rule. In 1988 more than 1.3 million workers were legally paid less than $3.35. Among the groups that can be paid less than the minimum are certain disabled workers, some trainees, and students (in limited numbers per establishment) working in retail services and agriculture. They are the vanguard of the class of super-exploited workers that the Right so desperately wants to expand.

Yet many poor young people have a different idea. Faced with the dismal prospect of a job at a ridiculously low minimum wage, they often take the other option open to them: a life of crime. When George Bush visited Harlem in 1989 to promote his anti-drug campaign, a teenager identified only as Walter set the president straight. "I'm not working for $125 for a whole week. At McDonald's? Flipping hamburgers?" Walter said indignantly. "One hundred dollars a week? That ain't no money. I can make that in 15 minutes selling drugs."

The Real Family Agenda

If an economic policy such as keeping down the minimum wage can undermine a social policy like the anti-drug effort, so can the opposite occur. There is a good chance that the Bush administration's social crusade to restrict women's right to abortion will backfire on the drive to curb federal spending. In the short term, Bush saved some money in 1989 by cruelly vetoing legislation to provide Medicaid funding for abortions in cases of rape and incest. But he may pay much more in the long run.

The so-called right-to-life movement, cultivated by the Bush administration and encouraged by the Supreme Court in its 1989 *Webster* ruling, is notorious for having little regard for life after birth. Yet if abortion is effectively outlawed, and forced childbearing becomes the norm, then it will be much more difficult for the government to deny responsibility for seeing to it that those unwanted children are provided for. Washington lawyer Lloyd Cutler has suggested that a refusal by the government to support such children could be construed as "a denial of equal protection to the compelled mother and her unwanted child, or a taking of the mother's body for a public purpose without just compensation.''

The inconsistency between the Right's vocal opposition to abortion on moral grounds and its silence on the issue of who will care for the unwanted children is but one way in which the conservative social agenda is out of touch with reality. Throughout the 1980s these crusaders stood in defense of a family type, the nuclear variety, that was rapidly becoming extinct. Their movement succeeded in overshadowing the real crisis that had gripped America's women and children: the feminization and juvenilization of poverty, the persistence of second-class status for female workers, and the dim prospects for young people entering the labor force. These are the family issues that must take center stage in the 1990s.

· NINE ·

Tarnishing the Golden Years

Louise W., age 73, lives by herself in a single furnished room on the third floor of a rooming house located in a substandard section of the city. In this one room, she cooks, eats and sleeps. She shares a bathroom with other lodgers. Widowed at 64, she has few friends remaining from her younger years. . . . When the weather is warm enough, she ventures down the long flight of stairs about once a week for a walk to the corner and back.

—*from a 1960 Senate report on the problems of the aged*

RETIRE IN STYLE! Pine Lakes Country Club, Fort Myers, Florida. Imagine . . . acres of lakes, 18 holes of golf, tennis, heated pool, a lakeside jacuzzi, 24-hour manned security, and a clubhouse & recreation complex that is unbelievable!

—*from a 1989 advertisement in* Modern Maturity *magazine*

IF the new consensus of social observers is to be believed, there is no place for a discussion of the elderly in a book on declining living standards. The aged, we are told, are no longer living lives of quiet desperation, eking out an existence from meager savings and modest retirement benefits. Far from being poor, the over-65 set are said to reside in Fat City, thanks to a combination of generous Social Security payments, hefty private pensions, and appreciating financial assets. Those who proclaim an Age of Affluence also posit an Affluence of the Aged. In the words of the Reagan administration: "Thirty years ago the elderly were a relatively disadvantaged group in the population. That is no longer the case."

On the contrary, declares the new conventional wisdom, the elderly are relatively advantaged, so much so that they are depicted as gluttons, greedily slurping up much more than their fair share of society's resources. Conservatives and neo-liberals complain that nearly 30 percent of federal outlays go to the aged—a group that, by some measures, now experiences less economic hardship than the rest of the population. An article in the *New Republic* declared: "Something is wrong with a society that is willing to drain itself to foster such an unproductive section of its population."

The more clever elder-bashers seek to blame the old for the disturbing increase in the percentage of children living in poverty and other problems of the young. One business magazine has claimed that "an enormous intergenerational transfer of wealth and income" is responsible for lowered living standards among those not yet retired. Generational conflict is said to have broken out, and the upper hand is held by the elderly population, with its formidable lobbying apparatus in Washington and its huge bloc of voters. As the elderly component of the population rises, and especially when the baby-boomers reach their golden years, the prognosis is for out-and-out civil war between the generations.

A Public Policy Success Story

Rising anti-elder sentiment has its roots in some undeniable facts. The living conditions and general status of the old have improved considerably in recent decades, both in absolute terms and relative to the remainder of the population.

This is seen first in physical well-being. The large majority of the elderly are in good-enough shape to take care of themselves without assistance; only about one in six elderly people are mildly to severely disabled. Only about 5 percent of the aged are in nursing homes at any given time. Life expectancy at age 65 increased from 13.9 years in 1950 to 16.9 years in 1987.

As for financial matters, the median income of elderly family units increased more than 98 percent, in constant dollars, from 1950 to 1980. Over the same period the ratio of household income to the poverty line rose considerably faster for the aged than for others. One study in the mid-1980s even went so far as to argue that once an elaborate series of adjustments were made, after-tax household income per capita for the elderly was higher than that of the nonelderly.

"I hear all these retired folks complaining that they don't have this and don't have that," 74-year-old Ralph Hunter told a reporter in 1983. "I'm not pinched." Revealing that he received a total of $1,000 a month from Social Security, a private pension, and a part-time job, Hunter said he was unable to find ways to spend all his income.

Dramatic improvements can also be seen regarding poverty levels. The percentage of the elderly who are poor has dropped sharply in the postwar era, sinking from about 60 percent in 1950 to about 13 percent in the mid-1980s. By some alternative measures of poverty that take into account the value of noncash benefits, the elderly rate may have been as low as 2.1 percent in 1987. Reviewing this evidence, an economist at the Urban Institute called the improvement in the status of the elderly "one of the greatest success stories of public policy."

Neither Villains nor Victims

Case closed? Well, not exactly. There are various reasons why we cannot be too sanguine about the conditions of the current elderly population or those who will be reaching retirement age in the years to come. It should be said at the outset that even if the improvement in their living standard were unambiguous, that is no reason for attacking the elderly. For decades the aged lived in miserable circumstances; if they have now achieved some modicum of comfort, that is a cause for celebration, not laments about "wasting" social resources on a "nonproductive" population. There is no justification for the tendency to think that any group that has ceased to be victims must automatically become villains.

The first fact that diminishes the record of improvement is that the median income of elderly families is still far below that of families headed by younger persons. In 1988 the numbers were $21,705 versus $34,728. Social scientists attempt to explain away this gap in one of two ways. Either they argue, in theoretical terms, that the elderly have willingly traded income for "leisure." Or else they say that once you take into account the variety of government benefits, the condition of the elderly looks much better indeed.

As for the income-leisure trade-off, it is true that many older people want to or are compelled to shift from the labor force to the ranks of the retired, which means trading a wage for retirement benefits which are usually considerably smaller. What is not true is that this substantial drop in income is somehow inevitable and acceptable.

Especially pernicious is the argument that the needs of the elderly are more limited, so the reduction of income is of no consequence. Aside from the odd senior citizen discount, the cost of living does not change once one reaches the magic age of 65. Much is made of the idea that food consumption tends to decrease with old age, but it is hard to imagine that making an enormous difference in overall costs, since any drop in intake is likely to be at least matched by price increases stemming from an inability to buy in bulk or the need to shop at smaller, higher-priced stores closer to home rather than more distant supermarkets.

The dubious assumptions about the reduced needs of the elderly are partly responsible for the decline in the official poverty rate of the aged. It is not widely known that the Census Bureau definition of poverty for the elderly is different from that of others. In 1988 the threshold for aged individuals was $5,674, compared to $6,155 for those aged 15 to 64; for two-person households the figures were $7,158 and $7,958. If the elderly were subjected to the same standard as others, their poverty rate would have been several points higher than the official 12 percent rate for 1988. Such a discrepancy is widened by the fact that the calculations used to determine the poverty level do not take into account the cost of items like health care, which represent a relatively large portion of spending by the elderly.

The other justification for lower incomes for the elderly, the in-kind benefits argument, involves some highly speculative estimates about the value of noncash government transfers. Responding to pressure from Congress, the Census Bureau now makes such estimates each year. The assumption that reduces the official elderly poverty rate the most is the "market value" technique. For the largest of the noncash programs, Medicare, this approach estimates the value received by each recipient by dividing the total benefits paid by the number of persons covered. This brings about a peculiar paradox: the sicker people are, and hence the more the government must spend on Medicare, the more "value" they receive. The more illness there is among the elderly, the higher is their supposed standard of living.

The alternative approach, that of "recipient or cash equivalent value," does not lead to a similarly absurd conclusion. However, it requires some dubious assumptions about what a person would pay for a service if he or she were not getting it from the government—which in the case of Medicare requires a leap of the imagination. Even the Census Bureau admits that the data used to compute the recipient values for medical benefits are "especially weak."

Economic Vulnerability

It is not enough to look only at the poverty population or the median when considering the well-being of the elderly. A disturbing fact about the aged is that their incomes are disproportionately clustered just above the official poverty level. "Economically vulnerable" is the term that is frequently used to describe the condition of those whose incomes are above the poverty line but less than twice that figure. In 1988 this meant elderly individuals with incomes from $5,674 to $11,348 ($218 a week) and two-person households with incomes from $7,158 to $14,316 ($275 a week).

A study by the Villers Foundation concluded that there were more than twice as many elderly people who were vulnerable as were poor, and that they represented nearly 30 percent of the aged population. By comparison, the vulnerability rate for those under age 65 was 19 percent. Taken together, the poor and vulnerable portion of the elderly population amounted to 42 percent.

Income distribution expert Timothy Smeeding has stated that those he calls the 'tweeners—the elderly with incomes that are low but just above the poverty level—"may in fact be worse off than those who have poverty level cash incomes." The reason is that their additional income makes them ineligible for housing subsidies, Medicaid (which provides more extensive coverage than Medicare), and Supplemental Security Income (which supplements Social Security old-age benefits). "When facing economic and/or health problems," Smeeding says of the 'tweeners, "the only way they can improve their well-being is to spend themselves down to penury and thereby qualify for means-tested cash and in-kind transfers."

The plight of the economically vulnerable is an indication that behind the overall averages and medians, the distribution of income among the elderly is highly unequal. In fact, it can be said that there are two worlds of the over-65 population. On the one side are the privileged elderly: those with substantial private pensions, savings, and investments who can afford to live out their remaining years with a fair degree of luxury. These are the people who inhabit the affluent "retirement communities" scattered throughout the Sunbelt.

Contrasted to these are more than 10 million elderly persons who depend almost exclusively on Social Security and other government benefits to survive. As the Villers Foundation report concluded, "Millions of the elderly are poor. Millions more are, if not officially impoverished, so close to it that any kind of unanticipated economic blow can knock them off the economic tightrope on which they struggle to walk."

This distribution of hardship occurs to a great degree along lines of sex and race. Among the elderly the economic condition of women living alone and of blacks is much more precarious than that of white males. In 1987 the official poverty rate for elderly women living alone was 24.8 percent, for elderly blacks 33.9 percent, and for elderly black women living alone it was a shocking 63.5 percent.

"I live on $307 a month, of which $217 of that goes into rent," testified Florence Rice, a black retired garment worker, at a 1986 public forum in New York. "Medical, I don't have any of that. I can't afford it. It is certainly too expensive. Some will say 'Why don't you get SSI?' I don't intend to subject myself to the humiliation and insults that we have to be subjected in order to collect SSI." SSI, Supplemental Security Income, is available only to the very poorest of the aged; in 1989 only seniors receiving less than $388 a month in Social Security benefits were eligible.

The class divide also occurs along the lines of age and health. The older groups within the elderly have markedly lower median income levels and substantially higher rates of poverty. Given that Medicare covers almost no nursing home costs, many of the disabled elderly find themselves heading rapidly for destitution. A 1987 congressional report found that 7 in 10 elderly persons living alone would find their income spent down to the poverty line after only 13 weeks in a nursing home. Within a year of entering a nursing home, more than 90 percent of these elderly persons would find themselves impoverished.

Out of Pocket, Out of Control

Medical costs are decisive for the living standards of all the elderly, not just those needing institutional care. The popular myth is that the health problems of the elderly have been wiped away by Medicare, but that is far from the truth.

First it is important to keep in mind that there are two components to Medicare. The Hospital Insurance program (Part A) automatically provides in-patient coverage for everyone collecting Social Security benefits and is funded entirely by payroll taxes. The Supplementary Medical Insurance program (Part B) is a voluntary plan that covers physician and out-patient services and is funded by participant premiums as well as general tax revenues.

Shortcomings in each of the two plans have placed a heavy burden on participants. In the hospitalization program, ceilings on benefits can bring about financial ruin for people suffering from a major illness. Even those with less serious ailments have been affected by the rapid rise in deductibles, which increased from $204 in 1981 to $540 in 1988 for the first 60 days of hospitalization; longer-term in-patients get stuck paying out more than $100 a day. To protect themselves from ruin in the event of serious illness, recipients are compelled to purchase additional coverage from private insurers, known as Medigap policies, that cost hundreds of dollars a year in premiums.

At the same time, many recipients have faced a deterioration in the quality of care as a result of new cost control efforts enacted by Congress in 1983. Under these changes hospitals are reimbursed fixed amounts for specific procedures according to a system of "diagnostic-related groups." If they can provide treatment for less than that amount, the hospital gets to keep the difference. This has created an incentive to shorten hospital stays, and there is evidence that many institutions are discharging patients prematurely—what critics call the "quicker but sicker" syndrome.

In Part B the limits on reimbursement levels and the lack of coverage for items like prescription drugs, dental care, eyeglasses, and hearing aids have resulted in substantial out-of-pocket expenses for recipients. Premiums jumped from $115 a year in 1981 to $298 in 1988—a 158 percent hike. Deductibles have also been going up.

The result of these shortcomings is that in 1984 (the most recent data available) elderly persons paid more than 25 percent of health costs out of their own pockets. In per capita terms this amounted to more than $1,000 a year (about three times the figure for the nonelderly), which was equal to about 15 percent of their income. What is astounding is that this is about the same percentage as the elderly were paying before Medicare was enacted in 1965. For all the ballyhoo about overblown Medicare benefits, the program has simply enabled the elderly to hold their ground with regard to the relative share of their income taken up by medical expenses.

There have been changes in recent years that alleviate some aspects of the problem. One of these is the campaign by senior organizations to pressure doctors to accept "assignment," an arrangement under which the physician agrees to bill Medicare directly and thus cannot charge fees above the standard rates. The percentage of doctors participating in assignment was pushed up sharply in the 1980s. By 1988 some 80 percent of Medicare claims were handled on an assignment basis, up from about 50 percent at the beginning of the decade. Yet many doctors agree to assignment for some patients and not for others. Only about 37 percent of physicians have committed themselves to use assignment for all of their cases.

In 1987 the Reagan administration, responding to an outcry over rising hospital costs, proposed a modest plan to give greater protection to Medicare recipients who experience catastrophic illness. The following year Congress passed a more ambitious bill, which included coverage for prescription drugs (above $600 a year) and 150 days a year of skilled nursing care while limiting a recipient's out-of-pocket hospital and physician costs to about $2,000 a year.

That was an improvement, but the method of financing the program created a new controversy. The $4-a-month premium for the expanded coverage (increasing to $10.20 by 1993) was not bad, but along with it went an annual 15 percent income tax surcharge on seniors, which was scheduled to rise to a maximum of $2,100 a year for a couple in 1993. Not long after the legislation was passed there was a ground swell of protest against the surcharge as more seniors learned of the additional cost they were being asked to bear. Contributing to their anger was the fact that premiums for Medigap policies, rather than declining as expected because of the expanded federal coverage, continued to rise.

Seniors are a potent political force, and members of Congress were made to feel the pressure. House Ways and Means Committee chairman Dan Rostenkowski was heckled in his home district in Chicago by a group of militant seniors who surrounded his car. The administration was also targeted. "The elderly complaints are rolling in, in tidal waves of immense proportion," admitted White House spokesman Marlin Fitzwater. By the autumn of 1989 the government was forced to act. The House voted to repeal the whole plan, while the Senate voted to eliminate the surtax while salvaging some elements of the law, including the annual limit on out-of-pocket hospital expenses. Congress adjourned at the end of 1989 without resolving the issue.

The postmortems on the demise of catastrophic coverage have

pinned the responsibility on higher-income seniors, who were to pay the lion's share of the surtax even though most of them already had the coverage offered by the federal government through their employer-sponsored retirement plans. Their protests gave new ammunition to the elder-bashers. An op-ed article in the _New York Times_ was entitled "Elderly, Affluent—and Selfish."

While the surtax protesters may not have concerned themselves with the medical-cost problems of poorer seniors, their rebellion was not entirely unjustified. For one thing, the surtax would not have served only to fund the expanded coverage. The projections were that the payments would have exceeded the cost of coverage and provided a surplus that the Bush administration was counting on to reduce the budget deficit. In addition, the surtax functioned as a risky "foot in the door" which could have been widened in future years to make Medicare recipients shoulder an even greater share of their health costs. If catastrophic coverage can be resurrected without the surtax, the "selfish" protesters may in fact have been acting in the long-term interest of all seniors.

Targeting Social Security

Another source of anxiety for the elderly has been the state of the old-age pension program of Social Security. It once was the case that attacks on Social Security were the domain of the crackpot Right. In the 1980s, as many reactionary ideas were adopted by "respectable" conservatives, it became fashionable to denigrate Social Security along with all other forms of nonmilitary federal spending. The idea that the government should guarantee a decent standard of living to all elderly persons sticks in the craw of those who believe that someone who does not work should not eat. Even the neo-liberals have gotten into the act. A 1985 article in the _New Republic_, suggesting that the typical Social Security recipient was "a wealthy widow [living] in an East Side luxury condominium," exclaimed: "The senior citizen's demands on federal taxpayers, on working Americans, their demands on their own children and grandchildren have grown far beyond what is fair and can reasonably be provided."

The irony is that this fulmination was issued not long after the federal government had acted to scale back benefits. An attempt early in the Reagan administration to abolish the minimum benefit for current recipients was defeated, but the floor was eliminated for new retirees.

In 1983, amid much talk about an impending collapse of the Social Security system, Congress passed legislation that delayed a cost-of-living adjustment for current recipients, made benefits partially subject to federal income tax, and hit future retirees by raising the eligibility age after the turn of the century. These changes, which were coupled with an increase in Social Security taxes on the working population, were enacted in a spirit of bipartisanship; in other words, both parties were scared silly at the prospect of a strong backlash from the elderly. Yet the "reforms" survived, in part because the doomsayers had done such a good job of convincing policymakers and much of the public that the alternative was bankruptcy.

It is true that Social Security benefits had been on the rise, thanks especially to a spurt of congressional largesse in the early 1970s and the indexing of benefits to the cost of living. This does not mean, however, that Social Security recipients are living quite so high on the hog. The 1989 average monthly benefit of $541 for retired workers was not exactly the basis for a life of luxury. Without other sources of income, those benefits were enough to bring recipients above the poverty level but keep them well within the ranks of the economically vulnerable.

The Pig in a Python

A cartoon displayed at the offices of a Washington lobbying organization showed an old woman pointing a gun at the head of a child holding a lollipop. "OK," grandma barks, "just drop it in the bag and no one will get hurt." The organization is called Americans for Generational Equity, and despite the crudeness of the cartoon AGE represents the slicker side of the anti-elderly movement. AGE, which was founded by Minnesota Senator David Durenberger and enjoys high-powered corporate and political backing, is in business to argue that society is spending too much of its resources on the elderly and that this is creating an intolerable burden on younger people.

We have seen how dubious is the notion of a giveaway to current retirees, but there is still a legitimate question about the ability of society to support the elderly in the decades to come. Concerns about the future are fueled by a simple demographic fact known informally as "a pig in a python"—the 75 million Americans born between 1946 and 1964. The baby-boom generation is making its way through the stages of life and by the second decade of the next century they will begin to reach retirement age. Just as they have put strains on the school system and other institutions, the boomers will stretch Social Security to its limits. Unless fertility rates increase sharply in the coming decades, a large number of beneficiaries will be seeking to collect benefits funded by a relatively small number of workers. Already the number of active workers per retiree has dropped from 8.6 in 1955 to 3.4 in 1987, and the ratio is expected to drop to about 2:1 by the year 2030.

It is worth stopping for a moment here and making clear that the Social Security system does not work the way many people think. Unlike a pension fund, the amounts contributed by workers in payroll taxes (and matched by employers) are not invested and held in trust until the worker reaches retirement age and can draw on it. Social Security is a "pay-as-you-go" program, which means that the taxes paid now are quickly spent on current recipients. Although beneficiaries like to think they are getting back "their money," those funds were expended long ago.

Critics of Social Security depict it as nothing more than a legalized Ponzi scheme, a con game which provides large returns for early investors but nothing for those who enter later. This portrayal is half true. Participants who retired during the first 40 or so years of the program did receive much more in benefits than they paid in taxes over their working years. Yet it is not inevitable that twenty-first-century retirees will get stung. Unlike a true Ponzi scheme, the Social Security system can continue to be self-sustaining, because the government can step in periodically to change the rules of the game.

As John Myles has pointed out, it makes no sense, as some conservative economists do, to talk of future benefit costs as unfunded liabilities that could lead to bankruptcy of the system. "There is no comparable discourse," Myles said, "about the 'American Defense Fund' going broke by the turn of the century as a result of the billions or trillions of dollars in unfunded liabilities accumulated by long term American defense commitments." The future of Social Security is a political question, not an actuarial one.

Congress made that quite clear in 1983 when it passed amendments modifying benefits and raising payroll tax rates. In fact, those tax hikes succeeded in dissolving the short and medium-term financing problems of the program. In the place of what were supposed to be imminent deficits, the Social Security trust fund began generating surpluses and is expected to continue doing so into the next century. Those surpluses will most likely be replaced by deficits when the baby-boom retirement era begins. Yet, as the Reagan era demonstrated, deficits need not stand in the way of essential government spending. The issue is whether, 25 years from now, the Social Security benefits of the new wave of retirees will be regarded as essential.

Groups like AGE are right that demography could bring about lower living standards and even generational conflict—but only if the current model of political economy prevails. If we remain with a system that continues to pit workers against recipients while giving business subsidies and the military a free ride, then we do indeed have much to fear as the baby-boom pig makes its way through the python.

Pension Piracy

The prospect for future retirees is also made bleaker by the condition of the private pension system. The obsession of corporate America with cutting costs and restructuring has produced an unprecedented assault on employee benefits that will result in fewer pension benefits for fewer people.

It was not long ago that social scientists were marveling at the role of private pensions, along with Social Security, in creating a new leisure class—the first generation of people who could enjoy high levels of income and health for a long period after the end of their work life. Pensions were so attractive in many cases that workers were retiring earlier.and earlier, and labor force participation rates for men in their 50s and 60s were declining. In 1977 the director of employee benefits at General Motors told a reporter: "There used to be a stigma to going out. He was over the hill. But now it's a looked-for status. Those retirement parties, they used to be sad affairs. They are darn happy affairs now."

Then the climate began to change. The first step was an ideological response to early retirement. This took the form of an attack on mandatory retirement ages. The right to continue working beyond 70 was placed ahead of the right to a decent pension as Congress was stampeded into passing legislation that abolished most mandatory retirement. Although this was presented as a boon to older workers who wanted to remain on the job, it served to usher in a period of diminished expectations with regard to retirement.

Next came a direct assault on the funds set aside for retirement benefits. In the early 1980s many companies awoke to the fact that a rising stock market had made the pension plans under their control technically overfunded, meaning that the current value of plan assets was well above the anticipated cost of future benefits for plan participants. Rather than seeing this as a desirable financial cushion, employers eyed the surpluses greedily.

One by one such companies as A&P, Occidental Petroleum, and Harper & Row moved to appropriate the "excess assets" by terminating the overfunded plans, using some of the money to establish new plans, and keeping the rest. Corporate America had found a pot of gold. Hundreds of companies went through the termination process, and the amount of assets appropriated by employers each year climbed to hundreds of millions of dollars, reaching a peak of nearly $7 billion in 1985. Cries of "pension piracy" prompted Congress to change the tax law in 1986 to make terminations somewhat less attractive, but in 1988 employers still captured some $2 billion in assets. The cumulative total of assets stripped from pension plans during the 1980s was more than $20 billion.

For workers the termination process was a double whammy. On the one hand, companies were taking control of huge sums of money that were in effect interest on deferred wages and which should have been used for the benefit of pension plan participants. What employers were doing was equivalent to the government seizing part of savings accounts during a period of high interest rates. No one would tolerate that, but companies unabashedly put forth the idea that the appreciated value belonged to them—a view that was supported by the Reagan administration.

At the same time, terminations hurt employees because the old plans, which were usually of the defined-benefit type, were most often replaced with defined-contribution ones. This means that participants will no longer be assured of a certain level of benefits commensurate with the cost of living at the time of retirement. All the risks, especially the risk that the assets of the fund may one day plunge in value, are shifted from management to labor. In about a third of reversions, participants end up with no new plan at all, and whatever benefits are due under the terminated plan are paid out through annuities or lump-sum distributions.

These maneuvers have played havoc with the retirement plans of countless workers like Lester Reynolds. After putting in nearly 30 years with Pacific Lumber Co., Reynolds was looking forward to his reward as the company was taken over by corporate raider Charles Hurwitz in 1985. But Hurwitz terminated Pacific's pension plan and used the surplus to help pay down the debt he incurred in buying the firm. To compensate the workers Hurwitz bought them annuities from First Executive Corp., an insurance company known for its heavy reliance on income from junk bonds. Worried about depending on this source for his retirement, Reynolds kept on working longer than he had planned, and joined a lawsuit filed in September 1989 to force Hurwitz and First Executive to buy a bond guaranteeing the annuities or to rebid them to another insurer.

Shrinking the Pot

The danger of serious underfunding in the future is heightened by the trend among companies to reduce their level of contributions to plans. Starting about 1980 the level of employer contributions to pension plans (as a percentage of wages and salaries) ended its steady postwar rise and turned sharply downward. "A reduced rate of contributions into private pensions funds," a Federal Reserve report noted dryly, "has had a positive effect on corporate earnings." Indeed, contributions have declined from about 25 percent of after-tax earnings in the late 1970s to only 10 percent in 1988.

Not only are companies reducing the size of the pot, they are also making it more difficult for workers to have access to the funds that remain. Changes in federal law have brought about some improvements in the vesting rights of workers who change jobs or are laid off, but there are still employers that break the rules.

One such company is Continental Can. In 1989 a federal judge found the company guilty of using a sophisticated computer system to track employees and lay them off before they could qualify for pension benefits. Judge H. Lee Sarokin found that in the mid-1970s managers at Continental devised what they called the BELL System (a reverse acronym for Lowest Level of Employee Benefits or Let's Limit Employee Benefits) to carry out the plan. Stating that the pension policy was "executed companywide at the specific direction of the highest levels of corporate management," the judge ordered Continental to begin negotiating settlements with the 2,500 former employees affected. One of those workers looking forward to some compensation was Ruth Arnold, who was laid off in 1980 after 15 years with Continental. "They have really ruined a lot of people," she said of her former employer. Arnold can attest to that first hand. She had earned $10 an hour at the firm's can factory in St. Louis; when Judge Sarokin's decision was announced, she was making $2.10 an hour plus tips at a Pizza Hut restaurant. "I hate it," she said of her current job. "It's degrading, but there just weren't any [good] jobs."

Employers have also been reducing future pension liabilities through legal means: offering coverage to fewer employees. One of the prime motivations for the increasing use of contingent labor is to be free of pension obligations. This unwillingness to make provisions for an employee's future is most prevalent among small companies. The boss of one of them casually told a reporter: "I figure people should work until they're 70 or 75"—at which time they presumably should die promptly. The success of this new spirit of employer indifference to the retirement needs of workers can already be seen in the overall rates of pension coverage. From 1979 to 1988 the percentage of wage and salary workers participating in pension plans declined from 50 percent to 44 percent. In the latter year there were 57 million people whose employers were making no provision for their retirement.

Broken Promises

The attack on retirement benefits continues apace. The latest foray is against retiree health coverage. Starting in the 1970s many large companies began promising that they would continue to pay for their employees' health benefits after they had retired. Just as private pensions supplemented Social Security, these benefits were supposed to make up for the shortcomings in Medicare. They were also used in many cases as an added inducement when companies were trying to get employees to take early retirement. Companies are now seeking to renege on these commitments. After LTV went bankrupt in 1986 the company sought to eliminate retiree health benefits, but was forced to drop the plan when the Steelworkers union called a strike in protest. Retirees without that kind of union support are not so lucky. Their companies may claim a unilateral right to restrict benefits now that costs are rising so rapidly.

The corporate position has been bolstered by a scare campaign in the business press consisting of articles with titles like "Sick Retirees Could Kill Your Company" and "The Killer Cost Stalking Business." The hysteria was heightened in 1989 when the Financial Accounting Standards Board proposed a rule that, starting in 1992, companies would be required to show part of the anticipated liabilities for retiree health costs as a current cost each year. This means that corporations, which in almost no cases have been setting aside money for these costs, would have to reduce reported earnings by a considerable amount.

Although estimates of the total corporate liabilities for retiree health have gone as high as $2 trillion, it is difficult to feel much sympathy for business. A large part of these expenses will probably relate to people who were forced into early retirement by companies preoccupied with cutting costs and reducing head count. The Fortune 500 are getting their comeuppance for disposing of employees like so much human refuse.

One of these victims was Charles Fletcher. In 1983 Fletcher had to retire when his employer, American Forest Products, was cutting back operations after being taken private. Fletcher gave back more than half his $22,500 in severance pay in exchange for what he believed to be a guarantee of lifetime health insurance for himself and his wife. In 1988, shortly after Fletcher learned he had leukemia, American Forest Products was sold to Georgia-Pacific, which moved to terminate coverage for AFP's retirees. Georgia-Pacific offered $25,000 in compensation, but that did not begin to pay for the medical expenses Fletcher would run up as a cancer patient.

A lack of compassion for big business should not obscure the fact that it is workers who are going to suffer from the steps companies take to deal with this problem. In fact, the corporate response to the health benefit crisis could be a turning point in the emergence of an entirely new business approach to retirement.

Corporate America has already switched from a position of encouraging early retirement to one of pressuring employees to postpone their departure from the job. In the late 1980s some companies also began rehiring retirees on a part-time or temporary basis to deal with labor shortages. The next logical step is for business to abandon its 70-year-old practice of providing pension benefits. If employers do try to shift the burden of retirement costs entirely to the government and to individual resources, the result would be disastrous. We have already seen the current limitations of the Social Security system and the uncertain outlook for the future. Asking people to rely on their savings would be ridiculous. The combination of high housing costs and stagnant real wages has made saving all but obsolete in the U.S.

Business would probably like to believe that the baby-boom generation will continue to exhibit its current fetish for work and that they will do so far beyond age 65, thus easing the pension burdens. It is possible that people will obediently forgo retirement and work until they drop dead. It is also possible that boomers will grow weary of toil and rise up in anger against a society that seeks to keep them from a comfortable reward. The result could be a new version of the Townsend Movement for universal pensions, which helped bring about the creation of the Social Security system in the 1930s. But this time the stakes would be much higher, and both government and business would find themselves besieged by a generation that will want its golden years to be 14-karat.

· *TEN* ·

No Longer Leading: The U.S.
and the World Economy

WASHINGTON, APRIL 28, 1997 (REUTERS)—Saying that he had "no choice but to bow to the inevitable," President Quayle announced today that the U.S. will accept the austerity program proposed by the International Monetary Fund and the Foreign Creditors Committee. Under the plan the U.S. will reduce its $700 billion budget deficit by 40 percent next year to reassure the international community that the Treasury will not default on the national debt, 65 percent of which is now held abroad.

Administration sources say that complying with the austerity plan will involve major cutbacks in domestic spending, including a 25 percent reduction in Social Security benefits. "We're going to catch hell from the elderly," said one high-level official, "but we've got to restore international investor confidence."

NOT long ago the idea of the United States losing its economic sovereignty was unthinkable. If anything, the U.S. was responsible for undermining the economic self-determination of much of the rest of the globe. The third world had been turned into a sprawling workshop for U.S. manufacturers, stuffed with debt by U.S. banks, and then subjected to U.S.-instigated austerity plans. By the late 1960s Europe was drowning in a wave of U.S. direct investment—what a widely read book by Jean-Jacques Servan-Schreiber called the "American Challenge." Canada resembled a wholly owned subsidiary of U.S. business.

By the middle of the 1980s the picture was substantially different. U.S. trade relations were out of kilter. Exports stagnated while imports, especially those from Japan and certain third world nations like Taiwan and Brazil, kept on rising. The U.S. share of world manufacturing trade fell to the lowest level in the postwar period and by 1987 was below that of Japan.

The federal government had to depend on huge inflows of foreign money to finance its budget deficit. Corporations and wealthy individuals from around the world began buying up American companies, office buildings, and farmland for what they regarded as bargain-basement prices. While the dollar remained the dominant international currency, its value rose and fell depending on foreign exchange markets in cities like Frankfurt, Zurich, and Tokyo as well as periodic intervention by foreign governments.

Bit by bit, the economic supremacy enjoyed by the U.S. since the end of the World War II was disintegrating. Despite the vigor of the American economy in some respects—employment levels, GNP growth, price stability—it was deteriorating in international terms. The widening dependence on foreign money and the inability of many domestic industries to compete with imports gave rise to a growing fear that the U.S. was losing control of its economic destiny.

Not only was the U.S. no longer able to dictate terms to the rest of the world, but there were disturbing signs that America was headed for a future like the one imagined above: a situation in which foreign powers, fed up with American profligacy, could impose from outside the kind of financial discipline the U.S. never had the will to embrace itself. In his widely discussed 1988 book, _Trading Places_, former Commerce Department official Clyde Prestowitz referred to the U.S. as "a colony-in-the-making."

Whose Binge?

Underlying much of the discourse on the ebbing of U.S. power is the assumption that the country deserves such a fate because we Americans have been living beyond our means. We have been on a "consumption binge," say the experts, spending far in excess of what we produce, borrowing much more than we save, gobbling up imported goods well beyond what we are able to sell abroad, dishing out social welfare benefits in amounts out of line with tax revenues. Thanks to international borrowing, says Brookings Institution economist Robert Z. Lawrence, the U.S. in the 1980s was able "to enjoy living standards higher than were warranted by national productivity." To end the dangerous run-up of debt and dependency, the same economists tell us, we must mend our ways. The orgy of consumption has to end, and America needs to relearn thrift and self-restraint. Instead of focusing on our own gratification, we must be mindful of the need to make the interest payments on the gargantuan debt accumulated in the 1980s. Harvard economics professor Benjamin Friedman suggests that bringing our financial house in order will require a reduction in living standards of at least 5 percent.

Looking around at conditions in the U.S., it is difficult to figure out who this "we" is who has been living so lavishly. Wage levels have been stagnating for years, beneficiaries of government social programs have been squeezed, families find that two incomes do not accord the same level of comfort one used to provide. It is undeniable that in aggregate terms America has been consuming more than it produces, but that does not imply universal extravagance. Wide portions of the population are demonstrating that it is possible for a country to live beyond its means without most of the population doing so. The U.S. economy did not get out of whack because the government was overcome by a wild urge to eliminate poverty, help underpaid workers, rebuild the educational system, and meet other social needs. The sighs of contentment after a long feast can instead be heard in the Pentagon, the tax-relieved upper-income brackets, and the suites of the Fortune 500.

Most Americans have enjoyed no tangible benefit from the ballooning of the trade and budget deficits, just as the vast majority of people in the third world gained little or nothing from the borrowing sprees of their governments in the 1970s. On the contrary, the economic imbalances in the U.S. have made things worse for many parts of the population: workers who have lost well-paid jobs because of imports, poor people who have lost benefits because of deficit reduction efforts, young families who have been unable to buy a home because of high interest rates. Yet the experts are right about one thing: when the rest of the world comes around to collect what it is owed, these are the people who will be stuck with the bill.

Importing Trouble

Vera Splawn of Spartanburg, South Carolina, was eating her breakfast one day in 1985 when the news came over the television: Spartan Mills had announced that because of import competition it was shutting down the textile operation where Splawn had worked for 67 years. Splawn, having reached the age of 81, was willing to retire sooner than planned, but for thousands of younger workers in the industry, mill closings have eliminated an essential source of income. The textile industry has been one of the sectors of the economy hardest hit by the flood of imports streaming into the U.S. market. By 1985 the value of textile imports was nearly $4 billion, triple the figure of the early 1970s; the number of production workers employed by the industry was down to 619 thousand—a drop of roughly 30 percent in a dozen years.

Many other areas of the domestic economy were also losing the battle against foreign producers. By 1988, even after a shift in exchange rates was supposed to have helped American exporters, the market penetration of imports remained remarkably high: 65 percent in footwear, 59 percent in TV and radios, 56 percent in textile machinery, 41 percent in machine tools, 26 percent in motor vehicles, and 22 percent in steel.

This foreign invasion of commodities left no doubt that the U.S. could no longer consider itself insulated from changes in the global economy. In the early postwar period international trade accounted for a tiny fraction of the gross national product; by the 1980s imports had reached more than 10 percent of GNP. Robert Reich has estimated that more than 70 percent of all the goods produced in the U.S. are actively competing with foreign-made products.

In this contest the performance of the U.S. took a sharp turn for the worse during the 1980s. The trade balance, which had hovered around zero during the previous decade (meaning that exports and imports were equal), plunged far into the red. The deficit climbed from $38 billion in 1982 to more than $170 billion in 1987 before it started to level off. This growing imbalance is not only a problem for that abstraction known as "the economy." It translates into hundreds of thousands of layoffs and declining living conditions for large parts of the domestic work force—effects that far outweigh whatever consumer benefits may have flowed from relatively inexpensive imports.

In a 1986 report for the National Commission on Employment Policy, Charles Stone and Isabel Sawhill of the Urban Institute found that the impact of trade on U.S. employment in the 1980s was quite different from the decade before. In the 1970s the jobs provided by production for export exceeded the jobs lost to imports; in 1979 the net gain was one million jobs. Only five years later the results were exactly the opposite. Some 7.5 million jobs were lost to imports, while export production provided only 6.5 million, creating a net loss of one million positions. Stone and Sawhill found that in the period from 1972 to 1979 there were only four industries in which trade conditions contributed to employment losses; in the following five-year span there were 51 industries in that category.

Another approach was taken by Faye Duchin and Glenn-Marie Lange in a 1988 study for the Economic Policy Institute. They estimated what would have been the employment effect of eliminating the record 1987 trade deficit; in other words, how many additional jobs would have been created if exports and imports were in balance. Duchin and Lange considered three scenarios: increasing exports to match imports, decreasing imports to the level of exports, and moving each half way toward the other. The results were dramatic. Each of the scenarios would have yielded about five million additional jobs—in a year when the average number of the unemployed was 7.4 million. Imports have an effect on the quality of jobs as well as the quantity. One study found that the jobs lost to imports paid 16 percent *above* the national average, while those gained from exports paid 6 percent *less* than the average.

When pressed about the employment effects of the import flood, free traders are apt to bring up the fact that the federal government does have a program for helping workers whose jobs are eliminated by foreign competition. That program, known as Trade Adjustment Assistance, was created by the Trade Expansion Act of 1962. Yet TAA has hardly been a cornucopia for American workers. For the first seven years of its existence, the requirements were so stringent that not a single person qualified for aid. The rules were loosened in 1969 but only a few thousand people a year were certified for benefits, which included funds for training, relocation assistance, and income maintenance beyond what was provided by unemployment compensation.

It was only after further liberalization in 1974 that the program reached meaningful dimensions. The number of workers certified each year shot up beyond 100 thousand; in 1980 the huge layoffs in the auto industry pushed the figure close to 700 thousand and caused TAA outlays for income maintenance to reach a record $1.6 billion. Apparently displeased that the program was providing substantial help for workers, the incoming Reagan administration targeted it for severe cutbacks in 1981. The income maintenance features were scaled down, and the number of workers certified slid back to the levels of the early 1970s—at the same time that the trade deficit was breaking new records. Congress, which was also complicit in the assault on TAA, actually allowed the spending authority for the program to lapse in late 1985. After a few months TAA was re-authorized, but the administration—specifically the Labor Department, which ran the program—continued to chip away at it by tightening up the certification process. Things changed somewhat when Bill Brock took over as Labor Secretary, but TAA remains little more than a Band-Aid measure for the import-induced hemorrhaging of jobs.

The "Fantastic Journey"

The wave of imports brought with it an equally powerful torrent of controversy about trade policy. On one side stood the free marketeers of the Reagan administration, who insisted that market forces would eventually straighten things out. Reagan himself best expressed the free trade theology in a 1985 speech to an audience that included corporate executives:

> All of history has taught, the freer the flow of world trade, the stronger the tides for human progress and peace among nations. I certainly don't have to explain the benefits of free and open markets to you. They produce more jobs, a more productive use of our nation's resources, more rapid innovation and a higher standard of living. They strengthen our national security because our economy, the bedrock of our defense, is stronger.

It should be noted that the second Reagan administration did bow a bit more to protectionist pressures; in 1987, for instance, the U.S. imposed stiff tariffs on some types of Japanese computers, television sets, and power tools. Yet the administration's trade policy was always half-hearted, and the free-trade rhetoric never changed. The 1989 *Economic Report of the President*, for instance, continued to insist that "imports do not destroy domestic jobs."

On the other side was a rising chorus calling for a government trade policy that went beyond benign neglect. One of the loudest voices came from organized labor, which was seeing firsthand the impact of imports on workers. In hard-hit industries unions formed dubious alliances with management to push an agenda consisting of "Buy American" exhortations and stricter import quotas. The spokesman chosen for the Crafted with Pride in the U.S.A. Council, formed by a group of companies and unions in the textile and apparel fields, was Roger Milliken, president of Milliken & Co., one of the most anti-union firms in the industry. Moreover, while the unions were waving the flag, many U.S. textile and apparel companies were themselves undermining domestic employment by importing large quantities of fabrics and moving ahead quickly on automating operations.

The problems with protectionism go beyond the fact that it tends to put labor in bed with management. First of all, there is a fair measure of hypocrisy. Politicians shudder with indignation over the obstacles the Japanese erect to limit the entry of American goods into their home market. Yet the U.S. itself has used a variety of import quotas, tariffs, and other barriers to protect domestic industries ranging from peanuts to book manufacturing. In fact, economists have estimated that these barriers have kept many prices artificially high, costing consumers tens of billions of dollars a year. It is true that the U.S. is considerably less protectionist than many other countries, especially Japan. Yet the fact that this country goes to some trouble to protect domestic producers (in some industries, at least), belies both the protectionists' image of the U.S. as the chump of global commerce and the free traders' depiction of America as keeper of the eternal flame of market forces in a world benighted by tariffs and quotas.

What is so frustrating about the usual terms of the debate is that both sides miss a crucial point. Nearly everyone speaks in terms of economic relations among countries, yet the most important players in world commerce are transnational corporations. While the U.S. trade position has deteriorated, the share of world exports of manufactured goods held by U.S.-based transnationals has remained remarkably steady. Those firms also account for more than 40 percent of U.S. merchandise imports, most of that coming from their overseas affiliates. The growth of U.S.-based transnationals has taken its toll on the American labor force. According to estimates by Norman Glickman and Douglas Woodward, foreign investment by U.S. companies has eliminated nearly three million American manufacturing jobs since 1977. Those companies now employ more than six million workers abroad.

Many of the third world countries that are painted as commercial threats to the U.S. because of their high volume of exports to this country are in fact little more than offshore manufacturing operations for American transnationals. Nowhere is this clearer than in the case of Taiwan. A substantial part of that country's $14 billion trade surplus with the U.S. is generated not by aggressive local exporters but rather by factories set up by the likes of General Electric, Digital Equipment,

Atari, and Mattel to produce goods for the U.S. market; or else by Taiwanese firms working exclusively under contract with American companies. "You can't really consider Taiwan an exporting nation," a trade official in the country once said, "Taiwan is simply a collection of international subcontractors serving the American market."

International subcontracting has become the rage among U.S. companies. The practice is no longer limited to manufacturers of labor-intensive products scouring the world for low-wage havens, as the semiconductor industry, for instance, started doing more than two decades ago. Now the watchword is globalization of production. Companies that sell around the world believe it is necessary to produce in many countries as well. In part this is still aimed at obtaining the cheapest labor, but other motivations also come into play: easier access to foreign markets, avoidance of trade barriers, and protection against swings in the value of the dollar.

Perhaps most "globalized" is the auto industry. The Big Three have split up the production process and dispersed component manufacturing plants to the four corners of the earth. Using both subcontractors and plants of its own, General Motors gets, for example, engines from Australia, ignition parts from Singapore, and anti-lock brakes from West Germany. Ford gets transmissions from France, cylinder heads from Italy, and trim from Mexico. Chrysler gets door hinges from South Korea, springs from England, and wheels from Brazil. Moreover, all three companies import entire vehicles from such countries as Japan, Mexico, and South Korea to sell under their name in the U.S. The director of a high tech engine plant built by a U.S. automaker in Mexico boasted that the facility brought together "U.S. managers, European technology, Japanese manufacturing systems, and Mexican workers."

While our captains of industry will assure us that these arrangements simply represent sound business judgment, the truth goes far beyond that. The rush of American-based companies to embrace the global factory is a sign that these corporations are outgrowing the United States. There is a tradition on the Left that regards the working class as inherently internationalist; "the proletariat has no country," declared the *Communist Manifesto*. Yet today it is business that is transcending national identity.

"The Multinational Corporation. The sun never sets on it," proclaimed an advertisement by Irving Trust, a bank later gobbled up by the Bank of New York. "U.S. business knows no boundaries. The profit motive has propelled it on a fantastic journey in search of new opportunities." Less poetic but more blunt was an executive of Colgate-Palmolive who told a reporter: "The United States does not have an automatic call on our resources. There is no mindset that puts this country first." In other words, the U.S. is just another stop on that "fantastic journey" that corporations make in quest of the ideal business climate. The fact that they may have been founded and matured in the U.S. and may have their headquarters here does not earn this country any special consideration. Americans have to compete like everyone else for some share of the investment capital of these cosmopolitan corporations.

America for Sale

The transnationals giveth, and the transnationals taketh away. The surest sign that the U.S. has been swept into the currents of global economy is that as American capital has been flowing out of the country, investment money from other nations has been flooding in. Over the past decade foreign companies, institutions, and wealthy individuals have decided that the U.S. is a safe place to park their assets. One reason is this nation's unwavering respect for private property. An executive of a Luxembourg steel company once said, "There's no other country in the world where you can invest money and have some assurance that it will still be yours 10 years later." Economic incentives, however, were mainly responsible for the rapid acceleration of foreign investment during the 1980s. High on the list was the fiscal condition of the country. The huge budget deficits generated by the Reagan administration's military buildup and corporate tax giveaways required massive public borrowing, and foreigners were only too willing to purchase government securities, at attractive real interest rates, by the truckload.

By the end of 1988 foreigners held nearly $100 billion of Treasury issues. It was this giant fix of foreign money that allowed the federal government to maintain the illusion of economic stability for so many years—an illusion that is beginning to crumble now that the U.S. is by far the largest debtor country in the world. In 1988 our net international investment position was in the red to the tune of $532 billion—more than $2,000 per capita. Corporate securities have been a lure as well, despite the stock market crash of October 1987. Foreign holdings of corporate bonds reached nearly 13 percent in 1988 and the share of equities was more than 6 percent.

Some overseas investors are not satisfied being one of many stock- or bondholders; they want to control the whole show, and as a result foreigners have played a major role in America's merger & acquisition free-for-all of the 1980s. Often the marriages are friendly, as in the $2.6 billion purchase of Firestone Tire & Rubber by Bridgestone Corp. of Japan. But foreigners have not shied away from hostile takeovers, as in Robert Maxwell's epic battle for Macmillan Publishing and the conquest of Pillsbury by Grand Metropolitan of Britain.

Overseas buyers have also snapped up American real estate, particularly prime commercial buildings in cities like New York, where such major Manhattan office towers as the Exxon Building, the headquarters of ABC, the Mobil Building, and 51 percent of Rockefeller Center are now owned by investors from Japan. David Hale, chief economist of Kemper Financial Services, has circulated a satirical but pointed proposal that the U.S. raise the money to pay off the national debt by selling Manhattan Island to the Japanese.

Kentucky Hunts with a Vengeance

Jackie Dixon sold his engine repair shop in Union City, Tennessee, in 1983 and moved 150 miles across the state to be part of the future of industrial America. He rearranged his life to take a job at an assembly plant built by Nissan Motor Co. as part of a wave of direct investment in the U.S. by Japan's automakers. After he pinched a nerve in his shoulder and was taken off the assembly line on doctor's orders, Dixon found himself taunted by supervisors and labeled a troublemaker. "It's a total nightmare," Dixon told a reporter. "I wish I had never seen the place. I wish I had never heard of Nissan."

Dixon's experience illustrates some of the worst features of what is perhaps the most significant sort of foreign investment for the American people: the establishment of manufacturing facilities in the U.S. by foreign corporations. While U.S. companies have been shifting capital out of the country in great quantities, leading to a substantial deindustrialization of America, many foreign firms have concluded there is still hope for manufacturing in this country. By the late 1980s foreign transnationals, led by those from such countries as Japan, West Germany, Sweden, and even South Korea, accounted for some 10 percent of manufacturing shipments in the U.S. and 8 percent of manufacturing employment.

The influx of foreign manufacturing investment has been in part a response to the outcry in the U.S. over the loss of jobs from imports. Companies from Japan and South Korea, in particular, saw the move as a way of getting around any trade barriers that the U.S. might erect and of muting the clamor for protectionism. Some of that rhetoric was quelled once it became clear that the investment would create jobs, but the overall reaction to this foreign invasion has been sharply divided. On one side have been revenue-hungry state and local governments rolling out the red carpet. Governors and mayors have traveled throughout Europe and Asia as enthusiastic salesmen for their states and cities; some have even established permanent offices abroad. By the mid-1980s this preoccupation with luring foreign money had officials falling over one another to make the most attractive offers to potential investors. An executive of Canada's Northern Telecom revealed: "I've been approached by every state except Alaska." A major part of the sales pitch consists of economic inducements like tax relief, subsidized training, and road improvements. "The day is over—the day of no incentives," Kentucky's governor has said. "If you don't have them, you're just out of the hunt." Kentucky hunts with a vengeance; the state provided a staggering $325 million in incentives to lure Toyota.

On the other side have been the jingoists who fear that foreigners are taking over America. "Unless there is some strict form of protectionism in this country we are not going to have an industrial base," warns June Collier, chief executive of an Alabama manufacturing firm and founder of Citizens Against Foreign Control of America. "Some people call what they are doing investment," Collier told the New York Times. "But it's buying. And when they buy, they control."

Other critics look with concern at the tendency of foreign-owned factories, especially those from Japan, to give most of their business to suppliers from their own country. The establishment of factories by the Japanese automakers in the U.S., for instance, has been followed by direct investments on the part of Japanese producers of auto parts. An analysis by Robert Kearns in the Chicago Tribune warned that the Japanese were following "a pattern of vertical development, literally a separate Japanese economy inside the American economy, with virtually every step—financing, construction, suppliers, distribution—under Japanese ownership or control."

Caught in the middle is labor. In many Rustbelt regions workers are willing to do anything for a job, and the nationality of the employer is irrelevant. This desperation was captured well in Gung Ho, a 1986 film about a Japanese buyout of a shutdown American auto plant: when a national union official tried to discuss the need for a contract before his members went to work for the new owners, he was booed off the stage by the rank and file.

In the film and in real life, the infatuation with the new employer soon fades, and the old class conflicts can return to the fore. Foreign companies are aware of this danger and to evade it they take great care in deciding where to put their plants and what kind of workers to staff them with. The favored applicant is a white male from a rural area who has not worked in a factory before. To make it easier to obtain such a labor force, foreign investors have taken a number of precautions. First, they locate their plants away from major metropolitan areas—in places like Georgetown, Kentucky, and Marysville, Ohio. Then they subject applicants to a grueling battery of examinations to test not only their aptitude but also their attitude toward work and labor-management relations. When Toyota began staffing its factory in Kentucky, it subjected applicants to as many as 25 hours of tests, workplace simulations, and interviews. A company personnel manager proudly told a reporter: "We're going to know more about these people than perhaps any company has known about people."

Two of the things they know about applicants right from the start are their race and sex, and there have been repeated allegations that foreign companies avoid hiring blacks and women. In 1988 Honda of America paid $6 million to settle a discrimination suit brought by a group of blacks and women who had unsuccessfully applied for jobs at the company's plants in Ohio. The fact that most of the plants built by foreign companies are in largely white areas means that even if they do not explicitly discriminate on racial grounds, few blacks will end up being hired. A black United Auto Workers local president in Detroit complained to a reporter about the tendency by foreign (as well as some domestic) auto companies to shift production to rural areas. In the past in Detroit "all blacks could get was bus boy, car wash, or a job in the auto factory," said Joe Wilson. "You can still get the bus boy, and you can still get the car wash. What's changed is that you can't get anything in the auto industry."

Little Utopias?

It is no coincidence that most of the foreign-owned factories have been placed in states with low rates of unionization—South Carolina, for instance—and have used nonunion contractors to build the facilities.

Weak or absent unions along with low wage rates have been among the main selling points used by government officials in their efforts to attract foreign companies. Much of the writing in the business press has tended to present Japanese-owned plants as little utopias, in which productivity shoots through the roof, workers and managers coexist in beautiful harmony while wearing the same white coveralls, and unions are superfluous. The reality has actually been much more complicated.

Most of the first wave of Japanese companies to set up shop in the U.S. showed an unwavering refusal to allow their plants to be unionized. Honda lost a legal battle to prevent workers from wearing union insignia on the job but resisted the United Auto Workers' organizing drive so adamantly that the UAW suspended the attempt in 1986. The motorcycle manufacturer Kawasaki repeatedly fired union supporters to intimidate workers from participating in organizing drives. In Tennessee, Nissan conducted a fierce campaign against the UAW, which paid off in 1989 when workers at the plant voted 2–1 against union representation.

In some instances the Japanese bought existing factories and inherited a collective bargaining relationship. At a television factory in Forrest City, Arkansas, Sanyo found itself in this position and tried to incorporate the union, the International Union of Electronic Workers, into the corporate family. The IUE chose to retain its independence, and when the company sought extensive work-rule flexibility and reduced medical benefits in 1985, the result was a bitter 21-day strike. Pickets carried signs reading "Japs Go Home" and "Remember Pearl Harbor" and violent clashes occurred at the plant gate. Sanyo managers were appalled, and one of them told a reporter: "I want the union to be strong, but I want it to be intelligently strong to help people instead of stirring things up." The company later scaled down production and moved some of the operations to Mexico.

A third type of labor relations can be found in those Japanese firms that have made peace with their unions, usually in cases where the Japanese have entered joint ventures with U.S. companies. Mazda located an assembly plant (sponsored in part by Ford) in Flat Rock, Michigan—only 15 miles outside of Detroit and thus in "union territory"—and indicated its willingness to cooperate with the UAW. The same approach has been taken at the General Motors-Toyota New United Motors Manufacturing Inc. (NUMMI) project in Fremont, California, and the Chrysler-Mitsubishi venture called Diamond-Star in Normal, Illinois.

The existence of such peaceful coexistence between unions and management is less a reflection of more enlightened policies by foreign companies and more a result of a new approach taken by labor, in particular the UAW. The Auto Workers decided that if they could not beat the Japanese, they would join them at their game of cooperation. Such Japanese management practices as the elimination of work rules, merging of job classifications, and the notorious principle of *kaizen* ("continuous improvement") have been embraced by the UAW in a Faustian bargain with foreign capital. Owen Bieber, president of the union, in effect signaled surrender in his statement hailing the establishment of collective bargaining at the Diamond-Star operation in late 1988. Instead of using the traditional term "workers," he adopted the vocabulary of the Japanese in welcoming the plant's "production and maintenance associates into the UAW family."

The danger of accepting the Japanese model is not only the ideological one of giving up the labor movement's traditional adversary role. It also has grave consequences for the well-being of workers. The issue is not immediately one of money. A study by the General Accounting Office found that Japanese auto plants in the U.S. pay starting wages and offer fringe benefits comparable to those of "native" factories. What is at stake, instead, is the quality of life on the job. While the Japanese are big on quality circles, those forums are primarily concerned with the quality of the product, not working conditions. The *kaizen* system has been widely criticized as a method of intensifying work toward the limits of human endurance. The drastic reduction of job classifications—from more than 90 in traditional General Motors and Ford contracts to two or three at Mazda and Honda, for instance— forces workers to perform at top speed in unfamiliar jobs and thus raises the chance of serious accidents.

Gladys Baines found herself in this position at the Nissan plant in Tennessee. One day in 1985, she was forced to fill in for some absent workers on a part of the assembly line she did not know well. Working hard to keep up, she seriously injured her back and had to be hospitalized. After she was released, Baines's doctor ordered her restricted to light work, but Nissan managers said there was no such thing at the plant, so Baines found herself out on the street. Nissan's attitude is that a worker who cannot perform 100 percent, regardless of the reason, is to be disposed of like a broken tool.

Nissan is not an isolated case. When Luis Orozco, a worker at NUMMI, the General Motors-Toyota joint venture in California, returned home one day from a dentist's appointment, his mouth swollen and sore from gum surgery, he got a phone call from a supervisor wanting to know why he was not back on the job. "You don't have a right to be sick," Orozco told a reporter. "They're too strict. There has to be some liberty. This country is based on liberty." Critics like Mike Parker and Jane Slaughter have called these practices "management by stress." Even *Forbes* magazine, which usually shows scant interest in the problems of workers, admitted that "strange noises are coming from the factory floors, complaints that constant improvement really means constant speedup."

Being Wicked Away from Home

Although foreign companies have provided employment in a number of job-hungry areas, on balance, the new wave of overseas investment has to be seen as contributing to the erosion of living standards for American workers. In a variety of ways these new employers, especially those from Japan, diminish the quality of working life: by freezing out much of the labor force (blacks, women, urban workers, and those experienced in factory labor); by diminishing individual liberty on the job in making workers conform to a rigid corporate culture; by putting productivity and quality control above all human considerations; and by making the job a situation of enormous stress.

Over the longer term, serious consequences will be felt from the fact that most foreign companies still resist acknowledging the collective bargaining rights of American workers. This is not limited to the Japanese. Some of the biggest sinners are European firms. The German chemical company BASF locked out 400 workers in Geismar, Louisiana, for more than three years. Other union-busters include Sweden's Electrolux, which bought U.S. appliance makers Tappan and White Consolidated, and France's Carrefour, which entered the supermarket business in the U.S. Ironically, many of these firms have civilized relations with unions in their home countries. But they seem to think that one of the perks of investing in the U.S. is not having to recognize the rights of workers here. An AFL-CIO economist has suggested that the reason for this is that these corporations feel they do not have to worry about their image when they operate abroad. "It's like when people travel," he said. "They do things away from home that they'd never do at home."

Quite telling is the case of a steel mill in Delaware. In 1988 the bankrupt Phoenix Steel Corp. was purchased by the China International Trust and Investment Corp., an arm of the government of the People's Republic of China. The United Steelworkers union, which had represented the Phoenix workers, helped the new owner obtain exemptions from some state environmental regulations and received what the union interpreted as a commitment that Phoenix workers would be given preference in hiring for the new operation. Yet it soon became clear that the Chinese were inclined to hire only a limited number of the Phoenix workers and were trying to keep the operation nonunion. "The world is changing," the president of the operation told a reporter. "The Chinese are just as capitalistic as anyone."

To the extent that foreign firms contribute to the erosion of the power of organized labor, they are laying the groundwork for erosion of workers' material living standards in the future. For the moment, many foreign firms are paying wages competitive with domestic companies, in large part in order to eliminate a financial incentive for workers to vote union. Yet once the union threat is further diminished, there is every reason to believe that foreign companies will abandon this "generosity." The problem is intensified by the fact that many domestic firms are using Japanese labor policies as a model in reforming their own workplaces. As one autoworker has put it, "Once they take your power away they come after your money."

The Deposed Aristocracy

One almost forgets that only a few years ago, the standard view was that Americans enjoyed a highly privileged status with regard to the rest of the world. Mainstream analysts seemed to think this was our God-given right, while many on the Left bemoaned the complicity of U.S. workers with employers that subjected their foreign work force to "super-exploitation." The traditional Marxist theory of working class impoverishment was put aside in favor of the idea that U.S. workers constituted a kind of labor aristocracy thanks to the fruits of imperialism.

During the 1980s that aristocracy was deposed. The corporate assault on wages turned American workers into cheap labor, compared with much of the rest of the industrialized capitalist world. By 1988 there were eight countries in Europe and Scandinavia with hourly compensation levels higher than those in the U.S. In West Germany, Switzerland, and Norway the compensation level exceeded that of the U.S. by 30 percent or more. Even Japan, that supposed paradise of moderate wages, has been catching up; in 1988 its hourly compensation levels were 91 percent of those in the U.S., compared to 48 percent in 1975.

Bit by bit U.S. workers are facing conditions that were once limited to the third world: stagnant real wages, precarious work status, tyrannical foreign employers, and woefully inadequate government services. The early signs of this trend were evident to Richard Barnet and Ronald Muller when they were writing *Global Reach*, their pathbreaking book on transnational companies. Warning that the rise of the global factory and the international economic crisis were leading to a "LatinAmericanization of the United States," Barnet and Muller wrote: "Compared with what most of the world endures, these indicators of a decline in the standard of living are perhaps barely worth talking about. But in the context of American expectations of something bigger and better each year, they are significant indeed." That was written more than 15 years ago. Today the signs are much clearer, and the notion that U.S. living standards are slipping can be put forth with much less hesitation.

In abstract terms, the narrowing of the gap between living conditions in the first and third worlds is desirable. The problem is that it is occurring more as a result of the impoverishment of Americans than from the enrichment of those in the developing countries. The rise of the global factory has contributed to this by forcing American workers to compete with their counterparts not only in Japan and Western Europe but also in Brazil, South Korea, Taiwan, and even poorer nations. Under the banner of international competitiveness, the U.S. work force is held responsible for labor-cost differentials with countries that are only beginning to industrialize and that are often run by governments willing to impose virtually any hardship on the population in the name of development. "Until we get real wage levels down much closer to those of the Brazils or Korea," stated an executive of Goodyear Tire & Rubber, "we cannot pass along productivity gains to wages and still be competitive."

The result is beneficial neither to Americans nor to the third world—and that is exactly what the transnationals want: constant rivalry between workers everywhere. They also want there to be confusion on the trade issue. While there are still unions and others pushing a "Buy American" ideology, the global factory has made it extremely complicated to identify the nationality of a product. American companies make products abroad and sell them in the U.S. under familiar brand names. Foreign firms produce goods in the U.S. and sell them here to customers who assume they were made abroad. Akio Morita, chairman of Sony, recalled an encounter with a bewildered American consumer: "One of my American friends recently said to me, 'Akio, I bought an American TV rather than a Japanese TV because we have a terrible trade deficit. I found out later that the American set was made in Taiwan, and the Sony set I wouldn't buy was made in the United States."

The risks in giving in to the logic of globalization and international competition were expressed well in a 1986 staff report of the House Committee on Energy and Commerce:

> While realism requires flexibility in the face of international competition, the U.S. cannot agree to abandon its standard of living. . . . If we permit ourselves to become locked into the competitive 'race to the bottom' we will inevitably lose control over the most basic social and political aspects of our national life.

These words have apparently had little impact on policymakers or the business world. While transnationals fight among each other in the quest for the top, most of the rest of us remain trapped in that self-defeating race to the bottom.

ELEVEN

Prosperity Regained?

If you dream alone, it's just a dream.
If you dream together, it's reality.
—*Brazilian folk song*

THESE days there is not much collective dreaming in America. The erosion of living standards and the increase in economic insecurity have brought about a climate of quiet frustration and cynicism. People have been caught between official pronouncements that these are the best of times and their personal realization that life is getting tougher every day. The contradictory evidence is having an immobilizing effect: most Americans do not see a way out of this dilemma and consequently have grown wary of any change at all. While people in other parts of the world, notably Eastern Europe, are boldly confronting their oppression, the U.S. feels like a political backwater.

Yet this social and political paralysis cannot last much longer. Although the crisis of the Soviet bloc has given U.S. capitalism an ideological boost, domestic ills are becoming more difficult to disguise. The spell of the 1980s is beginning to wear off, and people are awakening to an increasingly unpleasant reality. Although there are prominent voices still preaching complacency—or suggesting that even greater austerity is necessary for our national survival —it is not too soon to be planning an entirely different agenda. Sooner than we expect, we may be in a position to tear down capitalism's Berlin Wall: the barrier between people's income and their needs.

Regaining the Initiative

One of the obstacles in formulating a program of radical change is that the political center of gravity shifted so far to the Right during the 1980s. The movement of liberals into the territory of the conservatives created a vacuum at one end of the spectrum of conventional politics. This void ended up being filled by many people who call themselves leftists or progressives. As most Democrats joined with the Right in the assault on social spending, the Left (broadly defined) became the defenders of the welfare state, government paternalism, and the rest of the Roosevelt legacy. Throughout the 1980s, much of the Left did little more than denounce the budget cutbacks initiated by the Reagan administration and for the most part acceded to by Democrats in Congress. The Left, which in the 1960s took great pains to criticize and challenge the liberal establishment, became the last bastion of the New Deal tradition.

Falling into this trap was probably unavoidable. There was an immediate need to challenge the repressive fiscal policies of the era and the encouragement given to abusive employers. Someone had to stand up for workers and the poor. Yet the time has come to move beyond this simply defensive posture. It is no longer enough to defend endangered government benefits and protections. In light of the restructuring of capitalism taking place, it may be a hopeless cause. At the same time, one of the prime motivations of social spending in the 1960s—pacifying an increasingly restive poor population—no longer seems urgent to the powers that be. The fact that the poor could be squeezed as much as they were in the 1980s without more than an occasional outbreak of looting during a blackout has convinced policymakers that rebellion from below has ceased to be a threat.

The Left's defense of the remnants of liberalism is also a problem because it has allowed the Right to present itself as the purveyor of new ideas. Figures like Georgia congressman Newt Gingrich, seizing on widespread frustration with bureaucracy, talk of empowering people against government and of creating a "conservative opportunity society." Jack Kemp, supply-side apostle and now Secretary of Housing and Urban Development, is pushing housing vouchers and tenant ownership of public housing, as well as continuing with his never-ending crusade for enterprise zones.

Big business is being touted as another source of policy innovations. Some large companies have, indeed, taken initiatives with regard to low-cost housing, education, and literacy, prompting one observer to speak of "Business Roundtable Socialism." It is naive to think that corporate America and its advocacy groups like the Business Roundtable are about to put social needs before the pursuit of profit. The social activism of business is not a solution to America's ills but simply a symptom of how much government has abdicated its role. Yet it is significant that the idea of business as savior is even in circulation.

The Left has to regain its position as the source of ideas on the cutting edge of political discourse. This means combining the sensibilities of the ecological movement with the traditional strongpoints of the New Left: concern for the poor at home and in the third world, and a critical attitude toward liberal institutions. The critique of government bureaucracy and of the repressive features of benefit programs originated in the New Left and was appropriated by the Right; now is the time to take it back.

This is not to say that government initiatives are passé. In some ways they are more crucial than ever. Yet they must be structured so that people, not bureaucrats, are empowered, and the programs must bring about fundamental social change rather than merely patching over some of the unfortunate side effects of free enterprise. The challenge for the 1990s is to find solutions that begin to free us from the tyranny of the market as well as of the state.

Setting the "Maximum Wage"

It is in the area of income and wealth that the need for government initiatives remains strong. Left to its own devices, the private economy tends to concentrate money in the hands of the few and discontent in the hearts of the many. The history of economic policymaking in the U.S. and Western Europe over much of the past century has been a series of attempts by political leaders to check this dangerous tendency while preserving the basic principles of capitalism. Social welfare expenditures, progressive taxation, and encouragement of collective bargaining made the distribution of income somewhat more equitable and thus reduced social tensions.

In the 1980s free-market ideologues like Reagan and Thatcher tried to turn back the clock, with disastrous consequences. Some of the worst features of nineteenth-century unbridled enterprise—poverty, precarious working conditions, child and home labor, repression of unions, corporate takeovers—began to reemerge. Once we are in a position to terminate this laissez-faire revival, the alternative will have to be more than a return to the liberal policies of previous decades. The complaints of the supply-siders notwithstanding, the tax system never accomplished a significant redistribution of income and wealth from the upper to the lower levels of the social pyramid. Direct government spending was a bit more effective in rectifying the imbalances, but aside from the Social Security system for the elderly, such programs were stigmatized and often underfunded.

A new and radical approach must involve not only a redistribution of income but also a redistribution of power. This means placing restraints on one of the most sacred yet pernicious principles of capitalism: the right of the wealthy to go on accumulating wealth without limit. For the past half-century the federal government has enforced some kind of minimum wage; now we need to establish a "maximum wage" as well.

The 1980s witnessed an unabashed grab for income and wealth by those controlling the country's private economy. Chief executives of large companies arranged to receive generous increases in pay and perks even when their firms were not doing well. In 1988 the average salary and bonus for CEOs at the largest companies was more than $1.1 million; when exercised stock options and other forms of long-term pay were added in, the figure topped $2 million. Walt Disney chairman Michael Eisner raked in $40 million. Junk bond king Michael Milken was making more than $500 million a year before he was brought down by federal prosecutors in 1989. The number of billionaires on the *Forbes* magazine list of the 400 richest Americans climbed from about a dozen in 1982 to 66 in 1989.

The accumulation of wealth at the top is totally out of control and must be reined in. It is unrealistic to expect America to become economically egalitarian in the foreseeable future, but there has to be some limit on the portion of the country's riches being concentrated in a few hands. Beyond a certain point, income and wealth levels have nothing to do with incentives and serve only as socially irresponsible ego gratification for the likes of Donald Trump.

Using tax policy has proven futile in bringing about this sort of change. What we need to consider is some kind of absolute limit on income. Chief executives should be paid no more than some multiple—say 20 times—of the average pay of their employees. Wealthy individuals should not be allowed to accumulate more than some multiple—perhaps 1,000—of the poverty line for a family of four. This would still allow overachievers to reach $10 million or so. If this does not satisfy the competitive urges of our entrepreneurs, we could allow them to accumulate larger fortunes, but on paper only. The super-rich could still take pride in their Forbes 400 ranking but not have to worry about what to do with unwieldy amounts of assets.

Admittedly, it would be difficult to enforce such ceilings on income and wealth. In the case of chief executives of publicly held companies, the federal reporting requirements would help in keeping tabs. Otherwise, we would have to depend on zealous federal investigators who would be using the Forbes 400 list for an entirely different purpose than its originators intended. There will, of course, be cheating, but the fact that overaccumulation of wealth will be illegal would put a check on the excesses of the rich and move us toward the kind of society we want to create.

"His Title Is His Humanity"

It is not enough to bring down the top; the bottom must be raised. Years of handwringing about the "underclass" have tended to obscure a simple fact: the complete abolition of poverty is well within the reach of this society. The total income deficit of the poor—that is, the total amount they would need to be brought just above the poverty line—is only about $50 billion. In other words, it would take only about 5 percent of the annual federal budget to end the worst forms of privation in America. Ten percent would begin to bring the formerly poor to a decent standard of living. Yet rather than putting it in terms of the federal budget, it might make more sense to say that funding that income deficit could be done by confiscating less than half the wealth of the Forbes 400.

The poor are not the only ones who require help. Something needs to be done about the tens of millions of workers with insufficient earnings. What the deteriorating economic conditions of the U.S. call out for is some sort of guaranteed annual income for everyone. Many workers can no longer depend on the labor market to provide the means for decent living standards. The U.S. has the resources to give every worker a financial cushion against the ups and downs of the private economy. This would enable workers to refuse the most exploitative jobs and thus force abusive employers to raise their wage rates and improve their working conditions to attract a labor force. It is only through the abolition of cheap labor that American business will be diverted from its current penchant for exploitation and turn back to the high-wage, high-productivity economy that is essential to the nation's future prosperity.

Whenever guaranteed income proposals have been put forth in the past, the two leading objections have been: we cannot afford it, and even if we could, it would undermine the incentive to work. When it comes to work, conventional social analysts tend to speak out of both sides of their mouths. To justify a society increasingly dominated by work, they insist that humans have a fundamental need to engage in productive activity. Yet at the same time, they are quick to insist that people, given the opportunity, will gladly give up the workaday world to sit home and collect government checks. Sorting out human motivation is complicated by the fact that capitalism transforms what should be a social and creative activity into a compulsory one essential for physical survival. A more benevolent economy would allow people to do meaningful work for its own sake and not under the threat of starvation.

The first step in this direction would be to present the guaranteed income plan as a true entitlement, like Social Security, rather than a variation on welfare, like the Family Assistance Plan introduced by the Nixon administration in 1969 and killed by Congress. As Doctor Leete described each individual's right to a share of social resources in the future society of Edward Bellamy's novel *Looking Backward*: "His title is his humanity. The basis of his claim is the fact that he is a man."

As for the ability of society to pay for a guaranteed income plan, it is important to keep in mind that affordability is ultimately a political rather than an economic concept. A half century ago it would have been unimaginable for the country to be spending the mammoth sums lavished on the military during the 1980s. We need to create the same urgency about a guaranteed income plan that the cold warriors conveyed about the needs of the Pentagon. The budgetary arithmetic is made easier by the fact that the easing of East-West tensions has created the conditions for a substantial reduction in military spending. While the Bush administration has downplayed the idea of a "peace dividend," the ending of the cold war presents an unprecedented opportunity for a radical reordering of America's budgetary priorities.

Relief for Domestic Debtors

Until a guaranteed income program can help people regain economic stability, some relief will be needed for those who went out on a limb to survive the rigors of the 1980s. This means helping families that went heavily into debt to try to maintain their living standards during a time of stagnating real wages. Everyone recognized that third world countries needed some assistance in meeting the crushing interest burden on their $1 trillion in foreign debt; the same consideration should be given to American consumers weighed down by the monthly vigorish demanded by Mastercard and Visa.

One of the few appealing things about Pat Robertson's 1988 presidential bid was his call for debt forgiveness based on the Biblical notion of a Jubilee year every half century. This kind of religious fundamentalism would do the country some good. Banks would be required to write off a significant portion of the debt amassed by consumers as uncollectible. For good measure, the banks (and the federal government) could also forgive student loans and the debts of small farmers. This could be called a gesture of appreciation by the financial community for the huge bailout of the savings and loan industry being shouldered by American taxpayers.

Curing Merger Mania

Along with the uncontrolled concentration of wealth, the other pathology of the 1980s that has to be cured is the mania for mergers and restructuring. Most of the corporate transformations of the past decade have had little to do with making companies more efficient. Hostile takeovers are battles between corporate managers seeking to protect their power and raiders looking to make a killing by busting up firms. Friendly mergers are often aimed simply at eliminating competition or satisfying a corporate urge for aggrandizement. Leveraged buyouts saddle firms with immense debt burdens. Internal realignments may cut costs but they do so at the expense of jobs, and they usually end up undermining the morale and productivity of those employees who remain.

What is even more maddening about these corporate maneuvers is that they are subsidized, and thus encouraged, by the federal government. Multi-billion-dollar takeovers and buyouts are possible because the players can deduct the interest they pay on the huge sums borrowed to carry out these deals. The $25 billion leveraged buyout of RJR Nabisco in 1989 by itself cost the Treasury billions of dollars in tax revenues. The solution is clear: end the tax deductibility of interest on debt incurred for buyout and takeover purposes. Without Uncle Sam's helping hand, merger mania will quickly die down.

Another approach is needed for the problem of plant shutdowns. In 1988 Congress enacted legislation requiring companies to give 60 days of public notice before a facility is closed. That's fine, but for workers and communities dependent on such facilities, being warned of an impending economic catastrophe makes it no less catastrophic.

What is needed is a way of forcing companies to take responsibility for dealing with the economic impact of their decision to pull up stakes. This means a system of reparations that firms would have to pay to communities and to displaced workers when a plant is shut down. In the same way that a company like Exxon is required to clean up the mess its oil spill caused off the coast of Alaska, so should a company be compelled to deal with the economic mess it causes when it deprives communities and workers of their source of tax revenue and earnings.

Making Contingent Labor Less Precarious

It is tempting to say simply that contingent labor should be outlawed. The potential for abuse when people are hired as part-time, temporary, leased, or free-lance workers is just too great. But what complicates the issue is that many workers want these kinds of flexible working arrangements rather than full-time, permanent situations. As long as women are stuck with major responsibility for housework and child-rearing, they will need these nonconventional job schedules. And once those chores are more equitably distributed between the sexes, more men will be clamoring for flexibility as well.

The trick, then, is for workers to get the flexibility they need without having to pay a high price in terms of substandard wages. Employers should be barred from paying part-timers, temps, and free-lancers less than they pay regular workers for the same job. Contingent workers also have to be assured of getting the fringe benefits they need. Those with a regular relationship with a single firm (for example, permanent part-timers) should be guaranteed benefits by their employer. These should be full benefits, at least as far as things like health insurance are concerned. The fact that someone works only a partial week does not diminish the cost of medical care. For those workers who are employed through an intermediary (agency temps), the middleman organization should be required to provide the benefits.

Equalizing the working conditions of permanent and contingent workers in individual firms is only part of the solution to the problem. On a larger scale what is required is a national commitment to providing flexibility and protection for all workers. What this means, first of all, is universalizing essential employee benefits. There are many full-time, permanent workers, as well as contingent ones, who lack medical insurance and pension coverage. In the absence of a national medical plan, and in light of the uncertainties of Social Security, employers should be required to make provisions for their entire labor force in these vital areas.

While precarious workers have to gain more protections, regular workers need more flexibility. One of the prime attractions of contingent labor for workers is the ability to control the scheduling of their workday, workweek, and work year. Full-time, permanent workers need some of this freedom as well. At the heart of this is the reduction of working time. The U.S. was once in the vanguard of the movement for a shorter workweek, but the issue has largely been forgotten. As a result, the standard week has been stuck at 40 hours for more than half a century. During this same period workweeks in Western Europe have continued to decline. European workers also enjoy more vacation and holiday time. The result is that the average American works more than 1,900 hours a year, while the average West German, for instance, works about 1,700.

The time has come for a redistribution of work as well as income. It is insane to have a society in which some people work ridiculously long weeks while others cannot find a job at all. Shortening the full-time workweek and expanding protected part-time employment would prop up employment levels in faltering industries while allowing people to handle family responsibilities more easily and to enjoy the nonwork aspects of life a bit more. It may also be the cure for the workaholism that afflicted so many white-collar types during the 1980s. No country can be said to have a high standard of living that works people (or causes people to work themselves) to the point of exhaustion.

Worktime also needs to be limited for young people. They should not be forced into the labor market at an early age, and when they do work they should receive strong protection against exploitation. Child labor restrictions need to be strengthened and enforcement intensified. Rather than being allowed to pay substandard wages to teenagers, employers should be required to pay a premium to hire young people. Society ought to discourage the employment of school-age young people, who should be in school and otherwise enjoying their youth rather than slaving in front of a hot grill in a fast-food outlet.

Union-Building, Not Busting

The problems of unions are so great that extensive reforms are needed to halt the precipitous decline of organized labor. Some of the changes are internal: unions have to rediscover their militant origins and back away from the self-defeating labor-management cooperation that is so much in vogue today. They also need to complete the transition from the cold war anti-communism that suffused the labor establishment in the 1950s to a spirit of international solidarity.

From the point of view of public policy, the biggest issues are the corrosion of the strike weapon and the ability of employers to undermine organizing drives. Faced with these problems, AFL-CIO president Lane Kirkland has toyed with the idea of calling for the abolition of the National Labor Relations Act (NLRA) so unions can freely slug it out with management. That would be fine if there were any signs that the current labor establishment had the stomach for such a brawl.

What makes more sense is to seek radical changes in the law. On the issue of strikes, Congress has to be made to give meaning to the right of workers, enshrined in the NLRA, to engage in collective action, including strikes, to pursue their economic interests. During the half-century since the passage of the act this right has repeatedly clashed with the right of employers, as affirmed by the Supreme Court, to continue operating during a walkout.

As a result, companies may not fire workers for going on strike, but they may hire permanent replacements (the polite term for scabs) to take over their jobs. Only in instances where the union can establish that the company had engaged in unfair labor practices do the workers have an absolute right to reclaim their jobs after the strike has ended. It is difficult to see any significant difference between this power of firms to replace strikers and a situation in which walkouts are simply illegal.

The solution is, as the labor movement has proposed, a law that would outlaw the use of permanent replacements during any kind of walkout. Even better would be legislation, like that which exists in Quebec, barring employers from operating during strikes. The original concept in the NLRA was that during a strike both sides faced difficulties: the worker lost wages, and the employer lost revenues because production was halted. The ability of companies to continue operating by hiring a new labor force upsets what was supposed to be a relatively even balance of power. The scales need to be brought closer to equilibrium once again.

As for organizing efforts, the lack of strong enforcement provisions in the NLRA, along with the promanagement tilt of the National Labor Relations Board in the 1980s, has crippled the efforts of unions to expand their ranks. Companies use delaying tactics in complying with the law, knowing that the penalties they may ultimately face will be insignificant compared to the hardships faced by workers while they wait for justice.

Two reforms are urgently needed. First, the NLRB should allow representation elections immediately after a union has gone public with an organizing drive. The usual delays most often serve only to give employers time to bring in anti-union consultants to pressure the workers to vote against the union. Second, there should be stricter penalties, including criminal sanctions, against firms that egregiously violate labor laws by firing union activists and otherwise intimidating workers. Serious labor law violators should be barred from receiving government contracts. It is only through reforms such as these that the NLRA can once again be a tool for union organizing rather than union busting.

Women and Children First

One of the main benefits of a guaranteed income program would be to eliminate the risk of poverty that confronts divorced women and their children. No one should have to remain in a bad relationship because of the economic consequences of leaving, and no one should have to suffer a precipitous decline in living standards after breaking up with a spouse. The enactment of tough laws to force divorced fathers (who may be facing financial difficulties of their own) to pay child support is not the ideal solution. Seeing to it that those children's needs are taken care of should be society's responsibility.

The guaranteed income scheme should compensate employed women, whether divorced or not, for the tendency of employers to pay them less than men. In fact, as long as women remain stuck with most housework and child-care responsibilities, they should receive *more* income than men. Nevertheless, society should take steps to relieve that burden. The most obvious step is the enactment of a comprehensive child-care program.

197

As for children, there is clearly a need for increased social spending on health care. The steady decline of infant mortality rates must resume, and immunization levels should be no less than 100 percent. All of this must come about in the course of establishing a national health care system. The urgency of meeting this long-overdue social need is becoming apparent even to the captains of industry who used to abhor the idea. The issue now is not whether such a system is required, but what form it should take. A major challenge of the 1990s will be to prevent the creation of a Swiss-cheese sort of national health plan—one filled with holes relating to eligibility and coverage.

Protecting the Nest-Egg

Every effort must be made to avoid returning to a situation in which becoming elderly means becoming poor, and those seniors who are in need ought to be brought up to a decent standard of living by addressing the shortcomings of Social Security. The burden of hefty out-of-pocket health care expenses for seniors also has to be lifted. Medicare should be made into a comprehensive insurance program in which all expenses are covered and paid by assignment.

In order to help finance these reforms, the regressive nature of the Social Security tax has to be changed. The ceiling on covered earnings ought to be abolished, and the tax should be levied on a progressive basis rather than as a flat rate.

As for private pensions, the biggest issue is who is going to control a nest-egg worth several trillion dollars. The corporate world panicked in 1989 when an obscure member of Congress proposed a measure, which got attached to the budget bill, giving employees an equal voice with management in decisions about the investment and administration of pension funds. "We want to see this bill dead," stated a spokesperson for an employer group. The measure was indeed killed, but the reaction of business indicated how much is at stake. Corporations have used their control of pension funds to seize "excess assets," either to protect against a takeover, to finance a move on another firm, or simply to fatten the balance sheet. Sometimes the funds are simply looted. Even when the funds are administered properly, their assets are often invested in the stocks and bonds of companies that engage in union-busting, sex and race discrimination, and other policies that are not in the interest of pension plan participants.

The Housing Solution

Ending corporate control of pension funds would not only protect plan participants; it could also provide the resources for solving another social problem: housing. There is no reason why pension assets should be overwhelmingly invested in corporate stocks and bonds. That money would do a lot more good if it were used to finance low-cost housing. Some funds that are under the partial control of unions have moved in this direction, but the amount of money involved is still small. Pension funds could ultimately take over the financing of all residential construction, and by keeping mortgage rates low they could bring down the overblown price of housing.

At the same time, something must be done to protect those who cannot afford to buy homes, even at subsidized prices. The federal government should end its quiet war against local rent-control regulations and take steps to protect the hundreds of thousands of tenants in federally subsidized housing scheduled to shift to a free-market basis during the 1990s. The safeguards enjoyed by those tenants should be grandfathered, and the federal housing programs decimated during the 1980s need to be rebuilt. The desire of Housing and Urban Development secretary Jack Kemp to convert public housing to tenant ownership is not entirely a bad idea. Yet the conversion should be done at no cost to tenants, and the transfer should not be completed until the government makes all necessary repairs. The program should also not be used as an excuse for ceasing construction of new subsidized housing.

A New Kind of Zoning Variance

Another of Kemp's projects, the creation of enterprise zones, is an idea whose time has come and gone. The notion that business needs special areas in which tax and regulatory burdens would be relieved may have had some appeal in the late 1970s, when the plan was first presented, but after a decade of serve-the-corporations policymaking in Washington, the last thing the country requires are more incentives for the private sector.

In fact, what makes more sense now is the creation of a different kind of zone: what might be called, to borrow a term from the 1960s, liberated zones. Rather than experimenting with greater liberty for business, we need to expand freedom for workers and the poor. This would involve the creation of noncapitalist spheres of economic and social activity, specifically worker and consumer cooperatives. Worker-owned companies and consumer co-ops, once heralded as the foundation stones of a new society, have largely been stripped of their radical potential. Big business has turned employee stock ownership plans into tax shelters and anti-takeover devices. Food co-ops, where they have survived, now are usually little more than offbeat places to shop. The excitement of nonprofit, nonhierarchical institutions has to be revived, and the viability of larger-scale cooperative networks has to be explored. Socialism may be out of fashion, but that does not mean that complete corporate domination of life is inevitable.

Reining In the Multinationals

As far as the international economy is concerned, there is little that a new political program, however bold, can do about the end of U.S. global might. Yet that need not be a problem. There is no reason for the U.S. (or any other country) to rule the world, and the American economy has to be made to work without relying on exploitation of weaker nations.

What is a problem is that many large U.S. corporations have outgrown their home country and are totally oriented to the requirements of international competition. There is nothing wrong with operating on a global basis per se; the problem arises when these firms use their far-flung facilities to weaken the bargaining power of workers and communities at home. The only way to prevent this is to put some limits on the international mobility of capital. The shifting of facilities and investments around the globe, as in a giant chess game, often serves no economic purpose and is done mainly to keep one step ahead of governments and unions. Whether done through tax policy or some other form of regulation, multinationals need to be held to a stricter standard of international conduct.

The same goes for foreign companies operating in the U.S. While there is no basis for hysteria about America falling under alien control, foreign direct investors have to be discouraged from introducing repressive working conditions in their factories. They also have to be forced to pay more respect to U.S. labor laws. In fact, if this country were serious about enforcing the NLRA, it would enact legislation providing for the confiscation of assets of foreign investors who flagrantly violate the act.

The Right Way of Bridging the Gap

Another international issue has to do with relative living standards. While conditions in the U.S. have been eroding, it is undeniable that the quality of life in the third world remains far behind. At the extreme, there are several hundred million people in Asia, Africa, and Latin America who are "absolutely poor," meaning that they do not ordinarily obtain enough food to prevent stunted growth and serious health risks. Those conditions constitute an international emergency that first world governments have never adequately addressed.

Yet the conditions of life are not so dire for the majority of people in the developing countries. In fact, as the pace of industrialization in the third world has accelerated over the past few decades, the relationship between living standards there and in the developed world has become more complicated. Goods made with cheap Asian and Latin American labor have poured into the U.S., upsetting America's trade balance and leading to the elimination of many industrial jobs. Third world workers are presented as a leading cause of the difficulties faced by the American labor force. Business leaders have implied, and sometimes come right out and stated, that U.S. workers must lower their living standards down toward that of their counterparts in countries like Brazil and South Korea. The corporate powers that be have their own solution to the discrepancy in international living conditions: making those in the developed countries poorer.

While rejecting this false egalitarianism promoted by business, the situation of the third world must be taken into account when deciding what to do about living standards in the U.S. The alternative is clear: American workers should not be made poorer; third world workers have to be made richer. One of the major ways of doing this is to encourage the development of aggressive labor unions in the third world and building stronger solidarity between them and the labor movement in the U.S. and other developed countries. Improving conditions in the third world is not only a moral issue. Bridging the gap between the first and third worlds will make it much more difficult for multinational corporations to play off workers in one area against those in the other.

Quality as well as Quantity

In analyzing economic trends there is an unavoidable tendency to focus exclusively on the quantitative dimensions of living standards, yet there are also grave problems relating to the form of consumption. The U.S. style of manufacturing and distributing goods, transporting people, and controlling the climate take a heavy toll on the environment. The ways in which Americans use physical resources have been cited as causes of ecological crises such as global warming, the depletion of the ozone layer, acid rain, and general despoiling of the land, sea, and air. It has been said, with some justification, that America's major product is garbage—more than 200 million tons of it each year.

Yet it is a mistake to attribute the accumulation of waste and pollution to a supposedly profligate population. It is not by popular demand that America is inundated with shoddy, disposable products and non-biodegradable packaging; nor is it the people's will that transportation and power systems should employ nonrenewable energy sources. In fact, the high-waste, high-pollution society is a sign of diminished rather than bloated living standards, which have to be judged in qualitative as well as quantitative terms. Having clean air to breathe, safe water to drink, and otherwise living in a nontoxic environment is as important—sometimes more important—than the size of one's gross income or net worth. It is better to have a cleaner environment than more money to pay for doctors to treat the ills brought on by a noxious world. The fact that these aspects of public health are becoming increasingly elusive is another indication that American living standards, broadly understood, are in crisis.

It is pointless to counterpose economic living standards to ecological conditions and conclude that the former must be reduced for the sake of the latter. If it is true that wasteful and polluting conditions do not make people rich, then it follows that impoverishing the population is not the solution to the environmental problem. In the early days of the ecology movement there was a tendency to condemn workers who put their job security before concern for pollution. Eventually, the two groups realized they had common concerns, especially when it came to dangerous conditions in the workplace. The same recognition needs to come about between environmentalists and the general population. Consumers are not the problem; the system of production and the corporations that run it are.

It is precisely this conclusion that business is trying to obscure in its recent discovery of the environment. "Caring for the environment used to be a chore. It is now a market opportunity," cheerfully reports the London *Economist.* "Manufacturers are churning out more and more green products, and retailers are finding that many can be sold at a premium." After defiling the planet for the past two centuries, business is now perfectly willing to sell us, at inflated prices, the means to make some token improvements. Corporations, in other words, are planning to carry out what environmentalists have only suggested: that people should reduce their economic well-being for the sake of ecology.

Yet that need not be the case. Quantitative improvements in the standard of living can go hand in hand with qualitative changes that enhance the standards of livability. This would require sacrifices from corporations rather than consumers. Rather than profiteering by charging more for "green" goods, business should be forced to absorb the costs of making the transition.

In addition, corporations that continue to pollute and contribute to the accumulation of waste should be made to pay a penalty for their sins. This is not simply a matter of beefing up the Environmental Protection Agency. For too long, the harmful side effects of industry on the environment have been treated as unfortunate "externalities" that do not show up in the national economic accounts. The impact of production on the environment should be made a part of accounting at both the national and the corporate level. Only when it is hit in its balance sheet will business really clean up its act.

A genuine move toward cleaning up the environment would be the first in a series of pathbreaking qualitative changes in the conditions of life. The environment is the classic "social good" that everyone enjoys collectively and without (for the most part) the mediation of money. Other examples include a high-quality public education system, safe (crimeless) streets, public health, and cultural institutions. In the long run, it is the enhancement of such collective goods rather than income levels that will be decisive in assessing standards of living. Ideally, money income should be a minor rather than the central element in determining the quality of life.

A Time for Utopia

Some of the preceding proposals may seem overly ambitious, but the aim is to dramatize the need to go beyond the usual confines of policy debates. The U.S. economy is undergoing dramatic restructuring, and things will continue to deteriorate until the forces of inequality and privilege are challenged. At the same time, the world is changing rapidly, and exciting opportunities are emerging. Recent events in Eastern Europe show that seemingly permanent institutions can crumble virtually overnight. The ending of the cold war has up-ended many of the assumptions about what is or is not possible in terms of economic and social policies. Such a situation calls for ideas that are bold, even utopian. Prosperity can be regained, but only if we fight for it.

· AFTERWORD ·

In late 1989, as *Prosperity Lost* was being completed, most private and government economists assumed that the purported boom of the Reagan years would extend into the new decade. The high priests of economics celebrated the fact that unemployment had been brought down to nearly 5 percent and that the gross national product continued to grow (albeit at a slower rate). "The United States enters the 1990s as a prosperous nation with a healthy and dynamic economy," crowed George Bush in his introduction to the *Economic Report of the President* released in February 1990.

It was not long before this cockiness began to collapse, thanks to a combination of fiscal politics and a long-overdue downturn in the business cycle.

The fiscal part of the sobering-up process was prompted by the June 1990 decision of President Bush, then under intense pressure to deal with the federal budget crisis, to abandon his stubborn "read my lips" opposition to new taxes.

Bush's reversal was significant for two reasons. First, it was a tacit acknowledgment that the supply-side program, which regarded tax cuts as a panacea, had failed. Simple budgetary arithmetic had replaced the voodoo-economic notion that lavishing money on the military and providing tax breaks for the wealthy somehow amounted to a sustainable fiscal policy.

The new policy also paved the way for a dramatic change in political discourse. As if their tongues had suddenly been untied, many Democrats began to question whether the fiscal recipe of the 1980s was still desirable. To an extent not seen since the 1930s, politicians began talking in explicit class terms.

The Democrats were emboldened in part by the publication in June 1990 of a book by a prominent Republican analyst that said many of the things they had lost the nerve to utter. *The Politics of Rich and Poor* by Kevin Phillips encouraged the kind of criticism of Reaganomics that had been disturbingly absent from the mainstream in the 1980s. Political figures such as New York governor Mario Cuomo began citing Phillips's critique of the "new plutocracy" with a gusto previously reserved for quotations from FDR.

This sentiment was intense enough to create some surprising results after President Bush and congressional leaders announced a deficit reduction plan at the end of September. The plan, which relied heavily on cuts in social spending (especially Medicare) and excise taxes on gasoline, alcohol, and other items, was widely rejected by rank-and-file members of Congress.

The budget debate was marked by extraordinary ideological confusion and frequent policy shifts, especially by the Administration. In the end, the strongest push came from members of Congress responding to the new populist mood. Or, as a *Wall Street Journal* headline bluntly put it: "Politicians Exploit Broad Public Support for Soaking the Rich."

The tax package that was finally enacted did exact heavier payments from those at the top of the income pyramid, although the effect on the monied classes was more of a sprinkling than a soaking.

Nonetheless, the mini populist revolt of 1990 helped destroy the legitimacy of trickle-down economics, and the Bush Administration has all but given up on its quest for a capital gains tax cut. However, the Social Darwinists have by no means given up gracefully. Just before the 1990 national elections, Bush lashed out at the Democrats, accusing them of trying to win votes by means of a "tax-the-rich, class warfare kind of garbage." Along the same lines, a review of *Prosperity Lost* in *The Wall Street Journal* accused the book of advocating a police state because of the call for a redistribution of income.

The assault on the economics of greed may have made conservatives grouchy, but the relatively progressive fiscal policies adopted in 1990 have barely put a dent in what remains an enormous problem. The legacies of the Reagan years are still with us, and the evidence of social polarization continues to mount, as evidenced by the following:

- The Census Bureau's annual report on the distribution of income published in September 1990 showed that inequality continues to break new records.

- The latest calculations by the House Committee on Ways and Means found that during the 1980s the poorest fifth of families suffered a 2 percent decline in inflation-adjusted income, while the richest fifth enjoyed a 20 percent gain.
- New data on household wealth showed a similar pattern. The median household experienced a drop in net wealth from 1984 to 1988 (in constant dollars). The only group to show a rise was the very rich.
- The Bureau of Labor Statistics reported that between 1985 and 1989 some 4.3 million workers who had been on the job at least three years had been displaced because of plant shutdowns, corporate streamlining, or economic slowdown.
- Cuts in federal aid have forced many cities and states to depend more on their own levies to fund social programs—and these taxes are notoriously regressive. A 1991 study by Citizens for Tax Justice found that a typical poor family pays some 13.8 percent of its income in state and local taxes, while the very wealthiest families pay 7.6 percent.
- The Department of Health and Human Services reported in 1991 that life expectancy for blacks declined for the fourth year in a row in 1988.

It is important to keep in mind that these statistics relate to a period when officially the economy was still growing. The symptoms of social erosion became even worse when a new affliction appeared on the scene: the return of the business cycle.

During the 1980s, many economists jumped to the conclusion that the traditional ups and downs of capitalism had been conquered. Repeating the self-deception that was common in many previous boom times, they decided that the U.S. economy could defy the law of gravity and go on expanding indefinitely.

Even when clear telltale signs of a downturn began to appear in mid-1990, top federal policymakers went through numerous verbal contortions to avoid admitting that a recession was upon us. As late as November of that year, Fed chairman Alan Greenspan refused to use the r-word in congressional testimony, speaking instead of a "meaningful downturn." The following month Treasury Secretary Nicholas Brady chose another euphemism: a "significant slowdown." Many economists inside and outside the federal government attributed the downbeat signs to the crisis in the Persian Gulf and argued that they would soon disappear.

When the business cycle scorekeepers at the National Bureau of Economic Research signaled that a recession had begun the official rhetoric began to change. The Administration admitted the country was in a slump; nonetheless, the spin doctors were promoting the message that the pain would be dull and brief. In February 1991 President Bush himself tried to minimize the significance of the crisis by speaking of "temporary disturbances and short-term setbacks."

Recessions, of course, are always temporary, but there was little basis for the Administration's promises of a speedy recovery. The fragility of the economy has been painfully evident in the rash of corporate bankruptcies (e.g., Pan American, Carter Hawley Hale), the failure of the Bank of New England and the wider banking mess, and the faltering of the insurance industry.

The intensity of the crisis has also been seen in the run-up of the unemployment rate, which reached 7.0 percent in June—the highest level in 5 years. Professional and managerial employees have been especially hard hit, even in companies like IBM, Digital Equipment, and Eastman Kodak, which have abandoned their no-layoff traditions. Many younger yuppies who began their careers during the Reagan go-go years are now having their first taste of joblessness.

The financial impact of job loss has been intensified by the poor state of the unemployment compensation system. The level of benefits remains woefully inadequate: the average weekly payment in 1990 was only $154—which in constant dollars was lower than the amount during the last recession in 1982–83. And because of tightened eligibility requirements, only about one out of every three unemployed persons qualifies for payments.

The duration of benefits is also inadequate. Most states have been providing a maximum of 26 weeks of benefits because complicated federal rules stand in the way of implementing the extended benefits provided for in the law. Every month several hundred thousand people exhaust their benefits without finding another job.

The Bush Administration has resisted calls for strengthening the unemployment compensation system and is hoping that a combination of eased credit and crossed fingers will get the country through the crisis.

By the time these words appear in print, it is possible that the recession will have ended. This will no doubt be accompanied by the usual celebrations of the resilience of American capitalism. If the recovery includes a significant rise in employment, it will indeed provide some relief for those currently caught between the paucity of jobs and the deficiency of jobless benefits.

Yet what the past dozen years have shown is that the business cycle is no longer the key determinant of the actual economic condition of much of the country. The tendency for living standards to erode during both up and down phases is a crisis that the practitioners of economics-as-usual cannot solve. Daring new initiatives are the only hope for preventing the 1990s from becoming as frustrating as the last decade.

July 23, 1991

INTRODUCTION

p. 1 "We snap on the TV": The ad, headlined "And the Walls Came Tumbling Down," was published, for example, in the *New York Times* on December 7, 1989.

p. 2 "real wages will have to fall": Jeffrey Sachs, "How America Can Help Poland Make History," *Washington Post*, October 29, 1989, p.B2.

p. 2 "The most difficult challenge": Alan Murray, "Polish Economic Plan Is Boldly Capitalistic," *Wall Street Journal*, December 4, 1989, p.1.

p. 4 "We've got enormous budget problems": Quoted in David E. Rosenbaum, "Spending Can Be Cut in Half, Former Defense Officials Say," *New York Times*, December 13, 1989, p.B14.

p. 4 "It was necessary to accept sacrifices": Joseph Stalin, *Questions of Leninism* (1939), quoted in Paul A. Baran, *The Political Economy of Growth*, New York: Monthly Review Press 1957, p.278.

p. 5 "the root malady": Peter G. Peterson, "The Morning After," *The Atlantic*, October 1987, pp.43–69.

p. 5 Brookings volume: Barry P. Bosworth et al., *Critical Choices: What the President Should Know About the Economy and Foreign Policy*, Washington: Brookings Institution 1989.

CHAPTER ONE

p. 7 Details about Kistler and MacKay: Betsy Morris, "Why 3 Grown Men from Pennsylvania Live on a Billboard," *Wall Street Journal*, December 9, 1982, p.1; Steve Swartz, "Billboard Squatters Both Called Winners and Are to Descend," *Wall Street Journal*, June 6, 1983; Tom Lowry, "5 Years Ago, 3 Men Got on a Billboard," *Allentown Morning Call*, September 20,

1987, p.A1; and a phone conversation with Ronald Kistler, September 9, 1989.

p. 8 "The whole world marvels": The Editors of *Fortune*, *The Changing American Market*, Garden City, NY: Hanover House 1955, p.13.

p. 8 "The most obvious fact": Quoted in Oxford Analytica, *America in Perspective: Major Trends in the United States Through the 1990s*, Boston: Houghton Mifflin 1986, p.57.

p. 8 "the challenge of abundance": Robert Theobald, *The Challenge of Abundance*, New York: Clarkson N. Potter 1961.

p. 8 "the possibility of economic satiety": Roy Harrod, "The Possibility of Economic Satiety," in Committee for Economic Development, *Problems of United States Economic Development*, vol.1, New York 1958, p.207.

p. 9 study showing that the portion of national income going to the rich was declining: Simon Kuznets, *Share of Upper Income Groups in Income and Savings*, New York: National Bureau of Economic Research 1953.

p. 9 the concept of social class "nearly valueless": Robert A. Nisbet, "The Decline and Fall of Social Class," *Pacific Sociological Review*, Spring 1959; quoted in Paul Blumberg, *Inequality in an Age of Decline*, New York: Oxford University Press 1980, p.17.

p. 9 "a huge new moneyed middle-income class": Editors of *Fortune*, *op. cit.* p.52.

p. 11 family income data: U.S. Bureau of the Census, *Money Income of Households, Families, and Persons in the United States: 1987*, Series P-60, No.162, February 1989, p.38.

p. 11 this "sudden break in trend": Frank Levy, *Dollars and Dreams: The Changing American Income Distribution*, New York: Russell Sage Foundation 1987, p.17.

p. 11 data on multiple jobholding: U.S. Bureau of Labor Statistics, "Multiple Jobholding Reached Record High in May 1989," press release, November 6, 1989.

p. 12 Leroy Montgomery's hours: Carlee Scott, "Americans Turn to Leading Double Lives," *Wall Street Journal*, December 1, 1989.

p. 12 surveys find that Americans have declining amounts of leisure time: A Harris survey, cited in *Time*, April 24, 1989, p.58, found that the leisure time enjoyed by the average American has shrunk 37 percent since 1973.

p. 12 real income of families with children: Sheldon Danziger and Peter Gottschalk, *How Have Families with Children Been Faring?* Institute for Research on Poverty, University of Wisconsin-Madison, Discussion Paper No.801–86, January 1986, p.6.

p. 12 "an economic disaster": Children's Defense Fund, *Vanishing Dreams: The Growing Economic Plight of America's Young Families*, Washington 1988, pp.3,4.

p. 13 intergenerational downward mobility: Frank Levy, "Incomes, Families, and Living Standards," in Robert E. Litan, Robert Z. Lawrence and Charles L. Schultze, eds., *American Living Standards: Threats and Challenges*, Washington: Brookings Institution 1988, p.116.

p. 13 studies that find rising income: see, for example, U.S. Congress, Congressional Budget Office, *Trends in Family Income: 1970–1986*, Washington, February 1988. Census figures can also be criticized for understating property income, but that is not usually addressed by the revisionists.

p. 13 among the more careful of these revisions: Stephen Rose and David Fasenfest, *Family Income in the 1980s: New Pressure on Wives, Husbands, and Young Adults*, Washington: Economic Policy Institute, Working Paper No.103, November 1988.

p. 14 quintile shares: U.S. Bureau of the Census, *op. cit.* p.42.

p. 15 "the egalitarian push": John Cobbs, "Egalitarianism: Threat to a Free Market, *Business Week*, December 1, 1975, p.62.

p. 15 Gini ratios: U.S. Bureau of the Census, *op. cit.* p.42.

p. 15 estimates by House Ways and Means: U.S. Congress, House Committee on Ways and Means, *Background Material and Data on Programs Within the Jurisdiction of the Committee on Ways and Means: 1989 Edition*, Washington: U.S. Government Printing Office 1989, pp.986, 994.

p. 15 "correct" family income: Levy, *op. cit.* p.196.

p. 16 a 1989 study: Fabian Linden, Gordon W. Green, Jr. and John F. Coder, *A Marketer's Guide to Discretionary Income*, a joint study by the Consumer Research Center of the Conference Board and the U.S. Bureau of the Census, 1989.

p. 16 30 percent of American households: U.S. Bureau of the Census, "Discretionary Income Totals Almost $320 Billion, Census Bureau-Conference Board Study Shows," press release, May 25, 1989.

p. 16 "an endangered species": Lester Thurow, *The Zero-Sum Solution: Building a World-Class American Economy*, New York: Simon & Schuster 1985, p.61.

p. 16 study on the shrinking middle: Michael W. Horrigan and Steven E. Haugen, "The Declining Middle-Class Thesis: A Sensitivity Analysis," *Monthly Labor Review*, May 1988, p.3. An excellent analysis of the Horrigan and Haugen study appeared in *Left Business Observer*, No.21, September 6, 1988, p.4.

p. 17 Hamlet's story: Jane Seaberry, "Middle-Class Dream Fades for Some," *Washington Post*, January 4, 1987, p.A1.

p. 17 General Tire & Rubber: Robert S. Greenberger, "More Workers Resist Employers' Demands for Pay Concessions," *Wall Street Journal*, October 13, 1982, p.1.

p. 17 "Money isn't the answer": Amanda Bennett, "Wage Increases Stay Surprisingly Modest Amid Labor Shortages," *Wall Street Journal*, August 29, 1988, p.1.

p. 18 *New York Times* articles: The first one appeared on September 8,

1987, p.A1 and the second on August 4, 1989, p.D1; both were written by Louis Uchitelle. The piece on wages and productivity, by the same author, was "As Output Gains, Wages Lag," June 4, 1987, p.D1.

p. 18 hourly wage rates of nonsupervisory workers: The 1989 figure came from a statistical table in the *Monthly Labor Review*, March 1990, p.92. The historical comparison was made from a table in the 1990 *Economic Report of the President*, Washington: Government Printing Office 1990, p.344.

p. 18 usual gross weekly earnings: The 1989 figure came from a statistical table in the *Monthly Labor Review*, March 1990, p.93. The historical comparison was made from a table in the 1990 *Economic Report of the President*, p.344.

p. 18 earnings of black male workers: Calculated from data in *Employment and Earnings*, January 1990, p.219.

p. 18/19 much of the improvement for salaried employees: Lawrence Mishel and Jacqueline Simon, *The State of Working America*, Washington: Economic Policy Institute 1988, p.13.

p. 19 "real rate" of joblessness: Phone conversation with Calvin George of the National Committee for Full Employment, September 13, 1989.

p. 19–20 index of inequality in earnings: Bennett Harrison and Barry Bluestone, *The Great U-Turn: Corporate Restructuring and the Polarizing of America*, New York: Basic Books 1988, p.118.

p. 20 additional evidence of earnings polarization: Robert M. Costrell, *The Effects of Industry Employment Shifts on Wage Growth: 1948–1987*, a study prepared for the Joint Economic Committee, August 1988.

p. 20 "a study reaching just that conclusion": Barry Bluestone and Bennett Harrison, *The Great American Job Machine: The Proliferation of Low Wage Employment in the U.S. Economy*, a study prepared for the Joint Economic Committee, December 1986.

p. 20 a propaganda sheet: *The White House Economic Bulletin*, September 2, 1988.

p. 20 "they later did new calculations": Barry Bluestone and Bennett Harrison, "The Growth of Low-Wage Employment: 1963–86," *American Economic Review*, May 1988, p.124 and Harrison and Bluestone, *op. cit.* pp.121–23.

p. 21 "I want my Maypo": Quoted in Peter T. Kilborn, "Darman Issues Warning on 'Self-Indulgent' U.S.," *New York Times*, July 21, 1989, p.D1.

p. 21 personal consumption expenditures: *Survey of Current Business*, July 1989, p.98.

p. 21 $14,000 wristwatches: Lindley H. Clark, Jr., "Consumers Keep Doing Their Thing, Helping Economy Chug Along," *Wall Street Journal*, September 7, 1989, p.1.

p. 21 trend in per capita disposable personal income: Calculated from data in *Survey of Current Business, op. cit.*

p. 21 labor income has been falling: William A. Cox, *Measures of Real Earnings Since 1970*, U.S. Library of Congress, Congressional Research Service, October 17, 1988, p.18.

p. 21/22 labor income per worker: *Left Business Observer, op. cit.*

p. 22 total consumer credit: The 1990 *Economic Report of the President*, Washington: Government Printing Office 1990, p.382.

p. 22 "I'm really living beyond my means": Barbara Rudolph, "Mounting Doubts About Debts," *Time*, March 31, 1986, p.51.

p. 22 the number of personal bankruptcies: Charles A. Luckett, "Personal Bankruptcies," *Federal Reserve Bulletin*, September 1988, p.591.

p. 22 personal savings: The 1989 *Economic Report of the President*, p.339.

p. 22 "We're saving to get out of debt": Pamela Sebastian, "Baby Boomers Find It Hard to Save Money; Will They Do It Later?" *Wall Street Journal*, February 13, 1989, p.A10.

p. 22 "There is no wealth but life": John Ruskin, *Unto This Last* (1862), sec.77, cited in *Bartlett's Familiar Quotations*, 14th edition, Boston: Little, Brown 1968, p.698.

p. 23 median holdings of financial assets: "Survey of Consumer Finances, 1983," *Federal Reserve Bulletin*, September 1984, p.679.

p. 23 net worth of families: "Survey of Consumer Finances, 1983: A Second Report," *Federal Reserve Bulletin*, December 1984, p.863.

p. 23 "a much higher profile report": U.S. Congress, Joint Economic Committee, *The Concentration of Wealth in the United States: Trends in the Distribution of Wealth Among American Families*, July 1986.

p. 24 "it was quite possible that the 'correction' was made solely for political purposes": From a methodological point of view it certainly was a mistake for the survey to weight that one individual so heavily. The problem is that there are so few of the super-rich and they do not tend to be cooperative when it comes to inquiries about their wealth. The account of the wealth controversy draws heavily on "Scandal at the Fed? Doctoring the Numbers on Wealth Concentration," *Dollars & Sense*, April 1987, p.10.

p. 24 "the Census Bureau came out with its first report": U.S. Bureau of the Census, *Household Wealth and Asset Ownership: 1984*, Series P-70, No.7, July 1986.

p. 24 "quiet riots": Fred R. Harris and Roger W. Wilkins, eds., *Quiet Riots: Race and Poverty in the United States*, New York: Pantheon 1988, p.xiii.

p. 24/25 "Let's talk about differences in living standards": Walter Joelson, chief economist at GE; quoted in Louis Uchitelle, "Narrowing a Wage Gap," *New York Times*, June 26, 1987.

p. 25 "Our parents feel sorry for young people today": Aaron Bernstein, "Warning: The Standard of Living Is Slipping," *Business Week*, April 20, 1987, p.49.

CHAPTER TWO

p. 26 "The gentlemen from Citibank": This account of the meeting appeared in U.S. Congress, House Committee on Banking, Finance and Urban Affairs, *Securities and Exchange Commission Staff Report on Transactions in Securities of the City of New York*, Washington: Government Printing Office 1977, pp.2–3.

p. 27 "When the box was opened": John Darnton, "When He Turns to Banks, They Now Tend to Say No," *New York Times*, March 30, 1975.

p. 27 "shock therapy": "Transcript of Mayor Beame's Speech Describing an Austerity Budget for the City," *New York Times*, May 30, 1975, p.8.

p. 28 "I have to have a complete assurance": Quoted in Damon Stetson, "New York City to Press Labor Pacts; Simon Stresses a Freeze on Wages," *New York Times*, June 21, 1976.

p. 29 black/white earnings in 1959: Calculated from data in U.S. Bureau of the Census, *Money Income of Households, Families, and Persons in the United States: 1987*, Series P-60, No.162, Washington: Government Printing Office 1989, pp.110–11.

p. 29 "I Have a Dream": The quote is taken from the text of the speech printed in Lewis Copeland and Lawrence W. Lamm, eds., *The World's Great Speeches*, 3rd enlarged edition, New York: Dover Publications 1973, p.751.

p. 30 "We're gonna lay down our shufflin' shoes": Milwaukee County Welfare Rights Organization, *Welfare Mothers Speak Out*, New York: Norton 1972, p.16.

p. 30 "a lever to pry loose more money": Irwin Ross, "Those Newly Militant Public Workers," *Fortune*, August 1968, p.104.

p. 31 "a desire to regulate business more closely": Daniel Yankelovich, "The Real Meaning of the Student Revolution," *Conference Board Record*, March 1972, p.13; quoted in David Vogel, *Fluctuating Fortunes: The Political Power of Business in America*, New York: Basic Books 1989, p.57.

p. 31 "challenging the institutions in which the democratic capitalist order is rooted": "Special Report on Youth," *Fortune*, January 1969, pp.68,70.

p. 31 "The major objection to the capitalist class": Greg Calvert and Carol Neiman, *A Disrupted History: The New Left and the New Capitalism*, New York: Random House 1971, p.101.

p. 33 "an escape valve": Norman Pearlstine, "UAW Uses GM Strike to 'Educate' Workers, Pull Together Factions," *Wall Street Journal*, October 29, 1970, p.1.

p. 33 "not guilty by reason of temporary insanity": "Hell in the Factory," *Time*, June 7, 1971, p.39.

p. 33 pessimistic conclusions: *Work in America, Report of a Special Task Force to the Secretary of Health, Education and Welfare*, Cambridge, MA: MIT Press 1973, p.19.

p. 34 "an excess of democracy": Michel Crozier et al., *The Crisis of Democracy*, New York University Press 1975, p.113.

p. 34 "discipline in the factories": Michal Kalecki, "Political Aspects of Full Employment" (1943), in *Selected Essays on the Dynamics of the Capitalist Economy, 1933–1970*, New York: Cambridge University Press 1971, p.141.

p. 35 "We need a sharp recession" and "healthy respect for economic values": both were quoted in Leonard Silk and David Vogel, *Ethics and Profits: The Crisis of Confidence in American Business*, New York: Simon & Schuster 1976, p.64. Silk and Vogel were allowed to attend a series of gatherings of executives organized by the Conference Board on the condition that quotes from participants would remain unattributed.

p. 35 "a balance-of-work-ethic deficit": Felix G. Rohatyn, "New York City Mirrors the U.S.," *Business Week*, March 27, 1978, p.12.

p. 35 "a prolonged period of programmed economic stagnation": Samuel Bowles, David M. Gordon and Thomas E. Weisskopf, *Beyond the Waste Land: A Democratic Alternative to Economic Decline*, Garden City, NY: Doubleday 1983, p.111.

p. 36 "what is being tested in New York City": L.D. Solomon, "For New York, a Time of Testing As the Nation Looks On," *New York Times*, February 21, 1976.

p. 37 "Such an outpouring of consumer legislation": Vogel, *Fluctuating Fortunes, op. cit.* p.38.

p. 37 "Among the companies pleading guilty to this offense": *Report of the Watergate Special Prosecution Force*, Washington: Government Printing Office 1975, pp.73–75.

p. 38 "a ghostly heap of rubble": Walter Guzzardi Jr., "Business Is Learning How to Win in Washington," *Fortune*, March 27, 1978, p.53.

p. 38/39 "Mobil stepped up the level of ideological confrontation": See for example, the ads, headlined "Business: Last Haven for Radicals" and "Regulators: the New Reactionaries," which ran in the *New York Times* on June 29, 1978 and July 6, 1978, respectively.

p. 39 "a businessmen's liberation movement": Herbert Stein, "Businessmen of the World, Unite!" *Wall Street Journal*, June 12, 1978.

p. 39 "with a little money they hear you better": Thomas B. Edsall, "Business Learns to Play New Politics," *Baltimore Sun*, February 25, 1980, p.A7; quoted in Michael Pertschuk, *Revolt Against Regulation: The Rise and Pause of the Consumer Movement*, Berkeley: University of California Press 1982, p.60.

p. 39 "public policy has become increasingly responsive to the needs and desires of industry": Philip Shabecoff, "Big Business on the Offensive," *New York Times Magazine*, December 9, 1979, p.134.

p. 40 "would do everything but cure dandruff": Robert Kuttner, *Revolt of the Haves: Tax Rebellions and Hard Times*, New York: Simon & Schuster 1980, p.245.

p. 40 "capital formation has entered the lexicon of 'good' words":
Quoted in *ibid.* p.246.

CHAPTER THREE

p. 45 "The prosperity of the middle and lower classes": Cited in Robert
Kuttner, *Revolt of the Haves: Tax Rebellions and Hard Times*, New York: Simon
& Schuster 1980, p.230.

p. 46 "Sound the trumpets": Walter Heller, "The Kemp-Roth-Laffer Free
Lunch," *Wall Street Journal*, July 12, 1978; reprinted in Arthur B. Laffer and
Jan P. Seymour, eds., *The Economics of the Tax Revolt*, New York: Harcourt
Brace Jovanovich 1979, p.46.

p. 47 "turbo-charged Keynesianism": "Tory King, Whig Policies," *Econo-mist*, August 18, 1984, p.11.

p. 48 tax revenue statistics: Organisation for Economic Co-operation and
Development, *Revenue Statistics of OECD Member Countries, 1965–1981*, Paris
1982, p.68.

p. 48 effective tax rates for income groups: Joseph A. Pechman, *Who Paid
the Taxes, 1966–85?* Washington: Brookings Institution 1985, p.4.

p. 48 corporate tax rates: Joseph A. Pechman, *Federal Tax Policy*, 5th
edition, Washington: Brookings Institution 1987, p.150.

p. 49 "a Trojan horse to bring down the top rate": William Greider,
The Education of David Stockman and Other Americans, New York: Dutton
1982, p.49.

p. 50 General Electric's tax refunds: Craig A. Carter, "A Tax Study Busi-ness Doesn't Like," *Fortune*, November 26, 1984, p.33.

p. 50 corporate taxes as a share of federal receipts: U.S. Office of Manage-ment and Budget, *Budget of the United States Government, Fiscal Year 1990,
Historical Tables*, Washington: Government Printing Office 1989, pp.26–27.

p. 50 payroll taxes: Employers and employees pay equal percentages of
the worker's earnings for the Old Age, Survivors, Disability and Hospital In-surance program; employers alone pay the Unemployment Insurance tax.

p. 50 "no boon for the working poor": Marilyn Moon and Isabel V.
Sawhill, "Family Incomes: Gainers and Losers," in John L. Palmer and Isabel
V. Sawhill, eds., *The Reagan Record: An Assessment of America's Changing Do-mestic Priorities*, Cambridge, MA: Ballinger 1984, p.328. The studies in this
volume were sponsored by the Urban Institute.

p. 51 two brackets: Some taxpayers (including married couples with tax-able income between $71,900 and $149,250 in 1988) will actually face a rate
of 33 percent because of the phaseout of the lower-bracket rate and the per-sonal exemption for higher-income taxpayers.

p. 51 effective corporate tax rates: Citizens for Tax Justice, "Corporate
Tax Abuses Wane," press release, October 26, 1989.

p. 51 "which Ed Meese once labeled 'immoral' ": quoted in Herbert H. Denton, "Progressive Income Tax Is 'Immoral,' Meese Says," *Washington Post*, May 8, 1982, p.A6.

p. 52 "essentially unchanged for most income groups": U.S. Congress, Congressional Budget Office, *The Changing Distribution of Federal Taxes, 1975–1990*, Washington, October 1987, pp.47–48. The lowest income group refers to the bottom decile (tenth) in the distribution of family income.

p. 52 "encourage the entrepreneurial spirit": quoted in Alan Murray, "Capital-Gains Tax Bill Would Spur Asset Sales More than Investment," *Wall Street Journal*, September 29, 1989, p.1.

p. 52 "90 percent of the benefits": Citizens for Tax Justice Fact Sheet, February 10, 1989.

p. 53 "the little people pay taxes": Paul Moses, "Witness Taxes Leona's Patience," *New York Newsday*, July 12, 1989, p.5.

p. 54 the total benefits available to a typical AFDC family: D. Lee Bawden and John L. Palmer, "Social Policy: Challenging the Welfare State," in Palmer and Sawhill, eds., *op. cit.* p.193.

p. 54 "a 1978 article calling for the abolition of welfare": David A. Stockman, "Welfare *Is* the Problem," *Journal of the Institute for Socioeconomic Studies*, Autumn 1978, p.39.

p. 54 "a total reduction of about 17 percent": Bawden and Palmer, *op. cit.* p.186.

p. 54 "557,000 additional people into poverty": "Congress Study Finds Reagan Budget Curbs Put 557,000 People in Poverty," *New York Times*, July 26, 1984, p.A19.

p. 55 "They are deliberately trying to kill the program": Physician Task Force on Hunger in America, *Increasing Hunger and Declining Help: Barriers to Participation in the Food Stamp Program*, Boston: Harvard School of Public Health, May 1986, p.56.

p. 55 the effectiveness of benefit programs: Center on Budget and Policy Priorities, *The Decreasing Effectiveness of Government Benefit Programs, 1979–1987*, Washington, September 1988, p.1 and table 1.

p. 56 the ranks of the working poor: U.S. Bureau of the Census, *Money Income and Poverty Status in the United States: 1988*, Series P-60, No.166, Washington: Government Printing Office 1989, table 21, p.66.

p. 56 "male confidence and authority": George Gilder, *Wealth and Poverty*, New York: Basic Books 1981, p.114.

p. 56 "Congress accepted the administration's call": The repeal of the "30 and a third" formula applied to recipients on the rolls four months or more.

p. 56 "snatching benefits from some one million people": U.S. Congress, House Committee on Ways and Means, *Background Material and Data on Programs Within the Jurisdiction of the Committee on Ways and Means, 1989 edition*, Washington: Government Printing Office 1989, p.1121.

p. 57 "I was really hurting": Spencer Rich, " 'Safety Net' Strands Thinner Under Reagan," *Washington Post*, November 27, 1988.

p. 57 "you can't have an antique car": Physician Task Force on Hunger in America, *Hunger Reaches Blue Collar America*, Boston: Harvard School of Public Health, October 1987, p.14.

p. 57 "a new class war": Frances Fox Piven and Richard A. Cloward, *The New Class War: Reagan's Attack on the Welfare State and Its Consequences*, New York: Pantheon 1982, p.39.

p. 57/58 "scrapping the entire federal welfare and income-support structure": Charles Murray, *Losing Ground: American Social Policy, 1950–1980*, New York: Basic Books 1984, pp.227–28.

p. 58 "by 1988 the figure was down to 32 percent": Isaac Shapiro and Marion E. Nichols, *Unprotected: Unemployment Insurance and Jobless Workers in 1988*, Washington: Center on Budget and Policy Priorities, August 1989, p.2.

p. 58/59 "You just pray you're not going to get caught": Burt Schorr, "Reagan Cutbacks Help to Trim Welfare Rolls But Hurt Some Needy," *Wall Street Journal*, November 16, 1982, p.1.

p. 59 "In only a handful of states": Carmen D. Solomon, *Aid to Families with Dependent Children (AFDC): Need Standards, Payment Standards, and Maximum Benefits for Families with No Countable Income*, Washington: Congressional Research Service, September 7, 1988, pp.30–31.

p. 59 "Families in the top quintile had an average gain of nearly 19 percent": U.S. Congress, House Committee on Ways and Means, *op. cit.*, p.1004.

CHAPTER FOUR

p. 61 rise and fall of the flat-iron plant: This account comes from Gilda Haas, *Plant Closures: Myths, Realities and Responses*, Boston: South End Press 1985, pp.4–11.

p. 61 "the jobs of more than 100,000 GE employees have been annihilated": INFACT, *INFACT Brings GE to Light*, Boston 1988, p.25.

p. 61 The Morse story: Dan Swinney, "UE Local 277's Strike at Morse Cutting Tool," *Labor Research Review*, vol.1, no.1, Fall 1982, p.4. In 1989 Gulf+Western changed its name to Paramount Communications Inc. The more recent Morse developments are taken from Jane Slaughter, "Morse Tool Workers Win One More Fight Against Plant Closing," *Labor Notes*, August 1987, p.1.

p. 63 manufacturing's share of total employment: *Employment and Earnings*, January 1989, p.83 and January 1990, p.238.

p. 63 "500" employment decline: Calculated from figures in the *Fortune 500 Double 500 Directory: 1980*, p.23 and the April 23, 1990 issue of *Fortune*, p.339. In 1989 the employment figure was 12.5 million. Figures on the earlier trend are from Linda Snyder Hayes, "Twenty-five Years of Change in the Fortune 500," *Fortune*, May 5, 1980, p.94.

p. 63 "systematic disinvestment": Barry Bluestone and Bennett Harrison, *The Deindustrialization of America: Plant Closings, Community Abandonment and the Dismantling of Basic Industry*, New York: Basic Books 1982, p.6.

p. 64 "a definite future": Portwood's story is told in Dale Russakoff, "A Worker's Search for Job Security," *Washington Post*, July 5, 1987, p.A1.

p. 64 "Labor costs are the big thing": Originally quoted in *Akron Beacon Journal*, February 29, 1971; requoted in Richard B. McKenzie, *Restrictions on Business Mobility: A Study in Political Rhetoric and Economic Reality*, Washington: American Enterprise Institute 1979, p.42.

p. 65 destruction of Sunbelt jobs: Bluestone and Harrison, *op. cit.* pp.30,272.

p. 65 later estimates on dislocation in the South: Francis W. Horvath, "The Pulse of Economic Change: Displaced Workers of 1981–85," *Monthly Labor Review*, June 1987, p.6.

p. 65/66 "beneficiaries of the competitive process": Richard B. McKenzie, *Fugitive Industry: The Economics and Politics of Deindustrialization*, San Francisco: Pacific Institute for Public Policy Research 1984, p.87.

p. 66 "it is not a tragedy": James Cook, "The Molting of America," *Forbes*, November 22, 1982, p.163.

p. 66 "You don't eat a steak": Woolaghan's story is described in Denise Mitchell, "Jobbing Down," *Union* (magazine of the Service Employees International Union), September/October 1987, p.22.

p. 67 "a cut of at least 20 percent": U.S. Bureau of Labor Statistics, "BLS Reports on Worker Displacement," press release, December 9, 1988.

p. 67 " 'luxuries' like fresh fruit": The Baudendistels' story is told in Paul Blustein, "Some Swing-Voter Groups Miss Out on Prosperity," *Washington Post*, September 22, 1988.

p. 67 "no longer had coverage": Horvath, *op. cit.* p.11.

p. 67 "a growing body of research": see, for example, M. Harvey Brenner, *Estimating the Effects of Economic Change on National Health and Social Well-Being*, study prepared for the U.S. Congress, Joint Economic Committee, 1984.

p. 67 "I sat down with my wife": Margaret Engel, "Plant's Closing Exacts a Toll on Workers' Spirits," *Washington Post*, January 3, 1984.

p. 67 suicide rates: Bluestone and Harrison, *op. cit.* p.65.

p. 67 the total value of mergers and acquisitions: John Paul Newport, Jr., "A New Era of Rapid Rise and Ruin," *Fortune*, April 24, 1989, p.80.

p. 68 "he's not doing his job": "Surge in Restructuring Is Profoundly Altering Much of U.S. Industry," *Wall Street Journal*, August 12, 1985, p.1.

p. 68 "it will prove a permanent revolution": Myron Magnet, "Restructuring Really Works," *Fortune*, March 2, 1987, p.38.

p. 68 "damaging their future vitality": Ralph E. Winter, "Trying to Streamline, Some Firms May Hurt Long-Term Prospects," *Wall Street Journal*, January 8, 1987, p.1.

p. 69 "total settlements worth nearly $100 million": Matthew Winkler, "Ten Primerica Executives' Parachutes Gilded in $98.2 Million Severance Pact," *Wall Street Journal*, November 29, 1988, p.A10.

p. 69 "crossed an invisible line": John Greenwald, "Where's the Limit?" *Time*, December 5, 1988, p.67.

p. 69 "Someone has to stop American employees being sacrificed": Tom McNutt; quoted in "UFCW Sues Haft Family for Injury to Bradlees Workers from Takeover Bid," *Labor Relations Week*, November 16, 1988, p.1081.

p. 70 "We cannot continue on this path": "Final Report," in Martin K. Starr, ed., *Global Competitiveness: Getting the U.S. Back on Track*, New York: Norton 1988, p.300.

p. 70 "The U.S. is abandoning its status": Quoted in Norman Jonas, "The Hollow Corporation: The Decline of Manufacturing Threatens the Entire U.S. Economy," *Business Week*, March 3, 1986, p.57.

p. 70/71 "one of the greatest changes" and "not a requisite": both are quoted in Stephen S. Cohen and John Zysman, *Manufacturing Matters: The Myth of the Post-Industrial Economy*, New York: Basic Books 1987, p.5.

p. 71 "Manufacturing matters mightily": *Ibid.* p.3.

p. 71 "have been remarkably stable": The 1988 *Economic Report of the President*, Washington: Government Printing Office 1988, p.62.

p. 71 "the manufacturing share of GNP had fallen": Lawrence Mishel, *Manufacturing Numbers: How Inaccurate Statistics Conceal U.S. Industrial Decline*, Washington: Economic Policy Institute 1988. See also the same author's "Of Manufacturing Mismeasurement," *New York Times*, November 27, 1988.

p. 71 "There probably has been some overestimation": quoted in Louis Uchitelle, "Strength in Manufacturing Overstated by Faulty Data," *New York Times*, November 28, 1988, p.D1.

p. 72 "healthy adaptability": Susan Lee and Christie Brown, "The Protean Corporation," *Forbes*, August 24, 1987, p.77.

p. 73 "the gap in average earnings": *Employment and Earnings*, January 1990, pp.122–23.

p. 73 "one-fifth of the increase in overall wage inequality": Bennett Harrison and Barry Bluestone, *The Great U-Turn: Corporate Restructuring and the Polarizing of America*, New York: Basic Books 1988, p.120.

p. 73 unionization rates: "Union Members in 1989," Bureau of Labor Statistics press release, February 7, 1990.

p. 74 "badly paid, unchanging": Emma Rothschild, "Reagan and the Real America," *New York Review of Books*, February 5, 1981, p.13.

p. 74 "those occupations expected to lead the pack": George Silvestri and John Lukasiewicz, "Projections of Occupational Employment, 1988–2000," *Monthly Labor Review*, November 1989, p.60.

p. 74 "He thinks I'm stupid": Bryan Burrough and Carol Hymowitz, "As Steel Jobs Dwindle, Blue-Collar Families Face Vexing Changes," *Wall Street Journal*, August 8, 1986, p.1.

p. 74 "a point of diminishing returns": quoted in Richard B. McKenzie, *The American Job Machine*, New York: Universe Books 1988, p.47.

p. 75 "communities are carelessly discarded": Bluestone and Harrison, *op. cit.* p.12.

CHAPTER FIVE

p. 77 The testimony of Ward and Packard: U.S. Congress, House Committee on Government Operations, *Rising Use of Part-time and Temporary Workers: Who Benefits and Who Loses?* Hearing held May 19, 1988, Washington: Government Printing Office 1988.

p. 78 "A business magazine headlined its story": Michael A. Pollock and Aaron Bernstein, "The Disposable Employee is Becoming a Fact of Corporate Life," *Business Week*, December 15, 1986, p.52.

p. 78 "one out of every four workers": Richard S. Belous, "How Human Resource Systems Adjust to the Shift Toward Contingent Workers," *Monthly Labor Review*, March 1989, p.10.

p. 78 irregularity of employment: Gareth Stedman Jones, *Outcast London: A Study in the Relationship Between Classes in Victorian Society*, Harmondsworth, England: Penguin Books 1971, p.64

p. 79 "job-hunting early in this century": Leon Stein and Philip Taft, eds., *Workers Speak: Self Portraits*, New York: Arno 1971, p.74; cited in David Montgomery, *Workers' Control in America*, New York: Cambridge University Press 1979, p.36.

p. 79 "streetcorner men": Elliot Liebow, *Tally's Corner*, Boston: Little, Brown 1967, pp.58,212.

p. 79 "poor employment prospects for blacks": *Report of the National Advisory Commission on Civil Disorders*, New York: Bantam Books 1968, especially ch.7.

p. 80 "It is a curious irony": Sar A. Levitan and Richard S. Belous, *More than Subsistence: Minimum Wages for the Working Poor*, Baltimore: Johns Hopkins University Press 1979, p.17.

p. 80 "a third of the teaching force": William Serrin, "Up to a Fifth of U.S. Workers Now Rely on Part-time Jobs," *New York Times*, August 14, 1983, p.1.

p. 81 "a study of low-wage day labor pools": Southern Regional Council, *Hard Labor: A Report on Day Labor Pools and Temporary Employment*, Atlanta 1988, p.31.

p. 81 "It's a phenomenal economic and social event": quoted in Dale Russakoff and Cindy Skrzycki, "Growing Pains in the Contingent Work Force," *Washington Post*, February 11, 1988, p.A1.

p. 81 "going to become more fluid": prepared testimony of Conference Board economist Audrey Freedman, printed in U.S. Congress, House Committee on Government Operations, *op. cit.* p.36.

p. 81 "this lower level of smaller plants": transcript of the NBC television documentary "The Japan They Don't Talk About," broadcast April 22, 1986, p.7.

p. 82 "There are so many ranks": Satoshi Kamata, *Japan in the Passing Lane: An Insider's Account of Life in a Japanese Auto Factory*, New York: Pantheon Books 1982, p.11.

p. 82 "part of the family": Robert C. Wood, "Japan's Multitier Wage System," *Forbes*, August 18, 1980, p.53.

p. 82 unionization of part-timers: *Employment and Earnings*, January 1990, p.231.

p. 82 short-term hires at Mazda: Mike Parker, "Mazda Moves Toward Two-Tier Wage System," *Labor Notes*, December 1988, p.5.

p. 83 increase in part-timers from 1954 to 1977: William V. Deutermann, Jr. and Scott Campbell Brown, "Voluntary Part-time Workers: A Growing Part of the Labor Force," *Monthly Labor Review*, June 1978, p.3.

p. 83 "You can't build a lifestyle": Deborah C. Wise and Aaron Bernstein, "Part-time Workers: Rising Numbers, Rising Discord," *Business Week*, April 1, 1985, p.62.

p. 84 The People Express and Spiegel cases: 9to5, National Organization of Working Women, *Working at the Margins: Part-time and Temporary Workers in the United States*, Cleveland 1986, p.17.

p. 84 Mellon Bank terminations: John J. Sweeney and Karen Nussbaum, *Solutions for the New Work Force: Policies for a New Social Contract*, Cabin John, MD: Seven Locks Press 1989, p.62.

p. 84 median hourly wage for part-timers: Unpublished data from the U.S. Bureau of Labor Statistics covering only those workers paid on an hourly basis.

p. 84 "Part-timers account for more than half of those workers earning the minimum wage": This and many of the other statistics on part-timers come from Sar A. Levitan and Elizabeth A. Conway, "Part-timers: Living on Half Rations," *Challenge*, May–June 1988, pp.9–16.

p. 84 "One study summed up the conditions aptly": *Ibid.* p.9.

p. 85/86 "expected to increase more than 60 percent": Valerie A. Personick, "Industry Output and Employment: A Slower Trend for the Nineties," *Monthly Labor Review*, November 1989, p.37. The percentage is based on the moderate growth scenario.

p. 86 "as high as 18 million": estimate by Mitchell Fromstein, president of Manpower Inc., cited in David Kirkpatrick, "Smart New Ways to Use Temps," *Fortune*, February 15, 1988, p.110.

p. 86 "companies of Silicon Valley": Deborah C. Wise, "Part-time Workers: Rising Numbers, Rising Discord," *Business Week*, April 1, 1985, p.63.

p. 86 Weyerhaeuser temp pool: Louis Uchitelle, "Reliance on Temporary Jobs Hints at Economic Fragility," *New York Times*, March 16, 1988, p.D4.

p. 86 "We'd rather have a distant relationship": quoted in Kirkpatrick, *op. cit.* p.111.

p. 86 "a temp agency executive was able to gloat": quoted in Sarah Oates, "Temporaries Become Big Business," *Washington Post*, July 7, 1985, p.K5.

p. 86 temp earnings: Harry B. Williams, "What Temporary Workers Earn: Findings from a New BLS Survey," *Monthly Labor Review*, March 1989, p.4.

p. 86/87 benefits for temps: U.S. Bureau of Labor Statistics, *Industry Wage Survey: Temporary Help Supply, September 1987* (Bulletin 2313), Washington: Government Printing Office 1988.

p. 87 Workers and No Temporaries: Mark Vorreuter, "Fighting Fast-Growing Temp Industry," *Guardian*, July 29, 1987, p.9.

p. 87 "rent-a-boss business": Selwyn Feinstein, "More Small Firms Get Help from Rent-a-Boss Services," *Wall Street Journal*, January 25, 1989, p.B1.

p. 87 "a typical day in 1988": This account is drawn from Southern Regional Council, *op. cit.* pp.11–12. The name Johnny Tartt is a pseudonym given to the worker by the author of the report. The figures on typical take-home pay are from p.18 of the report, and the quote about "flesh peddling" appears on p.10.

p. 88 "Marvin Selter claims": Bureau of National Affairs, *The Changing Workplace: New Directions in Staff and Scheduling*, Washington 1986, p.34.

p. 89 "an estimated 500 thousand leased employees": Telephone conversation with Joseph Honick, Executive Director of the National Staff Leasing Association, January 3, 1990.

p. 89 "we have been able to keep out the union": quoted in Jaclyn Fierman, "Employees Learn to Love Being Leased Out," *Fortune*, April 1, 1985, p.80.

p. 90 "invisible threads": Karl Marx, *Capital* [1887], New York: International Publishers 1947, p.465.

p. 90 "tenement on Macdougal Street": Mary Van Kleeck, *Artificial Flower Makers*, New York: Survey Associates 1913; excerpted in Rosalyn Baxandall, Linda Gordon and Susan Reverby, eds., *America's Working Women*, New York: Vintage Books 1976, p.161.

p. 90 "It's not for Social Security": Hardy Green and Elizabeth Weiner, "Bringing It All Back Home," *In These Times*, March 11–17, 1981, p.8.

p. 91 "the coat retailed for $950": Maria Laurino, "Are Exploited Workers Turning Norma's Rags to Riches?" *Village Voice*, February 3, 1987, p.12.

p. 91 "the work is always there waiting for you": Osha Gray Davidson, "Doing Home Work Down on the Farm," *Nation*, July 17, 1989, p.87. Sarah Johnson is a pseudonym.

p. 91 "millions of dollars are involved": Pete Carey and Michael Malone, "Black Market in Silicon Valley," *San Jose Mercury-News*, August 31, 1980, p.1A.

p. 91 "toxic solvents that had to be heated on the kitchen stove": Rebecca Morales, "Cold Solder on a Hot Stove," in Jan Zimmerman, ed., *The Technological Woman: Interfacing with Tomorrow*, New York: Praeger 1983; and Naomi Katz and David S. Kemnitzer, "Fast Forward: The Internationalization of Silicon Valley," in June Nash and Maria Patricia Fernandez-Kelly, eds., *Women, Men, and the International Division of Labor*, Albany: State University of New York Press 1983.

p. 91 "It is almost like a typhus epidemic": Marilyn Webb, "Sweatshops for One: The Rise in Industrial Homework," *Village Voice*, February 10–16, 1982, p.24.

p. 92 "you only need to earn a third as much": Nadine Brozan, "Swapping Strategies at Forum on Family," *New York Times*, August 2, 1982, p.A13.

p. 92 Blackwell's situation: Philip Mattera, "Home Computer Sweatshops," *Nation*, April 2, 1983, p.390.

p. 93 "It brings work to your office. Not people": quoted in *ibid.*

p. 93 "the electronic cottage": Alvin Toffler, *The Third Wave*, New York: William Morrow 1980, ch.16.

p. 93 California lawsuit: Bob Shallit, "8 Ex-Employees Sue Insurance Firm," *Sacramento Bee*, January 26, 1986, p.C15.

p. 94 "irregularities in nearly all the companies examined": Internal Revenue Service press release, March 2, 1988.

p. 94 Italian decentralization of production: Philip Mattera, *Off the Books: The Rise of the Underground Economy*, New York: St. Martin's Press 1985, ch.7.

p. 95 "yeoman democracy": Michael J. Piore and Charles F. Sabel, *The Second Industrial Divide: Possibilities for Prosperity*, New York: Basic Books 1984, p.306.

p. 95 earnings in small firms: U.S. Small Business Administration, *The State of Small Business 1986*, Washington: Government Printing Office 1986, p.248.

p. 95 benefits in small firms: U.S. Small Business Administration, *The State of Small Business 1987*, Washington: Government Printing Office 1987, p.137.

p. 95 "small businesses hire more young workers": U.S. Small Business Administration, *The State of Small Business 1985*, Washington: Government Printing Office 1985, p.255.

p. 96 "we only work for ourselves": Jeffrey J. Hallett, "Work and Business in a New Economy," in Employee Benefit Research Institute, *Business, Work & Benefits: Adjusting to Change*, Washington 1989, p.33.

p. 96 "several million Americans on a limb": "America's Next Jobless," *Economist*, February 6, 1988, p.15.

p. 96 "pays a considerable price": U.S. Congress, Office of Technology Assessment, *Technology and the American Economic Transition: Choices for the Future*, Washington: Government Printing Office 1988, pp.381–82.

CHAPTER SIX

p. 99 Wilt and Martin stories: "Profiles in Courage: Displaced Workers in Lock Haven," *The Paperworker* (newspaper of the United Paperworkers International Union), April 1989, pp.8–9.

p. 100 "This is the worst antiunion, antilabor period in my lifetime": quoted in Alexander L. Taylor III, "Labor Gets a Working Over," *Time*, December 19, 1983, p.48.

p. 100 "the management revolution": Don Nichols, "The Management Revolution and Loss of Union Clout," *Management Review*, February 1988, p.26.

p. 101 "real wages in 1864": W.S. Woytinsky, *Employment and Wages in the United States*, New York: Twentieth Century Fund 1953, pp.582–83.

p. 101 "prosperity for the few": Norman J. Ware, *Labor in Modern Industrial Society* (1935), New York: Russell & Russell 1968, p.91.

p. 101 "He paid me three dollars a week": Leon Stein, ed., *Out of the Sweatshop: The Struggle for Industrial Democracy*, New York: Quadrangle 1977, p.29.

p. 102 "workers who switch from nonunion to union jobs": Richard B. Freeman and James L. Medoff, *What Do Unions Do?* New York: Basic Books 1984, pp.46–47.

p. 102 "the differential was 49 percent": calculations made from data in *Employment and Earnings*, January 1990, pp. 233–34.

p. 102 "the role unions play in lowering inequality": Freeman and Medoff, *op. cit.* ch.5.

p. 103 "That additional constituency is sizable": *Ibid.* p.34.

p. 103 "we consider IBM a good company": Hank Gilman, "IBM Dissidents Hope for Increased Support As Work Force is Cut," *Wall Street Journal*, January 13, 1987, p.1.

p. 104 "The threat of unions has prompted better wages": Peter Perl, "The Lifeline for Unions: Recruiting," *Washington Post*, September 13, 1987.

p. 104 Reuther statement: quoted in Derek C. Bok and John T. Dunlop, *Labor and the American Community*, New York: Touchstone Books 1970, p.362.

p. 105 "rolling back unionism": The statement, made by U.S. Steel chairman Roger Blough, is quoted in Mike Davis, *Prisoners of the American Dream*, London: Verso 1986, p.123.

p. 105 GE plants in the Sunbelt: *Ibid.* p.121.

p. 105 Texas Instruments anti-union indoctrination: Beth Nissen, "At Texas Instruments, If You're Pro-Union, Firm May Be Anti-You," *Wall Street Journal*, July 28, 1978, p.1.

p. 105 union share of the labor force in 1940s and 1950s: These are figures from the Bureau of Labor Statistics presented in Michael Goldfield, *The Decline of Organized Labor in the United States*, Chicago: University of Chicago Press 1987, p.10.

p. 105 "By the late 1970s": Richard B. Freeman, "Contraction and Expansion: The Divergence of Private Sector and Public Sector Unionism in the U.S.," National Bureau of Economic Research Working Paper No. 2399, October 1987, p.1a.

p. 105 "these four trends": Henry S. Farber, "The Extent of Unionization in the United States," in Thomas A. Kochan, ed., *Challenges and Choices Facing American Labor*, Cambridge, MA: MIT Press 1985, p.22.

p. 106 decline in organizing effort: Freeman and Medoff, *op. cit.* p.229.

p. 106 "I don't know, I don't care": quoted in *U.S. News & World Report*, February 21, 1972, p.27.

p. 106 "I don't feel like it's fair": "Former Textile Workers Approve a $5 Million Pact," *New York Times*, December 15, 1980.

p. 107 "unfair labor practice charges against employers jumped more than 750 percent": Paul Weiler, "Promises to Keep: Securing Workers' Rights to Self-Organization Under the NLRA," *Harvard Law Review*, vol.96 no.8, June 1983, p.1780.

p. 107 "One would have assumed": *Ibid.* p.1779.

p. 107 "We will show you how to screw your employees": quoted in Goldfield, *op. cit.* p.193.

p. 108 "the productivity surplus": Richard Edwards and Michael Podgursky, "The Unraveling Accord: American Unions in Crisis," in Richard Edwards et al., eds., *Unions in Crisis and Beyond*, Dover, MA: Auburn House 1986, pp.31–32.

p. 108 "Among those employers reported to have used the consultants": Kinsey Wilson and Steve Askin, "Secrets of a Union Buster," *The Nation*, June 13, 1981, p.725.

p. 108 "combined revenues of more than $500 million": Center to Protect Workers' Rights, *From Brass Knuckles to Briefcases: The Changing Art of Union-Busting in America*, Washington 1979, p.7.

p. 108 "until the painted lines on the floor were gone": Tony Dunbar and Bob Hall, "Union Busters: Who, Where, When, How & Why," *Southern Exposure*, Summer 1980, p.28.

p. 109 "Nothing to be ashamed of": Peter Perl, "Seminars on 'Deunionizing' Have Become Commonplace," *Washington Post*, September 13, 1987, p.H2.

p. 109 "destruction of individual freedom": quoted in a report of the House Labor-Management Subcommittee, entitled "Failure of Labor Law: A Betrayal of American Workers," the full text of which was published in the Bureau of National Affairs' *Daily Labor Report*, October 4, 1984, pp.D6–7.

p. 110 "backlog reached a record high": "NLRB Reports Case Backlog at Lowest Level Since 1978," *Labor Relations Week*, August 2, 1989, p.731.

p. 110 "depleted his bank account": Steven Greenhouse, "Labor Board Stirs Up a Storm," *New York Times*, February 5, 1984.

p. 110 "Let us go mano a mano": Cathy Trost and Leonard M. Apcar, "AFL-CIO Chief Calls Labor Laws a 'Dead Letter,' " *Wall Street Journal*, August 16, 1984, p.8.

p. 111 "go out and find another job": quoted in Kim Moody, *An Injury to All: The Decline of American Unionism*, London: Verso 1988, p.166.

p. 112 "the key element of our whole growth plan": Roy J. Harris, Jr., "More Concerns Set Two-Tier Pacts With Unions, Penalizing New Hires," *Wall Street Journal*, December 14, 1983, p.33.

p. 112 "I can't afford to stay in a good hotel": Agis Salpukas, "For Lower-Wage Tier, the Squeeze Is Tighter," *New York Times*, July 21, 1987, p.D22.

p. 112 "It makes me mad": Aaron Bernstein, "The Double Standard That's Setting Worker Against Worker," *Business Week*, April 8, 1985, p.70.

p. 113 "very bitter toward the paper": Bill Keller, "Workers Who Start— and Stay—at the Bottom," *New York Times*, August 19, 1984.

p. 113 "we are taking advantage of the bargaining climate": "A Management Split over Labor Relations," *Business Week*, June 14, 1982, p.19.

p. 113 "something we're not entitled to": Carol Hymowitz and Thomas F. O'Boyle, "Steelworkers, Management Grope for a Way to Reduce Labor Costs," *Wall Street Journal*, October 6, 1982, p.35.

p. 113 "the evidence is overwhelming that concessions do not prevent the closing of plants": quoted in Moody, *op. cit.* p.185.

p. 113 "Concessions do not save jobs": Barbara Reisman and Lance Compa, "The Case for Adversarial Unions," *Harvard Business Review*, May–June 1985, p.29.

p. 113 "nearly three-quarters of all major contracts": Linda A. Bell, "Union Concessions in the 1980s," *Federal Reserve Bank of New York Quarterly Review*, Summer 1989, p.46.

p. 114 "remained below 4 percent": William M. Davis, "Major Collective Bargaining Settlements in Private Industry in 1988," *Monthly Labor Review*, May 1989, p.35. The figures refer to first-year adjustments in private sector contracts covering 1,000 or more workers.

p. 114 "it won't be that way for the younger people who get our jobs": Ralph E. Winter, "Even Profitable Firms Press Workers to Take Permanent Pay Cuts," *Wall Street Journal*, March 6, 1984, p.1.

p. 116 "200,000 unionized workers were turned nonunion": "Death by Deceit," *Economic Notes*, March–April 1989, p.1.

p. 116 "We are emphatically not going out of business": "Wilson Foods Seeks Chapter 11 Protection Citing Labor Costs, Cuts Wages Up to 50%," *Wall Street Journal*, April 25, 1983.

p. 117 "I'm too old and tired": Tom Lewiston and Tim Wise, "Locked Out by Lockheed," *Dollars & Sense*, December 1987, p.17.

p. 117 unionized share in 1989: U.S. Bureau of Labor Statistics press release, February 7, 1990.

CHAPTER SEVEN

p. 118 "well in excess of any other capitalist nation": National Center for Health Statistics, *Health, United States, 1988*, Washington: Government Printing Office 1989, p.151.

p. 118 "I just need Emma's health care paid for": American Cancer Society, *Cancer and the Poor: A Report to the Nation; Findings of Regional Hearings Conducted by the American Cancer Society*, 1989, p.24.

p. 119 "the 31 million Americans": U.S. Bureau of the Census, *Health Insurance Coverage, 1986–88*, Series P-70, No. 17, Washington: Government Printing Office, March 1990, p.2.

p. 119 "some 19 million persons face financial barriers": Robert Wood Johnson Foundation, Special Report Number Two/1987, p.5.

p. 119 "some 65 percent are covered by employer health plans": U.S. Congress, Congressional Research Service, *Health Insurance and the Uninsured: Background Data and Analysis*, Washington: Government Printing Office, May 1988, p.95.

p. 119 percentage of workers without coverage: *Ibid.* p.96–97. Coverage by earnings level: *Ibid.* p.99.

p. 120 blacklisting entire occupations: Milt Freudenheim, "Health Insurers, to Reduce Losses, Blacklist Dozens of Occupations," *New York Times*, February 5, 1990, p.1.

p. 120 "adverse outcomes": Paula Braveman et al., "Adverse Outcomes and Lack of Health Insurance Among Newborns in an Eight-County Area of California, 1982 to 1986," *New England Journal of Medicine*, August 24, 1989, p.508.

p. 120 "refused to let his children participate in sports": See Lisa Belkin, "The Man with No Money to Buy Health Insurance," *New York Times*, September 27, 1988.

p. 120 underinsured for catastrophic illness: U.S. Congress, House Select Committee on Aging, *America's Uninsured and Underinsured: A Nation at Risk of Inadequate Health Care and Catastrophic Costs*, Washington: Government Printing Office 1986, p.4.

p. 120 "Some 15 percent of families": Congressional Research Service, *op. cit.* p.124.

p. 121 Information on the 1989 Hay/Huggins Benefits Report: telephone conversation with Mike Carter of Hay/Huggins on October 19, 1989.

p. 121 cancellation of coverage for AIDS patients: Constance Mathiessen, "Unsurance," *Hippocrates*, November–December 1989, p.39.

p. 121 "decided to proceed without authorization": N.R. Kleinfield, "When the Boss Becomes Doctor," *New York Times*, January 5, 1986, p.F1. After being contacted by the *Times* the company said it would reimburse the Andrees for their additional cost.

p. 122 "the average health insurance premium paid by employers": Figures are from the consulting firm Noble Lowndes, cited in Albert R. Karr and Mary Lu Carnevale, "Facing Off Over Health-Care Benefits," *Wall Street Journal*," August 11, 1989, p.B1.

p. 122 drop in the portion of workers whose premiums were paid entirely by their employer: Bradley R. Braden, "Increases in Employer Costs for Employee Benefits Dampen Dramatically," *Monthly Labor Review*, July 1988, p.5.

p. 122 J.C. Penney and First Interstate cases: Glenn Kramon, "Companies Shift Bigger Share of Health Costs to Employees," *New York Times*, November 22, 1988, p.1. The Circle K policy was described in Kenneth B. Noble, "Company Halting Health Plan on Some 'Life Style' Illnesses," *New York Times*, August 6, 1988, p.1.

p. 122 "This is a Rambo strategy": Glenn Kramon, "Employers Test New Ways to Shift Risk on Health Costs," *New York Times*, June 27, 1988, p.1.

p. 124 Mercer and Heckert quotes: Milt Freudenheim, "Calling for a Bigger U.S. Health Role," *New York Times*, May 30, 1989, p.D1.

p. 124 "this albatross around your neck": Karr and Carnevale, *op. cit.*

p. 124 "America is falling behind": National Health Care Campaign, *Paying More, Getting Less: How U.S. Health Care Measures Up*, Washington, December 1988, p.25.

p. 124 decline in black life expectancy: Philip J. Hilts, "Growing Gap in Life Expectancies of Blacks and Whites Is Emerging," *New York Times*, October 9, 1989.

p. 125 The situations of the Owl and Gilbert: Pauline Yoshihashi, "Remotely Affordable," *Wall Street Journal*, May 19, 1989, Gimme Shelter supplement, p.R18.

p. 125 The plight of the Tottens: Dan Cordtz, "You Can't Buy a House Anymore," *Financial World*, December 13, 1988, p.42.

p. 125 decline in home ownership rates: Joint Center for Housing Studies, Harvard University, *The State of the Nation's Housing 1989*, Cambridge, MA, 1989, p.12.

p. 126 "down payment burden": *Ibid.* p.11.

p. 126 total cost of owning: *Ibid.* p.22.

p. 126 foreclosure and delinquency rates: telephone conversation with the Mortgage Bankers Association, October 2, 1989.

p. 126 "I don't have enough money for a house": Joan Kelly, "Comeback Kids," *New York Newsday*, March 25, 1989, p.II–2.

p. 126–27 Census figures and "You think you've done your bit" quote: Alison Leigh Cowan, "Parenthood II: The Nest Won't Stay Empty," *New York Times*, March 12, 1989, p.1.

p. 127 vacancy rates in New York: Michael A. Stegman, *Housing and Vacancy Report: New York City, 1987*, City of New York, Department of Housing Preservation and Development, April 1988, p.47.

p. 127 median rents: Joint Center for Housing Studies, *op. cit.* p.24.

p. 127 "In New York nearly one household in four": Stegman, *op. cit.* p.116. The figure is actually for gross rents, which include utility costs.

p. 128 "the number of inexpensive housing units": Paul A. Leonard, Cushing N. Dolbeare and Edward B. Lazere, *A Place to Call Home: The Crisis in Housing for the Poor*, Washington: Center on Budget and Policy Priorities and the Low Income Housing Information Service, April 1989, p.7. Low-income rental units are defined as those priced below $250 a month; low-income households are those with incomes below $10,000. Both figures are in constant 1985 dollars.

p. 128 "between 650 thousand and 4 million persons": David C. Schwartz and John H. Glascock, *Combating Homelessness: A Resource Book*, American Affordable Housing Institute, Rutgers University, n.d. [1989], p.19.

p. 128 "emergency shelter and food facilities were being overwhelmed": United States Conference of Mayors, *A Status Report on Hunger and Homelessness in America's Cities: 1989*, Washington, December 1989.

p. 128 "the main social factors": U.S. General Accounting Office, *Homelessness: HUD's and FEMA's Progress in Implementing the McKinney Act*, Washington, May 1989, p.32.

p. 128 "I was stunned": B. Drummond Ayres, Jr., "Wooed by Jobs, and Now Homeless," *New York Times*, July 26, 1989.

p. 129 new HUD commitments for rental assistance: Leonard et al. *op. cit.* pp.28,29.

p. 129 "less than a third of renter households below the poverty line": *Ibid.* p.27.

p. 129 "contracts covering more than 700 thousand units": *Ibid.* p.38.

p. 129 "people who are politically well known had an absolute entree": Philip Shenon, "Ex-HUD Aide Tells of Role Played by Major Republicans," *New York Times*, June 23, 1989, p.1.

p. 130 "when the grocery shelves are empty": Peter Drier, "Communities, Not Carpetbaggers," *Nation*, August 21/28, 1989, p.199.

p. 130 "the key that opened the golden door": text of Ronald Reagan's radio address for April 30, 1983, as transmitted on UPI.

p. 131 "the race was being led by Sarah Lawrence": Deirdre Carmody, "Colleges Caught in Tuition-Student Aid Squeeze," *New York Times*, April 5, 1989.

p. 131 average charges for tuition: College Board press release, August 10, 1989. These figures are weighted according to the enrollment of the schools.

p. 131 rise in the total cost of attendance: The College Board, *Trends in Student Aid: 1980 to 1989*, August 1989, p.11.

p. 131 rise in college enrollment: U.S. Bureau of the Census, *Education in the United States: 1940–1983*, CDS-85-1, July 1985, pp.49,52.

p. 132 "the figure had been increased somewhat": College Board, *Trends*, *op. cit.* p.7.

p. 132 forms of student aid: *Ibid.* p.9.

p. 132/133 "students borrow more than they used to": Janet S. Hansen, *Student Loans: Are They Overburdening A Generation?* U.S. Congress, Joint Economic Committee, December 1986, p.i.

p. 133 "now we're playing the ultimate trump card": quoted in "IRS Will Help U.S. to Collect Student Loans," *New York Times*, August 7, 1985, p.1.

p. 133/134 Calvin's story and "they're not deadbeats" quote: Gary Putka, "Troubling Statistics on Student-Loan Defaults Yield No Agreement on Explanation or Solution," *Wall Street Journal*, March 15, 1988, p. 74.

p. 134 enrollment figures: telephone conversation with the school enrollment branch of the Census Bureau, March 13, 1990.

CHAPTER EIGHT

p. 135 testimony of Tennant and Hudson: U.S. Congress, House Select Committee on Children, Youth and Families, *Children and Families in Poverty: The Struggle to Survive*, hearing held February 25, 1988, Washington: Government Printing Office 1988, pp. 18,210.

p. 136 divorces: The latest rate, 21.2 per 1,000 married women in 1986, is from *Monthly Vital Statistics Report*, vol.38, no.2, supplement, June 6, 1989. The estimate on the number of marriages ending in divorce was obtained from a telephone conversation with the Marriage and Family Statistics Branch of the U.S. Bureau of the Census, October 26, 1989.

p. 136 births to unmarried women: telephone conversation with the National Center for Health Statistics, October 26, 1989.

p. 136 female-headed households: U.S. Bureau of the Census, *Household and Family Characteristics: March 1988*, Series P-20, No.437, Washington: Government Printing Office, May 1989, pp. 115–16.

p. 136 children living with one parent: U.S. Bureau of the Census, *Studies in Marriage and the Family*, Series P-23, No.162, Washington: Government Printing Office, June 1989, pp.13–14.

p. 136 female labor participation rate: U.S. Bureau of Labor Statistics, "Labor Force Participation Unchanged Among Mothers with Young Children," press release, September 7, 1988.

p. 136 "the classic nuclear family": Calculated from data in U.S. Bureau of the Census, *Household and Family Characteristics, op. cit.* pp.3,96.

p. 136 "families break down": George Gilder, *Wealth and Poverty*, New York: Basic Books 1981, p.17.

p. 137 "today it is family break-up": U.S. Congress, House Select Committee on Children, Youth and Families, *A Domestic Priority: Overcoming Family Poverty in America*, hearing held September 22, 1988, Washington: Government Printing Office 1988, p.15.

p. 137 median income of women: U.S. Bureau of the Census, *Money Income and Poverty Status in the United States: 1988*, Series P-60, No.166, Washington: Government Printing Office 1989, pp.3,42–43.

p. 137 PAR index: Randy Albelda, "Women's Income Not Up to Par," *Dollars & Sense*, July–August 1988, p.6.

p. 137 "the income of women fell an average of 30 percent": Greg J. Duncan and Saul D. Hoffman, "Economic Consequences of Marital Instability," in Martin David and Timothy Smeeding, eds., *Horizontal Equity, Uncertainty, and Economic Well-Being*, University of Chicago Press 1985, table 14.A.4.

p. 138 "divorce is a financial catastrophe" and "we ate macaroni and cheese five nights a week": Lenore J. Weitzman, *The Divorce Revolution*, New York: Free Press 1985, p.339.

p. 138 "only 3 percent of the total were actually receiving payments": U.S. Bureau of the Census, *Child Support and Alimony: 1985*, Series P-23, No.154, Washington: Government Printing Office, March 1989, p.6.

p. 138 average child support payments: *Ibid.* pp.3–4.

p. 138 Jensen's story: Tamar Lewin, "New Law Compels Sweeping Changes in Child Support," *New York Times*, November 25, 1988, p.A1.

p. 139 "an underclass of women and children": Weitzman, *op. cit.* pp.352,355.

p. 139 "15 percent of them remained below the poverty line": U.S. Bureau of the Census, *Money Income and Poverty Status, op. cit.* p.74.

p. 140 "explained only 35 percent of the wage gap": Greg J. Duncan, *Years of Poverty, Years of Plenty: The Changing Fortunes of American Workers and Families*, Institute for Social Research, University of Michigan 1984, p.158.

p. 140 "failure to measure all of the gender differences": The 1987 *Economic Report of the President*, Washington: Government Printing Office 1987, pp.220, 225.

p. 141 "the influx of women provided a cheap pool of labor": Karen Pennar and Edward Mervosh, "Women at Work," *Business Week*, January 28, 1985, p.80.

p. 142 "sometimes all of it goes to the grocery store": quoted in Alison Leigh Cowan, "Women's Gains on the Job: Not Without a Heavy Toll," *New York Times*, August 21, 1989, p.A14.

p. 142 "my day never ends": *Ibid.*

p. 142 "the gap would shrink even more in the future": U.S. Bureau of the Census, *Male-Female Differences in Work Experience, Occupation and Earnings: 1984*, Series P-70, No.10, Washington: Government Printing Office, August 1987, p.3.

p. 143 "due to the decline in the real earnings of men": National Committee on Pay Equity, "Briefing on the Wage Gap," press release, September 18, 1987.

p. 143 "men faced a 1 percent loss": Frank Levy, "Incomes, Families, and Living Standards," in Robert E. Litan, Robert Z. Lawrence and Charles L. Schultze, eds., *American Living Standards: Threats and Challenges*, Washington: Brookings Institution 1988, p.124.

p. 143 "so I'm cutting your salary in half": cartoon reprinted in the *Washington Post*, January 27, 1985, p.C4.

p. 143–44 "the rate had risen as high as 22.3 percent": U.S. Bureau of the Census, *Money Income and Poverty Status, op. cit.* p.60.

p. 144 "found the U.S. to have the highest level of child poverty": Timothy Smeeding, Barbara Boyle Torrey and Martin Rein, "Patterns of Income and Poverty: The Economic Status of Children and the Elderly in Eight Countries," in John L. Palmer, Timothy Smeeding and Barbara Boyle Torrey, eds., *The Vulnerable*, Washington: Urban Institute Press 1988, pp.96,113.

p. 144 "if we do not rise off our national rear end": Marian Wright Edelman, foreword to *A Vision for America's Future*, Washington: Children's Defense Fund 1989, p.xvi.

p. 144 "the first society in history": quoted in Andrew H. Malcolm, "New Generation of Poor Youths Emerges in U.S.," *New York Times*, October 20, 1985, p.1.

p. 144 infant mortality rates: Dana Hughes et al., *The Health of America's Children: Maternal and Child Health Data Book*, Washington: Children's Defense Fund 1989, p.95. The federal admission about not reaching its goal was reported in "U.S. Falling Short on Its Infant Health Goals," *New York Times*, July 10, 1988, p.17.

p. 144 "among black infants": Hughes et al., *op. cit.* pp.119–20.

p. 144 infants in homeless families: prepared statement of Jonathan Kozol in U.S. Congress, House Select Committee on Children, Youth, and Families, *op. cit.* p.28.

p. 144/145 international comparisons: *A Vision for America's Future, op. cit.* p.110.

p. 145 "the first increase in the low-birthweight rate": C. Arden Miller, Amy Fine and Sharon Adams-Taylor, *Monitoring Children's Health: Key Indica-*

tors, 2nd edition, Washington: American Public Health Association 1989, p.35. The 1985 rate was 6.8 percent.

p. 145 "more than 12 percent still received late care": *Profile of Child Health in the United States*, Alexandria, VA: National Association of Children's Hospitals and Related Institutions 1989, p.24.

p. 145 "some 25 percent are completely unprotected": Hughes et al., *op. cit.* p.48.

p. 145 "fewer than a dozen states": *Ibid.* p.71.

p. 145 "almost half of all poor children do not have Medicaid coverage": *Assuring Children's Access to Health Care: Fixing the Medicaid Safety Net*, Alexandria, VA: National Association of Children's Hospitals and Related Institutions, October 1989, p.1.

p. 145 "had not seen a physician in the previous 12 months": Hughes et al., *op. cit.* pp.33,61.

p. 145 "the insurance gap is even higher": *Ibid.* pp.44,45.

p. 145 "had not received vaccines": Miller et al., *op. cit.* p.64.

p. 145 "had not been fully immunized against polio": Hughes et al., *op. cit.* p.63.

p. 146 "ranging up to $10,000 per child" and "I was tearing out my hair": Tamar Lewin, "Day Care Becomes a Growing Burden," *New York Times*, June 5, 1988, p.22.

p. 146 "they pay an average of 22 percent": U.S. Bureau of the Census, "Child Care Costs Estimated at $14 Billion in 1986," press release, July 27, 1989, table 3.

p. 146 drop in Head Start enrollment: *A Vision for America's Future, op. cit.* pp.60,63.

p. 147 "in a culture dominated by laissez-faire ideology": Barbara Ehrenreich and David Nasaw, "Kids as Consumers and Commodities," *Nation*, May 14, 1983, p.597.

p. 147 "like living in the third world": Robert Reinhold, "California Receives Grade of 'D' in Study of Children's Condition," *New York Times*, June 29, 1989, p.A1.

p. 148 "The job was a monster": quoted in Froma Joselow, "Why Business Turns to Teen-Agers," *New York Times*, March 26, 1989, sec. III, p.6.

p. 148 "minors found to be employed illegally": " 'Sweatshops' and Child Labor Law Violations: A Growing Problem in the United States," presentation by William J. Gainer of the U.S. General Accounting Office at the Capitol Hill Forum on the Exploitation of Children in the Workplace, November 21, 1989, pp.5–6.

p. 148 "75 thousand children were working illegally": Michael Powell, "Illegal Labor Flourishes Again," *New York Newsday*, January 8, 1989, p.22.

p. 148 "the minimum wage has caused more misery": quoted in William

Serrin, "Plan for 2-Tier Minimum Wage to Stimulate Youth Employment Stirs Dispute," *New York Times*, November 18, 1980, p.B9.

p. 149 "to only 70 percent of the poverty line": Center on Budget and Policy Priorities, "The Bush Administration's Minimum Wage Proposal," press release, March 31, 1989.

p. 150 "were legally paid less than $3.35": Steven E. Haugen and Earl F. Mellor, "Estimating the Number of Minimum Wage Workers," *Monthly Labor Review*, January 1990, p.71.

p. 150 "That ain't no money": quoted in Larry Sutton, "Dear Prez, This Is Life," *New York Daily News*, June 23, 1989, p.5.

p. 151 "taking of the mother's body": Lloyd N. Cutler, "Pro-Life? Then Pay Up," *New York Times*, op-ed page, July 7, 1989.

CHAPTER NINE

p. 152 "lives by herself in a single furnished room": quoted in Michael Harrington, *The Other America: Poverty in the United States*, Harmondsworth, England, and New York: Penguin Books 1963, p.107.

p. 153 "that is no longer the case": The 1985 *Economic Report of the President*, Washington: Government Printing Office 1985, p.160.

p. 153 "willing to drain itself": Henry Fairlie, "Talkin' 'bout My Generation," *New Republic*, March 28, 1988, p.19.

p. 153 "an enormous intergenerational transfer": Subrata N. Chakravarty and Katherine Weisman, "Consuming Our Children?" *Forbes*, November 14, 1988, p.222.

p. 153 "are in good enough shape to take care of themselves": U.S. Congress, Senate Special Committee on Aging, *Aging America: Trends and Projections, 1987–88 edition*, Washington: n.d., p.99.

p. 153 "are in nursing homes": *Ibid.* p.118.

p. 153 "life expectancy at age 65": U.S. National Center for Health Statistics, *Health United States 1988*, Washington: Government Printing Office 1989, p.53.

p. 153 "median income of elderly family units": calculated from data in Susan Grad, "Incomes of the Aged and Nonaged: 1950–82," *Social Security Bulletin*, June 1984, p.7.

p. 153 "ratio of household income to the poverty line": Christine Ross, Sheldon Danziger and Eugene Smolensky, *Interpreting Changes in the Economic Status of the Elderly*, Institute for Research on Poverty, University of Wisconsin-Madison, Discussion Paper No.818–86, November 1986, p.5.

p. 154 "income per capita for the elderly was higher": Timothy M. Smeeding, *Full Income Estimates of the Relative Well-Being of the Elderly and the*

Nonelderly, Institute for Research on Poverty, University of Wisconsin-Madison, Discussion Paper No.779–85, September 1985, p.34.

p. 154 "I'm not pinched": Earl C. Gottschalk, Jr., "The Aging Made Gains in the 1970s, Outpacing Rest of the Population," *Wall Street Journal*, February 17, 1983, p.1.

p. 154 alternative measures of poverty: U.S. Bureau of the Census, *Estimates of Poverty Including the Value of Noncash Benefits: 1987*, Washington: Government Printing Office, August 1988, p.5.

p. 154 "one of the greatest success stories": John L. Palmer, "Financing Health Care and Retirement for the Aged," in *Business, Work, and Benefits: Adjusting to Change*, Washington: Employee Benefit Research Institute 1989, p.84.

p. 154 median income of elderly families: U.S. Bureau of the Census, *Money Income and Poverty Status in the United States: 1988*, Series P-60, No.166, Washington: Government Printing Office, October 1989, p.32.

p. 155 poverty line for the elderly: *Ibid.* pp.57,88.

p. 156 "especially weak": U.S. Bureau of the Census, *Estimates of Poverty*, *op. cit.* p.3.

p. 156 "the poor and vulnerable portion": *On the Other Side of Easy Street: Myths & Facts About the Economics of Old Age*, Washington: Villers Foundation 1987, p.24.

p. 156 "may in fact be worse off": Timothy M. Smeeding, *Nonmoney Income and the Elderly: The Case of the 'Tweeners*, Institute for Research on Poverty, University of Wisconsin-Madison, Discussion Paper No.759–84, December 1984, p.7.

p. 157 "can knock them off the economic tightrope": *On the Other Side of Easy Street*, *op. cit.* p.57.

p. 157 poverty rates for elderly women and blacks: U.S. Bureau of the Census, *Poverty in the United States: 1987*, Series P-60, No.163, Washington: Government Printing Office, February 1989, pp.29,86.

p. 157 "Medical, I don't have any of that": National Caucus and Center on Black Aged, *The Status of Black Elderly in the United States: A Report for the House Select Committee on Aging*, Washington: Government Printing Office 1987, p.16.

p. 157 "would find themselves impoverished": U.S. Congress, House Select Committee on Aging, *Long Term Care and Personal Impoverishment: Seven in Ten Elderly Living Alone Are at Risk*, Washington: Government Printing Office 1987, p.7.

p. 158 "about the same percentage the elderly were paying": U.S. Congress, Senate Special Committee on Aging, *op. cit.* pp.125,130 and *On the Other Side of Easy Street*, *op. cit.* p.26.

p. 159 assignment rates: telephone conversation with the U.S. Health Care Financing Administration, October 30, 1989.

p. 159 "the elderly complaints are rolling in": Martin Tolchin, "In Face of Protests, Bush Decides to Back Change in Medicare Plan," *New York Times*, September 13, 1989, p.A1.

p. 160 "an op-ed article": Phillip Longman, "Elderly, Affluent —and Selfish," *New York Times*, October 10, 1989.

p. 160 "far beyond what is fair": James Dale Davidson, "Social Security Rip-Off; the Poor Pay and the Rich Ride," *New Republic*, November 11, 1985, p.12.

p. 161 "an old woman pointing a gun": The cartoon was described in a box on AGE in Lee Smith, "The War Between the Generations," *Fortune*, July 20, 1987, p.82.

p. 162 "active workers per retiree": Board of Trustees of the Federal Old-Age and Survivors Insurance and Disability Trust Funds, *1988 Annual Report*, Washington: Government Printing Office 1988, pp.6,79.

p. 162 "There is no comparable discourse": John Myles, "The Trillion Dollar Misunderstanding," *Working Papers*, July–August 1981, p.25.

p. 163 "There used to be a stigma": Jerry Flint, "Early Retirement Is Growing in U.S.," *New York Times*, July 10, 1977, p.22.

p. 164 "reached a peak of nearly $7 billion": Mark J. Warshawsky, "Pension Plans: Funding, Assets, and Regulatory Environment," *Federal Reserve Bulletin*, November 1988, p.722.

p. 164 "the cumulative total of assets stripped": The 1988 and first-half 1989 figures came from a telephone conversation with the Pension Benefit Guaranty Corporation, November 1, 1989. The earlier numbers are from Employee Benefit Research Institute, *Pension Plan "Surplus": Revert, Transfer, or Hold?* Issue Brief No.88, Washington, March 1989.

p. 164 "In about a third of reversions": Larry Light, "The Power of the Pension Funds," *Business Week*, November 6, 1989, p.155.

p. 164/165 Reynolds's story: Jonathan B. Levine, "When the Safety Net Is Frayed," *Business Week*, November 6, 1989, p.158.

p. 165 "contributions have declined": Warshawsky, *op. cit.* pp.722–23.

p. 165 "the highest levels of corporate management": "Continental Can Cited for Illegal Scheme to Block Eligibility for Pension Benefits," *Labor Relations Week*, May 17, 1989, p.477.

p. 165 Arnold's story: George Landau, "Ex-Can Workers Win Battle But Not War," *St. Louis Post-Dispatch*, May 22, 1989, p.3A.

p. 166 "I figure people should work until they're 70 or 75": quoted in Gregory Stricharchuk, "Retirement Prospects Grow Bleaker for Many As Job Scene Changes," *Wall Street Journal*, August 26, 1987, p.6.

p. 166 "whose employers were making no provision": Employee Benefit Research Institute, *Pension Coverage and Benefit Entitlement: New Findings from 1988*, Issue Brief No.94, Washington, September 1989, p.7.

p. 166 "a scare campaign in the business press": *Fortune*, March 2, 1987 and *Fortune*, February 27, 1989.

p. 167 Fletcher's story: Carol J. Loomis, "The Killer Cost Stalking Business," *Fortune*, February 27, 1989, p.63.

CHAPTER TEN

p. 170 U.S. share of world manufacturing trade: General Agreement on Tariffs and Trade figures cited in Peter Truell, "All Exports Aren't Created Equal," *Wall Street Journal*, July 3, 1989, p.1.

p. 170 "a colony-in-the-making": Clyde V. Prestowitz, Jr., *Trading Places: How We Allowed Japan to Take the Lead*, New York: Basic Books 1988, p.308.

p. 170 "consumption binge": The term is used, for example, by Charles F. Stone in his chapter on international trade in Isabel V. Sawhill, ed., *Challenge to Leadership: Economic and Social Issues for the Next Decade*, Washington: The Urban Institute Press 1988, p.106.

p. 170 "living standards higher than were warranted": Robert Z. Lawrence, "The International Dimension," in Robert E. Litan et al., *American Living Standards: Threats and Challenges*, Washington: Brookings Institution 1988, p.28.

p. 171 "a reduction in living standards": Benjamin Friedman, *Day of Reckoning: The Consequences of American Economic Policy Under Reagan and After*, New York: Random House 1988, p.32.

p. 171 "where Splawn had worked for 67 years": Dudley Clendinen, "Textile Mills Squeezed in Modernization Drive," *New York Times*, October 26, 1985.

p. 172 textile imports and production workers: U.S. Department of Commerce, *1986 U.S. Industrial Outlook*, Washington 1986, pp.42–1 and 42–3.

p. 172 "market penetration of imports": U.S. Department of Commerce, *1989 U.S. Industrial Outlook*, Washington 1989. The figures are all estimates, and for motor vehicles and machine tools the estimates are for 1986, the latest ones provided in the report for those industries.

p. 172 imports as a percentage of GNP: Stone, *op. cit.* p.103.

p. 172 "are actively competing with foreign-made products": Robert Reich, *The Next American Frontier*, New York: Penguin Books 1984, p.121.

p. 172–73 "a net loss of one million positions": Charles F. Stone and Isabel V. Sawhill, *Labor Market Implications of the Growing Internationalization of the U.S. Economy*, Washington: National Commission for Employment Policy 1986, p.2.

p. 173 "there were 51 industries": *Ibid.* p.15.

p. 173 "employment effect of eliminating the record 1987 trade deficit": Faye Duchin and Glenn-Marie Lange, *Trading Away Jobs: The Effects of the U.S. Merchandise Trade Deficit on Employment*, Washington: Economic Policy Institute 1988, p.5. The exact numbers were 5.5 million in the first scenario, 4.8 million in the second, and 5.1 million in the third.

p. 173 "paid 16 percent above the national average": Stone, *op. cit.* p.113.

p. 173 "hardly been a cornucopia": The history of TAA and the data on the program come from U.S. Congress, Office of Technology Assessment, *Trade Adjustment Assistance: New Ideas for an Old Program*, Washington: Government Printing Office 1987.

p. 174 "all of history has taught": transcript of Reagan's speech appeared in the *New York Times*, September 24, 1985, p.D26.

p. 174 "imports do not destroy domestic jobs": The 1989 *Economic Report of the President*, Washington: Government Printing Office 1989, p.166.

p. 175 "kept prices artificially high": See Alan Murray, "As Free-Trade Bastion, U.S. Isn't Half As Pure As Many People Think," *Wall Street Journal*, November 1, 1985, p.1.

p. 175 transnationals' share of world exports: National Bureau of Economic Research figures cited in AFL-CIO Department of Economic Research, *America's Trade Crisis*, Washington 1988, p.37.

p. 175 "40 percent of U.S. merchandise imports": Obie G. Whichard, "U.S. Multinational Companies: Operations in 1987," *Survey of Current Business*, June 1989, p.29.

p. 175 "eliminated nearly three million American manufacturing jobs": Norman J. Glickman and Douglas P. Woodward, *The New Competitors: How Foreign Investors Are Changing the U.S. Economy*, New York: Basic Books 1989, pp.176,186.

p. 175 "employ more than six million workers": Whichard, *op. cit.*

p. 176 "You can't really consider Taiwan an exporting nation": quoted in Douglas R. Sease, "Taiwan's Export Boom to U.S. Owes Much to American Firms," *Wall Street Journal*, May 27, 1987, p.1.

p. 176 "a high-tech engine plant": The plant was described, but its parent company kept anonymous, in Harley Shaiken, "High Tech Goes Third World," *Technology Review*, January 1988, p.39.

p. 176 "The sun never sets on it": The ad was reproduced in Annette Fuentes and Barbara Ehrenreich, *Women in the Global Factory*, Boston: South End Press 1983, p.6.

p. 177 "There is no mindset that puts this country first": Louis Uchitelle, "U.S. Businesses Loosen Link to Mother Country," *New York Times*, May 21, 1989, p.1.

p. 177 "some assurance that it will still be yours": "Foreign Stake in U.S. Rises But Is Dwarfed by U.S. Stake Abroad," *Wall Street Journal*, July 3, 1978, p.1.

p. 177 "foreigners held nearly $100 billion": Russell B. Scholl, "The International Investment Position of the United States in 1988," *Survey of Current Business*, June 1989, p.42.

p. 177 "our net international investment position": *Ibid.* p.41.

p. 177 "foreign holdings of corporate bonds": Jeffrey M. Schaefer and David G. Strongin, "Why All the Fuss About Foreign Investment," *Challenge*, May–June 1989, p.31.

p. 178 "a satirical but pointed proposal": Daniel Burstein, "A Yen for New York," *New York*, January 16, 1989, p.26.

p. 178 "It's a total nightmare": The account is taken from John Junkerman, "Nissan, Tennessee," *The Progressive*, June 1987, p.16.

p. 178 foreign share of manufacturing shipments and employment: Jane Sneddon Little, "Foreign Investment in the United States: A Cause for Concern?" *New England Economic Review*, July–August 1988, p.54. The figures include existing plants that are bought by foreign interests as well as new facilities.

p. 179 "I've been approached by every state except Alaska": Thomas C. O'Donnell and Charles Gaffney, "The $10 Billion Sweepstakes: How States Woo Foreign Investment," *Business Week*, May 20, 1985, p.152.

p. 179 "you're just out of the hunt": Glickman and Woodward, *op. cit.* p.227.

p. 179 "provided a staggering $325 million": *Ibid.* p.230.

p. 179 "when they buy, they control": quoted in Jonathan P. Hicks, "The Takeover of American Industry," *New York Times*, May 28, 1989, sec. 3, p.1.

p. 179 "a pattern of vertical development": Robert Kearns, "Japan-America Inc.; Tokyo is Building a Separate Economy in This Country," *Chicago Tribune*, April 5, 1987, p.C1.

p. 180 "We're going to know more about these people": Richard Koenig, "Toyota Takes Pains, and Time, Filling Jobs at Its Kentucky Plant," *Wall Street Journal*, December 1, 1987, p.31.

p. 180 "you can't get anything in the auto industry": Jacob M. Schlesinger, "Shift of Auto Plants to Rural Areas Cuts Hiring of Minorities," *Wall Street Journal*, April 12, 1988, p.1

p. 181 Forrest City account: John A. Byrne, "At Sanyo's Arkansas Plant the Magic Isn't Working," *Business Week*, July 14, 1986, p.52.

p. 182 "into the UAW family": Doron P. Levin, "UAW Making Peace with Japanese in U.S.," *New York Times*, December 19, 1988, p.D5.

p. 182 "comparable to those of 'native' factories": U.S. General Accounting Office, *Growing Japanese Presence in the U.S. Auto Industry*, Washington 1988, ch.5.

p. 182 "drastic reduction of job classifications": *Ibid.* p.52.

p. 182 Baines's story: David Moberg, "Is There a Union in Nissan's Future?" *In These Times*, April 6–12, 1988, p.12.

p. 183 "There has to be some liberty": Neil Chethik, "The Intercultural Honeymoon Ends," *San Jose Mercury News*, February 8, 1987; reprinted in

Mike Parker and Jane Slaughter, *Choosing Sides: Unions and the Team Concept*, Boston: South End Press 1988, p.119.

p. 183 "management by stress": Parker and Slaughter, *op. cit.* ch.3.

p. 183 "strange noises are coming from the factory floor": Jerry Flint, "Constant Improvement? Or Speedup?" *Forbes*, April 17, 1989, p.92.

p. 183 "They do things away from home": Martin Tolchin and Susan Tolchin, *Buying Into America: How Foreign Money Is Changing the Face of Our Nation*, New York: Berkley Books 1989, p.165.

p. 184 "just as capitalistic as anyone": quoted in Martin Tolchin, "Union Takes on China-Owned Factory," *New York Times*, September 6, 1989.

p. 184 "they come after your money": Jane Slaughter, "Teaming Up — Against the Union," *International Labour Reports*, Summer 1988, p.10.

p. 184/185 international compensation costs: U.S. Bureau of Labor Statistics, *International Comparisons of Hourly Compensation Costs for Production Workers in Manufacturing, 1975–1988*, Report 771, August 1989, p.6.

p. 185 "LatinAmericanization": Richard J. Barnet and Ronald E. Muller, *Global Reach: The Power of the Multinational Corporations*, New York: Simon & Schuster 1974, p.215.

p. 185 "we cannot pass along productivity gains": quoted in Louis Uchitelle, "As Output Gains, Wages Lag," *New York Times*, June 4, 1987, p.D1.

p. 186 "I bought an American TV": Akio Morita, "How and Why U.S. Business Has to Shape Up," *New York Times*, June 6, 1987, p.27; quoted in Glickman and Woodward, *op. cit.* p.99.

p. 186 "competitive 'race to the bottom' ": quoted in David Gordon, "Do We Need to Be No.1?" *The Atlantic*, April 1986, p.106.

CHAPTER ELEVEN

p. 189 "Business Roundtable socialism": The phrase is attributed to Richard Belous of the National Planning Association in Robert Kuttner, "U.S. Business Isn't About to Be Society's Savior," *Business Week*, November 6, 1989, p.29.

p. 190 "Eisner raked in $40 million": Is the Boss Getting Paid Too Much?" *Business Week*, May 1, 1989, p.46.

p. 190 number of billionaires: *Forbes*, September 13, 1982, pp.102–4 and October 23, 1989, p.146.

p. 191 "only about $50 billion": Mark S. Littman, "Poverty in the 1980s: Are the Poor Getting Poorer?" *Monthly Labor Review*, June 1989, p.14.

p. 192 "His title is his humanity": Edward Bellamy, *Looking Backward, 2000–1887*, [1888], New York: New American Library 1960, p.75.

p. 195 "the average American works more than 1,900 hours": Robert K. Landers, "America's 'Vacation Gap,' " *Editorial Research Reports*, June 17, 1988, p.321.

p. 198 "We want to see this bill dead": quoted in Anise C. Wallace, "Bill Could Shift Control over Pension Funds," *New York Times*, August 28, 1989. The congressman was Peter J. Visclosky, Democrat of Indiana.

p. 202 "more than 200 million tons of it": John Schall, "Socialist Ecology, Capitalist Garbage," *Zeta*, June 1989, p.72.

p. 202 "It is now a market opportunity": The Perils of Greening Business," *The Economist*, October 14, 1989, p.75.

AFTERWORD

p. 206 "The Census Bureau's annual report": U.S. Bureau of the Census, *Money Income and Poverty Status in the United States: 1989*, Series P–60, No. 168. Washington, D.C.: U.S. Government Printing Office, September 1990, p. 30.

p. 207 "calculations by the House Committee": U.S. Congress, House Committee on Ways and Means, *Overview of Entitlement Programs: 1991 Green Book*. Washington, D.C.: U.S. Government Printing Office, 1991, p. 1184.

p. 207 "New data on household wealth": U.S. Bureau of the Census, *Household Wealth and Asset Ownership: 1988*, Series P–70, No. 22. Washington, D.C.: U.S. Government Printing Office, December 1990, p. 3.

p. 207 "Bureau of Labor Statistics": Diane E. Herz, "Worker Displacement Still Common in the Late 1980s," *Monthly Labor Review*, May 1991, p. 3.

p. 207 "Cuts in federal aid": Citizens for Tax Justice, *A Far Cry from Fair: CTJ's Guide to State Tax Reform*. Washington, D.C., April 1991, p. 18.

p. 208 "unemployment compensation system": U.S. Congress, House Committee on Ways and Means, *op. cit.*, pp. 466, 482.